Ayn Carrillo graduated from UCLA and Harvard and lives in Los Angeles where she writes screenplays for film and television and makes fun of herself in a relationship column for *Tu Cuidad* magazine. When she is not blogging at www.TheNaughtyKnitters.com she is working on her next book.

GOOD VIBRATIONS

Ayn Carrillo

CORGI BOOKS

TRANSWORLD PUBLISHERS
61-63 Uxbridge Road, London W5 5SA
A Random House Group Company
www.rbooks.co.uk

GOOD VIBRATIONS
A CORGI BOOK: 9780552155441

Originally published in the United States in 2007 under the title *Pornology* by
Running Press Book Publishers
First publication in Great Britain
Corgi edition published 2008

Excerpt from *Five-Minute Erotica,* edited by Carol Queen, in Chapter Two is
published by and appears courtesy of Running Press.

Acknowledgement is made to *Tu Ciudad* magazine, in which an excerpt from
Chapter Three first appeared in the column 'SEX y LA'.

All porn experiences and facts described in this book are real and were researched
by the author. Certain characters and situations have been altered for dramatic
purposes, or to protect the identities of real persons.

Neither Ayn Carrillo-Gailey nor Transworld Publishers nor any of their associates
shall be liable or responsible to any person or entity for any loss, damage, injury or
ailment caused, or alleged to be caused, directly or indirectly, by the information or
lack of information contained in this book.

A CIP catalogue record for this book
is available from the British Library.

Addresses for Random House Group Ltd companies outside the UK
can be found at: www.randomhouse.co.uk
The Random House Group Ltd Reg. No. 954009

The Random House Group Limited supports The Forest Stewardship Council (FSC),
the leading international forest certification organisation. All our titles that are
printed on Greenpeace approved FSC certified paper carry the FSC logo.
Our paper procurement policy can be found at
www.rbooks.co.uk/environment

Typeset in 10.5/15.5 Berkeley Book by
Falcon Oast Grpahic Art Ltd.

Printed in the UK by CPI Cox & Wyman, Reading, RG1 8EX.

2 4 6 8 10 9 7 5 3 1

To Samuel W. Gailey
for putting up with me on porn, *dread*lines, and too
much caffeine.

To Mom and Dad
who still do not know that I have written a book about porn.

CONTENTS

INTRODUCTION

So why is a good girl like me writing a book about porn? I'm well-educated, open-minded, serious about my career and the people I love, and I am certainly not obsessed with sex. That is probably why I was so reluctant to research all things porn. Did being interested in porn make me somehow cheap or "dirty," I wondered? Certainly smart, successful *men* aren't apprehensive about going to a newsstand and buying a *Playboy* magazine or renting a hard-core porn video at their local video store.

Admittedly, my first forays into porn were fueled by a boyfriend who accused me of being pornophobic. As usual I took criticism as a personal challenge. Obsessed with list-making, I jotted down every porn subject I was curious about and set out to explore it. It was also my girlfriends (mostly good girls) who encouraged me to explore the world of porn, calling me their spy on a reconnaissance mission to gather information that would make them more sexually savvy. In the beginning, I merely saw myself on a quest to understand men and their fascination with porn. Now, you might be reading this and thinking, "Oh, not my man," but yes, "your man," too. My research and interviews with dozens of men indicate that any woman who thinks that her significant other is not turned on by some porn is fooling herself.

In the end, I did learn a lot about men and their relationships with porn and sex, but what really surprised me was what I learned about myself, and how I improved *my* relationship with sex. For six months I basically became a *Good Girl Gone Wild*. I did things like attend blow job seminars, visit brothels, watch porn, test vibrators, read erotica, and much, much more. And, I had a few epiphanies on the way.

To start with, I realized that it doesn't do anyone any good to live off yesterday's orgasms, and that "cliterature"* is a far better coping tool for break-ups than Häagen-Dazs or buying shoes. The fact is that whether you are a single twenty-something exploring your sexuality for the first time, a married thirty-something with children trying to fit sex into a busy schedule, or a woman experiencing menopause, sex is a major part of everyone's life.

However, if you're a woman, you are likely to be more reluctant than a male reader or too strapped for time to do things like try a lap dance, patronize a sex store, research sex-enhancement products, or rent dozens of porn videos to figure out which one might improve your sex life. That's why I have gone out and embarrassed myself—so that you don't have to!

In your hands, *Good Vibrations* may be used to discover worthwhile products and places to improve your sex life without having to risk time or money testing these things yourself—a kind of *Zagat's Guide* to porn places and things, if you will. Or, if you're one of the many women frustrated with dating in a society where men prefer *Penthouse* to poetry, you may use it to explore men's fascination with porn. Or, you may simply read this book as it was originally meant to be: a laugh-out-loud chronicle of *One Good Girl's Exploration of All Things Naughty*. An exploration that is

---

*Erotic literature designed to help women masturbate.

constantly complicated by my break-ups with a string of insignif-
icant others, my fear that social evolution is based on survival of
the prettiest, hilarious diversions by The Naughty Knitters (a
group of friends I stitch and bitch with) and my best guy friend,
an out-of-the-closet metrosexual, and, of course, my neverending
search for a Mr. Right, which pitifully disintegrates into a search
for Mr. Right Now.

If, after reading this introduction, you are still reluctant to
explore my adventures in pornology because you are asking yourself, *"Will I still be a good girl after reading this book?"* The answer is
yes.

An informed Good Girl is still a Good Girl.

TEN SIGNS

THAT YOU ARE A GOOD GIRL WHEN IT
COMES TO MEN, SEX, AND PORN

1. You've considered looking up the word "orgasm" in the dictionary.

2. You feel guilty for faking it.

3. You are tempted to add a digit when giving
your sex tally to a new partner.

4. You prefer reading *House Beautiful* to *Penthouse*.

5. You wear thong underwear only to avoid panty lines,
not because you want to look sexy.

6. You thought dildos were only for women without boyfriends.

7. You still feel embarrassed when you buy condoms or
vaginal lubricant in a grocery store.

8. You think "dirty talk" during sex seems, well, dirty.

9. You let your inhibitions down with Tom only after three
or more shots of Jack.

10. Repeat the following three words: hot, throbbing, cock. If you didn't
say it out loud, you are definitely a Good Girl.

Chapter One
Generation XXX

Irritable boyfriend syndrome (IBS): *n. chronic condition characterized by frequent bouts of irritability, lack of interest in improving relationships, and irregular bowel movements*

Okay, I guess we're having sex. Not a lot of notice, but the lights are out, Greg is not snoring, and he has crawled on top of me. *Why does he always assume I want him on top?*

Oooh, wait a minute, that feels kind of good. He is actually using his hands in a way he never has before. . . . Damn it, he stopped—the hands thing must've been an accident. . . . All right, here we go again. . . . I need to get into this. . . . What is that noise? Did I forget to turn the stove fan off? No . . . is it . . . could it be . . . Greg's stomach? Can he really still be hungry? Oh, God, maybe he has gas! Wouldn't surprise me, he ate so fast. Okay, gas is distracting and not exactly a turn-on. Just stop thinking, Ayn! Maybe if I pretend I'm into sex tonight, that will get me more into it. Wow, he's really sweating. . . . He may fail creativity, but he gets an 'A' for exertion. . . . God, is he done yet?

Okay, here we go again, yes, yes. I even say, "Yes, yes" out loud to help matters. We are in sync now; I actually feel kinda good. Oooh, yes, yes, wheat-free waffles! Oh, no! Wheat-free waffles? Did I say that out loud?

Greg suddenly rolls off of me and turns on the light. *Crap*. I did say it out loud.

"What the hell was that?"

"Just a second." I take the pen and Post-its I always keep by my bedside and jot down "wheat-free waffles". "I've been trying to remember that all day. It's what I forgot at the store."

"Are you kidding me?"

"What?"

"We haven't had sex in two weeks and you just killed the mood."

"Well, I'm ready now. Getting that off my mind really freed me up."

"Forget it."

Greg rolls over and falls asleep in seconds, whereas I lay wide awake, staring at the ceiling, wondering why, after dating me for two years and living with me for the last month, he does not realize that I do not forget anything.

The next morning I am sitting in my pajamas in the kitchen doing what I always do while I eat breakfast: I make a list of the things I want to accomplish for that day. I also refer to the list I made the day before and transfer over any unfinished business.

When Greg enters the kitchen, he grabs the cup of coffee I made for him, eyes me making my list, and blatantly rolls his eyes. When we first started going out he would at least try to hide the eye rolls. *When did that change?*

"You know, you are the only person I know who plans to do only one thing a day," I tell him. "Everyone else makes 'To Do' lists."

"But don't you think your list-making tendencies are

borderline obsessive?" To illustrate his point, he opens a cupboard. Both of its doors are plastered with one very humongous list, which he reads from at random. "Under the heading of 'Travel': Climb a pyramid. See the Taj Mahal. White-water rafting."

"Those are checked off."

"... Spear fishing?"

I hate how he says it like it's beyond my capabilities. "It's good to have dreams," I say.

"'Household': Paint kitchen. Feng shui bedroom..."

"That's the *master* list," I try to explain. "The one I'm doing now is the daily list, which supplements the weekly lists."

He turns to the fridge and removes four Post-its. I grab them from him one at a time. "Yellow means I need to add it to my daily list, fluorescent green goes on the weekly, and blue is for the master list."

He holds up a hot pink Post-it that has "Shave legs" scrawled on it. "Hot pink means I have to take care of it immediately." He glances at my legs and does not argue this one.

"Hold up your hands," he says, trying to make a point. Reluctantly, I do so.

I have scribbled "Carpe Diet" on my left palm and "See other list" on my right.

"You're just mad about last night and taking it out on my lists," I tell him.

"Well, it's kind of a problem. Most women yell out things during sex like 'Yes, yes, come on, baby,' and you yell out 'wheat-free waffles,' or, what was it last time? 'Binder clips'?"

Actually it was just plain old "paper clips," but I don't tell him that because now I am mad.

I yell, "Yeah, well, you couldn't find my G-spot if I *MapQuested* it for you!" Actually, I don't yell this out loud, I just imagine doing it. Because I'm above that—for now. Meanwhile, I realize he is still complaining.

"You're obviously not in the moment during sex. You're constantly distracted!"

"Maybe I have ADD," I suggest.

"Yeah, right."

"My brother and mom have it," I insist. "That one doctor said maybe that's why I have trouble finishing my lists." (The truth is, Martha Stewart would have trouble finishing my lists.)

He grabs the soy milk from the fridge and takes a swig straight from the carton. It takes everything I have not to point out the Post-it on the carton that reads, "Use a glass, please."

"If you have ADD, why does it only happen during sex?" he asks.

"Maybe I have SADD."

He looks at me with one eyebrow raised.

"*Sexual* attention deficit disorder." I am half-joking, but he does not laugh.

"Now you're making up afflictions to excuse our sex life?" He rolls his eyes again. That's two times in ten minutes. "Why don't you just admit that you're not into sex?"

I thrust Friday's list at him, so ready to put him in his place. He reads it aloud. "'Floss teeth.' Do you really need to remind yourself to do that?"

"Not *that*. Read further down." He keeps reading while I continue. "And, if you knew anything about making lists, you would know that you should always put one item on your list that you know you can accomplish—it makes the rest of the list seem more doable."

"'Talk to Greg about last night,'" he says, still reading the list and getting more impatient.

"Give that to me!" I snatch the list back and check off "Floss teeth" and "Talk to Greg." Then I realize I handed him the wrong list. I hand him the weekly.

"The last item. Please read it."

"'Sex with Greg. Friday 10 p.m.-*ish*.'"

"See."

"Is that supposed to make me feel better?" He rolls his eyes *again*. We might be onto a record here. He puts the soy milk back in the fridge and turns to leave.

"Well? Is that all you're going to say or are your eye rolls some secret language, like the clicking of the Khoisan, that I'm just not fluent in?" The blank look on his face tells me that he has no idea what I'm talking about, so I make a few loud clicks with my tongue to illustrate—now he looks slightly afraid that I've lost my mind—and explain, "The Khoisan. They're the African tribe that communicates by clicking."

"You know what, I don't want to get into this. I'm late for work."

"You work at home!"

"So? I can still be late." With that he slams the door and heads out to his garage office.

I should be working, too, but I am now seriously distracted by our exchange. Actually, it doesn't take much to distract me. I wasn't kidding about the ADD. As a freelance writer, it usually takes me three or four hours of doing everything except writing—and a heavy dose of caffeine, equivalent to two cups of Kanaya green tea, two iced double soy lattes, or a pound of chocolate—before I can actually type or write my first paid word for the day.

After smearing a jar of Nutella chocolate hazelnut spread onto a plate of healthy and nutritious celery sticks, I start this particular writing session by searching for *Star* magazine. None of my friends would suspect that I read *Star* because it never appears in my living room on my knock-off Neutra coffee table perfectly fanned out with *Vanity Fair*, *Esquire*, *Jane*, *Harvard*, and *Saveur*. I only buy it because it is the perfect natural laxative.

There is something about the dramatic highs and lows of TomKat and Brangelina and "Knifestyles of the Rich and Famous" that makes me forget all of my own troubles and never provokes a single deep thought. After all, deep thoughts are constipating.

Greg has caught on to *Star*'s laxative powers, so now I constantly find it in his bathroom.

I search through the pile of magazines in his bathroom. *Sports Illustrated*, *Football Weekly*, *Xbox Magazine*, *Finally Legal*, *Fantasy Football Weekly*. Wait a minute. *Finally Legal*? My first thought is that it's a law magazine; then I remember we are talking about Greg here and what kind of law magazine puts a photo of a three-some on its cover? I keep looking. *Penthouse*? *Barely Legal*?

In disbelief, I glance through *Barely Legal*. I stare at a photo of a young woman—pretty if it weren't for overabundant makeup—on her hands and knees with two penises in her mouth. There are guys attached to the penises. I find myself wondering if she's ever shouted out a grocery item during sex.

I keep turning the pages, all kinds of thoughts going through my head. *My boyfriend reads porn? Wow, that has got to be the biggest penis I've ever seen. So, that's what a strap-on looks like? What does that girl have up her butt and why is she smiling about it? Will I ever get these images out of my head? Why are these pages stuck together? Aaaaggggh!* I throw the magazine down and flee the bathroom.

I march over to my desk and I do what I always do when a loved one makes me mad: I write a letter. A letter is kind of like a list except with full sentences and a lot more passion. My pen practically catches the paper on fire I am writing so fast and furiously.

In the letter I tell Greg that knowing that he ogles the women in these magazines makes me feel inadequate in all kinds of ways. His habit makes me wonder if he is misogynistic. I argue that porn objectifies women and sets back women's liberation and other feminist causes; I detail how it sets up false expectations (all of those boobs cannot be real) for looks, sex, and healthy relationships. I do not tell him the number one reason I do not want him reading porn: Seeing those photos makes me feel like my thighs are even more enormous than I already fear they are.

I head back to the garage where Greg conducts his so-called career and fling open his "office" door, catching him right in the middle of shooting a very large gun at a hulking figure in a ski mask who has his own gun pointed at Greg's head. Why he enjoys testing soon-to-be-released video games is beyond me.

"Since when do you read porn?" I ask as he continues pressing a zillion buttons on the control, causing an array of gunfire, explosions, and acrobatics in the video game.

"Uh, since always," he says without even a smidgen of guilt. "And, for the record, I don't read it, I just look at the pictures."

"*Barely Legal*? I can't believe this. I thought you were evolved. We met at a *Björk* concert!"

He rolls his eyes. (We definitely have a record now!)

I hand him the letter, confident that my passionate response to his porn habit will make him understand my point and empathize with smart women everywhere. We will grow together.

He puts the Xbox control down. After reading my letter, he looks up at me but says nothing.

"Well?"

With true wonder in his voice, he says, "Wow, you're really pornophobic."

"*Pornophobic?*" That's his response to my impassioned arguments about why porn is anti-feminist and misogynistic?

"Yeah, you know, you have an irrational fear of por—"

"I know what you mean. It doesn't make sense." I cut him off.

"Okay, have you ever read a *Playboy* magazine? Seen a porno?" he asks.

A long silence on my part as I search and search my memory banks.

"See? You're pornophobic," he practically shouts.

"Yeah, well, you're a *pornoholic*!" I yell and storm out.

I go to Barnes & Noble, where I always go to think, get away from things, and, okay, I admit it: I like to read magazines for free.

It's like someone is sending me signs. In the bookstore's front window, Jenna Jameson's *How to Make Love Like a Porn Star* is displayed right next to the Pulitzer-winning *Guns, Germs, and Steel* by anthropologist Jared Diamond, and apparently Traci Lords does Barnes & Noble, too. Her biography, *Underneath It All*, is on the best-sellers' shelf, and a coffee-table art book, *XXX: 30 Porn-Star Portraits*, is also front and center.

I open *XXX* and am surprised to see that real writers like Adam Gopnik, feminist Nancy Friday, and Salman Rushdie have contributed essays. In the magazine section of the store, I notice a handsome businessman picking up a *Playboy* as comfortably as I pick up the newest issue of *New York Magazine*.

Another sign: The cover article of *New York Magazine* is by David Amsden and happens to be all about porn and how it has seeped into the mainstream. *Wait a minute, porn is now mainstream?* As Amsden puts it, "Porn is not merely acceptable [nowadays], it's hip." I don't want to believe him, but as hard as I try to resist, I am a writer who cares what good writers think. And I so badly want to be hip.

In the Starbucks, where I go to finish the *New York Magazine* article, I run into a colleague's sixteen-year-old daughter, who comes from a good home and is an honor student. She gives me a big hug and when she stands back, I see that she is wearing a T-shirt that has "Porn Star" emblazoned across it. I feel as if I've been wearing porn blinders my whole life and suddenly Greg has pulled them off.

I find a dictionary and look up the word "porn." The definition is: "The depiction of erotic behavior or products (e.g. books, toys, movies, stage acts) intended to cause sexual excitement." This actual definition is not as intimidating as the common usage of the word, and the term "sexual excitement" definitely piques my curiosity.

Could Greg be right? Is there more to porn than I assumed? Could there be good porn? Why is it that smart, successful men (and Greg) are not apprehensive about porn, but I am?

Usually, much to the entertainment of my friends, when I'm curious about something, I don't blink an eye at checking it out. I have taken the Scientology exam, been to a Kabbalah meeting, attended NASCAR, sat front row at a bullfight in Spain, and visited a leper camp in India, all in the name of curiosity.

I call an emergency meeting of my knitting group, which sends beanies, booties, and sweaters to charities in third-world countries. It's also a reason to stitch and bitch with girlfriends. That's why, because most of our discussions revolve around sex, we have named ourselves "The Naughty Knitters."

Different Naughty Knitters—a typical L.A. mix of Caucasians, Asians, African Americans, half-Afs, Latinas, and Pac*-Lats (I am half Taiwanese-born Chinese—half Mexican) may attend every week, but in the core group, there are five of us who take turns discussing our love lives or lack thereof.

At this particular knitting session, after downing one too many margaritas and accidentally attaching a three-armed baby sweater that I am knitting to the sweater that I am actually wearing, I confess everything about my situation with Greg—the increasingly disappointing sex, his accusation that I am not into it, and last but not least, his penchant for porn.

The most vocal of our group is Victoria, a Puerto Rican fashion buyer who we call "Vee" even though she prefers "V-Lo." She is also one of the original *Girls Gone Wild* who is now more like the rest of us—a thirtysomething girl gone mild. She tells me

---

*Stands for Pacific Islander.

that I'm being too hard on porn.

"Everything I know about sex I learned from watching Nikki Tyler give blow jobs and Jenna Jameson take it up the ass," she says matter-of-factly.

"Exactly my point." I remind her. "You also almost got us kicked out of our hotel in the Bahamas for having sex with the cabana boy while he was supposed to be working."

"At least I got laid. You, on the other hand, finished *The Corrections* and a book of poetry."

I could argue that I let loose and got my hair corn-rowed by the locals, but I do not go there, because when Vee is drunk, which is often, you have as much chance of changing her mind as you would a tree stump's.

Paige, a happily married workaholic screenwriter who took up knitting with us to quit smoking, admits that she would love to know more about porn, but she's too busy to look into it and would not know where to start.

"The guys I've been dating are really into it," Vee tells us, steering the conversation back to her.

"How old is the newest guy?" asks Tricia, a music executive and an optimistic cynic when it comes to men.

"He's nineteen . . ." Vee says nonchalantly, then breaks into a grin, " . . . or he will be in a couple of months."

"I have eyeliner older than that," I tease her. Not that we aren't used to her dating younger guys; she's been doing this since her ex left her for a younger woman last fall. But this is the youngest by far. When it comes down to it, we are all happy for her; she's never looked better, and I think a few of us might even be envious of the sex she's having.

Vee, who has a one-track mind, shoves her yarn back in her bag and turns to me. "Back to porn. Haven't you ever wondered how a good girl can have bad girl sex?"

"Honestly," I reply, "what I'm wondering is why a good girl would *want* to have bad girl sex."

"You're such a goody two-shoes," laughs Vee.

"Great. Now you're on Greg's side and think I'm pornophobic."

"I'm just saying you are definitely a good girl when it comes to anything having to do with sex."

"Hey, I never said I was anti-sex, just anti-porn," I remind her.

"Yeah, it's not like Ayn's some Pollyanna saving herself for marriage," remarks Tricia.

"No. But she was the last of us to lose her virginity," adds Vee, who then demands to know, "When Greg asked you how many guys you've had sex with, did you or did you not add a digit?"

I just glare at her. Truth is, I was tempted to add a digit, but did not.

Maya, who is an assistant to a hot Hollywood producer (I'll call him Mr. X) known for his sexual escapades—which include hitting on Maya—nudges me. "You know, if you just admit you're curious, maybe Vee will shut up."

"Here, I'll start first," Vee announces as she prepares her third margarita, leaving out all of the ingredients except the tequila. "What I really want to know is how I can get my uptight boss a hooker if I only have two hundred dollars to spend."

Tricia jumps in. "How can I get my uptight *brother* a hooker if I only have fifty dollars to spend?"

"Wait a minute! Why would either of you even think of doing that?"

Vee looks at me, shaking her head. "See? Only a good girl like you would ask that."

Paige jumps in. "I want to know where guys hide their porn."

"My ex told me that he and his home boys have this thing they call 'Box of Porn,'" Vee announces. "It is actually a box of porn. You know, dirty magazines and videos, and every time one of them gets in a serious relationship they pass it off to someone who is single for safekeeping. When we divorced, they had to give it back to Andres."

Maya, who is a good girl like me when it comes to sex, tells us that Mr. X paid his last girlfriend to attend a blow-job seminar, then she confesses, "I came this close to signing up myself."

As I start to wonder how one would know if they sucked at giving blow jobs, I notice that the girls are all staring at me, as if they're part of some planned intervention to get me to admit I have a problem.

I down my drink and shout, "Okay, okay, I want to know more about porn!"

And then it all comes flooding out. "I want to know what guys really do at strip clubs. I want to walk into a sex store without feeling like a pervert. Are there hookers for women? What exactly is erotica? Will Internet porn turn me on? Is an orgasm really better with a vibrator?"

"Hey, you should write about this!" Paige intones. "Not that your 'timeless' period novel you've been writing for the last ten years isn't amazing, but it might be cool to write a book about something women like us really want to read."

Porn-to-Do

1. Visit a strip club

2. Watch Porn

3. Read erotica

4. Throw a sex-toy party

5. Visit a sex store

6. Enroll in blow-job seminar

7. Test vibrators

8. Read a Dirty Magazine

9. Consult a Sex Expert

10. Where do men hide their porn?

11. Check out a brothel

12. Meet a porn star

"Oooh, you can call it *The Good Girl's Guide to Porn*," shouts Vee.

"I love that title!" squeals Maya. Actually I do, too, but I don't admit it.

"You'll be like our own private spy," Tricia adds. "On a reconnaissance mission to find out why men are so obsessed with porn."

"How about, *Everything You Always Wanted to Know about Porn, But Were too Afraid to Ask*," I joke.

They laugh because that *is* funny and catchy.

Then in unison, we hold up our glasses and shout: "*Porn and the City!*"

At home, still buzzed, I defiantly decide to give porn a chance. I consider all of the things that meet the definition of porn, and happen to be legal, that I am curious about and I make, what else, a list.

I find Greg and hand him my newest list. He reads it and looks up at me, curious—an expression I have not seen on him in a long time.

"Are you drunk?" he asks. I am, but I shake my head no.

"Then what is this?"

"That's my 'Porn-to-Do' list."

Reading off the list, he recites with incredulity, "'Test vibrators'?"

Proud of myself, I answer, "Yep. Keep reading."

"You're going to meet a porn star? Is this some kind of joke?"

"No, I'm curious as to what they do and I'm going to find out."

"You're going to do all of these things? Yeah, right."

"Right." I say with a calm smile, but I'm thinking, *I'll show you!*

I take the list back and head to the living room, where I stare at the stacks of notes and printed pages on my desk that are the manuscript of my period novel, *La Dama*. And then, stack-by-stack, I box up a decade of writing and reflections until the top of the desk is completely cleared off.

Something about this feels really good. Maybe it is about time I tackle a new personal project, and with this one I have something to prove to Greg and to myself. With The Naughty Knitters as my sherpas, plenty more cocktails ahead to sustain me, and good ol' curiosity, I am excited to begin my next journey: *The Good Girl's Guide to Porn*.

WORLDWIDE ANNUAL PORN REVENUE

EXCEEDS $97 BILLION

Source: Internet Filter Review "from sources including Google, PBS, MSNBC, NRC, and WordTracker."

Chapter Two
You Glow, Girl

Cliterature: *n. erotic reading material used by women for masturbation*

It is eleven o'clock at night. I haven't done this in a long time—and it would be a lot more comfortable in bed—but for some reason I do not want Greg to know about this guilty little pleasure in which I am about to engage, so I have locked myself in my bathroom with the lights turned down low.

I am, of course, a little nervous that I might moan uncontrollably or shriek out loud with pleasure, but it should only take a few minutes, and when I really think about it, there's not much of a chance Greg will hear me: HE has fallen asleep on the sofa again, still gripping his Xbox control, and his snoring will surely drown out the sound of anything I might be doing.

Before I start, I look at what I have smuggled into the bathroom and marvel at how something as simple as stress-eating an enormous slice of coconut custard pie with an irresistible half-inch-thick graham cracker crust can make me forget the latest conflict with Greg—now officially known as *The Porn War*.

As I raise the first forkful to my mouth, I have a moment of guilt and consider just smearing the custard directly onto my thighs, since that is obviously where it and all of the chocolate croissants from my favorite French bakery, Le Provence, end up anyway. The fact is that my bottom half, never my better half, feels so out of shape lately that the last time I looked in the mirror I thought I was at a carnival funhouse. In other words, I feel as sexy as a slug, so porn, with its promises of "sexual excitement" has its work cut out for it.

After I lick off every last delicious graham cracker crumb and coconut flake from the plate—yes, I do moan out loud with pleasure—part of me entertains telling Greg that I was kidding about the whole investigating porn thing. *What was I thinking? Porn and the City?* I am a self-avowed good girl and Harvard grad who dreams of winning a Pulitzer; I am no Carrie Bradshaw. The proof? I do not drink Cosmopolitans (or any other pink beverages), I do not own a pair of Manolo Blahnik shoes (and wouldn't obsess over them if I did), and I do not have a neurotic relationship with my boyfriend (well, not most of the time).

But deep down, I *am* curious and I do not want to give into my fears or Greg's lowly assumptions about me. Also there is nothing quite like being peer-pressured into porn. Since our session of porn confessions, The Naughty Knitters have been egging me on in their own unique fashion: Vee sent me an encouraging message via a male stripper, who happened to take off his "policeman's uniform," despite my blushing protests, not just for me, but for Mrs. Splaver, my eighty-four-year-old neighbor, who was having our weekly tea with me at the time. Tricia sent flowers delivered with a giant Mylar penis balloon, which she was amused to find through the yellow pages. Paige sent me two adult videos, *Romancing the Bone* and *Shaving Private Ryan*, which she has never seen, but wants me to watch and tell her about. And Maya sent me a gift certificate she got online to a store called The

Pleasure Chest. She has never been, but can't wait for me to go.

I decide that if my nice girlfriends can find the time to be naughty, I can be naughty, too. I'll ease my way into porn, and the first thing I will tackle on my Porn-to-Do list will be reading erotica, which meets the definition of porn in that it's "designed to cause sexual excitement." I figure it's probably the least intimidating place to start my journey.

Of course, I will not mention to my book club that I am reading erotica. The group, which consists of five fellow Harvard alumni and one Yalie, consider, with few exceptions, anything less than a thousand pages to be fluff fiction. Needless to say, they are not aware that I subscribe to *Star* magazine, and I doubt they would ever read something titled *The Good Girl's Guide to Porn*. ("Chick lit," even if it is Ivy League chick lit, is the self-professed bane of their existence.)

I've also never confessed to them that there may have been more than one Sunday on which I've "glanced at" the Q&A section of *Parade* magazine.

Not sure where to start, I do a search for "erotica" on Amazon.com and get 775 results. Obviously I do not have time to read 775 erotica entries. I jot down the top five titles and head to the bookstore.

I end up at Brentanos, a smaller bookstore in Century City where I am less likely to run into someone I know. I don't know why, but I pretend that I am there for some real literature first. I pick up David Foster Wallace's magnum opus *Infinite Jest*, which is 1,088 pages, weighs 2.8 pounds, and has more than 400 footnotes (I know this because I bought and read it a month ago), Thomas Pynchon's *Mason & Dixon* (1.5 pounds and 784 pages, which I have also already read), and a non-fiction book—so that I look well-rounded—by Michio Kaku titled *Quantum Field Theory* (2.7 pounds, 808 pages). I'd rather not lug pounds of books around while I search for the erotica section, but the books in hand are the visual proof for anyone who happens to catch me browsing erotica that I am not a horny slut. I hate to stereotype, but I think it's safe to say that most horny sluts do not read David Foster Wallace, and they are certainly not interested in the sub-atomic phenomena and quantum chromodynamics that are covered in Kaku's work. The problem is the books are really heavy, and because I have to keep shifting them around so that my arms don't go numb, and I accidentally yell out like a banshee when I drop *Infinite Jest* on my foot, I end up drawing more attention to myself.

When I do find the erotica section, I momentarily put my other books down on the adjacent shelf (gay/lesbian literature) and quickly grab the five erotica titles I came for. Ordinarily, I would browse any book I am thinking about purchasing, but I don't in this case because part of me is worried that the erotica might give me the female equivalent of a hard-on in the middle of the bookstore, which would make me feel like a nymphomaniac.

At the register, I plop down my stack of books with the erotica paperbacks at the bottom of the stack, hoping that the cashier, a big guy with little affect, will just robotically scan everything without noticing the covers, but as soon as he scans *Five-Minute Erotica*, he pauses on the cover, which is a kinky photo of the bottom half of a woman in high heels as she removes a lacy blue g-string from beneath her mini skirt. He gives me the once over. I don't see it because I can't bring myself to look him in the eyes, but I can feel it. I am being judged. When he looks back at the books by Wallace, Pynchon, and Kaku, I do see his expression. He looks at me with one eyebrow raised. Out of the corner of my eye, I can feel the other cashier checking out my titles, too. *Great. Now, people don't just think I am kinky and horny and possibly a nymphomaniac because I am buying five erotica books, they think I'm chicken, too, because I am trying to hide the erotica by distracting everyone with my super smart books. I am a kinky, horny, nymphomaniac chicken slut.* I can only hope that my face does not look as red and hot as it feels. As if it helps matters, I snatch my receipt from the cashier and blurt out, "It's for research."

When I return with my pile of books, Greg checks them out and asks, "Does the Yawn Squad"—that's what he calls my book club—"know you're reading smut?"

"It's not smut," I answer and hold up one of the books, *Best American Erotica 2005*. "Jane Smiley has a piece in here—and, FYI, since I doubt *Barely Legal* includes book reviews, Smiley is a Pulitzer Prize–winning author."

Before I even finish my sentence, I am struck by the realization that I am standing up for porn. I quickly shake away the thought and take my erotic books over to my corner of the living room like a prizefighter going to his corner of the ring before the next round.

I feel slightly awkward reading erotic literature in the middle of the day and wonder how I should go about it. Should I lie down? Maybe pour a glass of wine, light some candles. In the end, I nix the wine because all I have on hand is cheap cooking wine, and pass on the candles, which seem like a weird idea in broad daylight anyway, and end up just lying on the sofa to read

A.N. Roquelaure's *The Claiming of Sleeping Beauty*. I am kind of excited about this one, because A.N. Roquelaure is a pseudonym for Anne Rice, the best-selling author of the much more mainstream *The Vampire Chronicles*.

The Claiming of Sleeping Beauty, which is the first book in a trilogy, is elegantly written, but, *Whoa!* The prince does not just kiss Sleeping Beauty to wake her, "He thrusts his sex into her," in a very un-fairytale-like manner (can anyone say rape?). Important note: Beauty is only fifteen years old!

Greg walks in while I am reading and asks how the erotica is. For some reason I am compelled to lie. "Great," I tell him.

"Then why are you cringing?"

I want to tell him I am cringing because when he asked his question, the main character was being subjected to the phallus-like handle of a whip being shoved up her anus. But I don't, because I don't want him to think I am being uptight.

The next night I have given up on reading erotica, which would mean that I have given up on my Porn-to-Do list, which would prove that he was right: I am pornophobic. My first clue that Greg is trying to sabotage me is that he has rented a rom-com. (I love a good romantic comedy. Greg once said that he would rather have his eyes pecked out by chickens than watch a rom-com with me.) My second clue is that he is suggesting that we cook an elaborate gourmet dinner from *Saveur* magazine. (I have been known to spend days preparing a five-course French dinner for fun; Greg has been known to eat TV dinners for five days in a row.)

His attempts to distract me only make me decide to go all out. I pick up *Five-Minute Erotica: 35 Passionate Tales of Sex and*

Seduction, which promises on its back cover to be an anthology that is at once "frisky and adventuresome, yet introspective and celebratory." It also guarantees that it will jump-start my libido, whether I share the tales with my lover or keep them my "sly little secret."

I draw a bubble bath, light some candles, and open a bottle of imported French wine that I bought for the special occasion. The first story is literally one page long and is a lot like sex with Greg; I can barely figure out what is going on before it is over.

There are several stories with protagonists who are middle-aged husbands and wives who have let themselves go, which is a big turn-off because I do not want to be reminded of reality (I've spent plenty of days letting myself go) and its mediocre sex. One of the stories, "Bad Kitty," even makes me feel embarrassed for the female protagonist, as it explicitly details a husband coming home and finding his wife dressed in a kitty costume, *purring* and *meowing* as she snuggles against him. The snuggles quickly turn to grinding until it builds to the point at which her husband gets so turned on, he starts—excuse my language—fucking her doggy style, or, more accurately, *kitty* style.

I have to admit I do get uncomfortable in a few of the stories, especially when they refer to body parts—*what the hell is a "mons"?**—such as "pussy," "cunt," and "anus" as easily as I use definite articles and pronouns.

Maybe I am uncomfortable because growing up, my father, an old fashioned Navy chief and Catholic who doesn't believe sex

---

*n. A protuberance of the human body, especially that formed by the pubic bones.

should be talked about (especially by daughters), never used the real words for sex-related body parts. In fact I wouldn't be surprised if he has never used the word "vagina" in his life. When we were kids, vagina was always "front fanny," my brother's penis was a "pee-pee," and "bopo" was the only word for butt. So, if my father were writing a passage for "Bad Kitty" it might read like this, *"I feel my pee-pee stirring as she wriggles her kitty bopo back and forth high in the air. . . . I turn her over and she claws at me with a loud hissssss, until I thrust my pee-pee into her front fanny."* You get the idea.

I start another story, which is a period piece that takes place during the Salem witch hunts. It quickly draws me in, as the witch hunt turns into a *cunt hunt*, and a young Puritan woman loses her virginity to a handsome man whose job is to strip-search her and scour her body for marks of the devil. I find myself wanting to turn the pages faster until Greg knocks on the door.

"Your dad's on the phone," he shouts from the other side.

"Can't you tell him I'm busy?"

"I did. He really wants to talk to you."

Ugh. "Fine. Come in."

Greg enters the bathroom and looks bemused at the sight of my bubble bath, the candles everywhere, and my half-drunk glass of wine. I guess it does look like I'm on the set of a Showtime after-hours series.

I grab the phone from Greg and hear my dad's voice on the other end.

"Hey, honey, Greg said you're reading. That's great. I always used to tell you kids reading is good for you."

Please don't ask me what I'm reading.

"So, what are you reading?" asks Dad.

"Oh, nothing you'd be interested in."

"You sure? I'm looking for a new book. It's official: I have now read every novel written by Tom Clancy, Richard North Patterson, and Robert Ludlum."

"Hey, Dad, you're calling past nine o'clock." He is usually in bed by now. "It must be kind of important."

"I was just wondering if you could tell your mom to stop telling people that I'm *retarded*."

"*What?*" This perplexes me because although my parents have recently filed for divorce, after 35 years of marriage, Mom is not the bitter type. "Wait a minute, Dad." Once I think about it, it starts to make sense. Mom—who is Chinese—has still not mastered the pronunciation of the letter "R," and for some reason I am the one in our family who is best at figuring out the mispronunciations in Mom's otherwise perfect English. "Dad, she's been telling people you're '*retired*.' It just comes out sounding like 'retarded.' You know, it's like that time when she asked if Greg could get her two *aspirin* and he brought her back two scoops of *ice cream*."

After a second, Dad agrees. "That would explain a lot."

I look over at Greg. He is sitting on the toilet, pants around his ankles, while reading my erotica. "Hey, Dad, can I call you back?"

I hang up and steal my book back from Greg. "What are you doing?"

"This is hot," announces Greg.

"Get out!"

"Are you turned on?"

"I was just talking to my father and you're using the toilet—I hope you're really just going number one—a foot away from my face. So, no, I am not exactly turned on right this minute. Can I please get back to my reading?"

"Fine." He leaves me alone, but the mood has been completely broken, and now my bath is cold.

The next day, I find that the stories and all of their sexuality have slowly seeped into my consciousness in unexpected ways. *Who knew that an ordinary trip to the grocery store could be so erotic?*

As I search for the items on my grocery list, I find myself drawn to other items as if I am seeing them for the first time. The bananas and cucumbers are especially provocative. And, when I reach for the whipped cream, I catch myself fantasizing about the hot guy standing next to me spraying it all over my body. When I see Vaseline, I think "lubricant," and as I walk down the ice cream aisle I notice my nipples getting hard and I feel turned on—and for once, not embarrassed.

I rush home, my bags filled with way more bananas and cucumbers than I could ever possibly need, so that I can read more erotica.

With the whole place to myself, I get comfortable on the sofa and read another story from *Five-Minute Erotica* titled "Subway." The story is about two strangers on a subway. The female heroine accidentally falls, for the second time, into the lap of a male stranger as the subway comes to another sudden stop between stations and the lights go out.

I like how the author describes the situation: *"The stranger's hands currently holding her waist, seemed to pause . . . Even through her skirt she could feel his obvious excitement . . . She hadn't been feeling very attractive of late, and this evidence of his lust left her . . . quite excited . . . She took one of his hands and, very deliberately (and before she could chicken out) placed it on one full breast. The other hand she nudged downward. . . secretly hoping he would get the hint."*

The stranger does get the hint, and the story builds nicely to the point where they are having sex, wishing it could last forever while at the same time fearing that the lights might come on suddenly and reveal their indiscretion to the other passengers.

I finish *Five-Minute Erotica*, put on my pajamas, and curl up in bed to read *Best American Erotica 2005*. By the time I get to the second story, I sense that something different—something even sexier—is going on here. Sometimes the writing is so good it is distracting; I find myself admiring the writing more than paying attention to the plot. Even though the plot usually, in the case of stories with female protagonists, goes something like: Woman feels detached, woman meets male stranger, woman gets laid. Or, in the case of the male protagonist: Man is feeling horny, man goes out with buddies, man ends up getting it on with buddy's female friend or buddy's two female friends.

I finish the entire book, accidentally skipping dinner to do so. As I put the book down at around 10 that night, I think, *Oh, crap, my period's started*. Then, just as I find a pad, I realize I had my period a week ago. Which means I am actually wet, as in turned on. *Should I wake Greg up?* I can hear him snoring in the bedroom. *God, I hope he remembered not to sleep on the new pillow shams. He ruined the old ones by doing that.*

Then I realize the reason erotica books must be small and paperback: They are obviously made to be held with one hand so that your other hand is free to masturbate. I turn the light down low and flip back to a couple of passages I had earmarked (without realizing at the time that I had done so).

I start to fantasize about myself in place of the protagonist in one particular story, which in this case means I am dressed to the nines in black leather. (Of course, I am much thinner and taller in my fantasy.) Visiting a sex club in Paris, I meet a good-looking and kind stranger who treats me to—what else?—fantastic sex. I don't even need to finish the story. My imagination completely takes over and within minutes I am grinding against a pillow between my legs, without even touching myself.

I get so turned on I feel like I am going to come at any moment. I feel lightheaded and increase the pressure between my legs. And I do come—in dizzying gasps!

Wow, reading really is *good for you!*

For the first time in a long time, I shut off the light and fall to sleep with a smile on my face.

The next night, Greg catches on when I turn down an invitation to get Italian ice cream with him.

"What do you mean you don't want a chocolate gelato?" He says this like I just refused something that I can't live without, like air or a car in Los Angeles.

"I told you, I'm too tired to go out." I'm lying, because all I really want to do is curl up in bed again and reread some of the stories in *Best American Erotica*.

"Okay, what the hell is going on?" He scrutinizes me. "You're glowing. Did you find a chocolate stash?"

"*You* can't even find a chocolate stash," I remind him.

Whoever lives with me takes on the responsibility of hiding any leftover chocolate or other equally bad goodies, so that I do not eat said leftovers, e.g. an entire bag of Oreos or M&Ms, or two-thirds of a Miss Grace's Lemon bundt cake all at once. (Carb bingeing is surprisingly easy to do when you work three feet away from your own kitchen.)

The problem with Greg having this responsibility is that he hides things too well. So well, in fact, that most of the time when I do need a chocolate fix, he can't remember where he hid the goods. Which means two things: First, I end up making a midnight run to 7-Eleven to buy more goodies that he will have to hide once again. And second, I am constantly finding the stashes when I am not looking for them; a few weeks ago while vacuuming under the sofa, I sucked up an entire bag of Reese's Pieces. Another time I found a piece of moldy pound cake behind the VCR.

"It's the *porn!*" he practically shouts.

"What are you talking about?" I play innocent.

"You've been totally nice to me, which usually means you've had a great orgasm or you've eaten your weight in chocolate. Except we haven't had sex this week, and you couldn't possibly reach the Ding-Dongs I hid in the attic. . . . Which means you've been *masturbating!*"

"Can you shout that any louder?" I whisper, bummed that he's onto me. "I don't think Mrs. Splaver across the street and her four-year-old grandson heard you."

"What do you like about it?" he asks with more earnestness in his voice than I've heard in a long time. Unfortunately, because he generally shows such a lack of interest in anything I like, we have considered breaking up several times during the last year. But at this moment, I ignore thoughts of our inevitable breakup because he looks so enthusiastic.

So enthusiastic that I give up keeping the erotica my "sly little secret" and decide to be generous and share.

I start to tell him about the stories, in general terms first. Then as I get more comfortable and see that he is not looking to make fun of me, I loosen up and describe in detail some of my favorite stories.

Ten minutes later, we are having sex!

And it's good sex, simultaneous orgasms included, which is surprising because we didn't even engage in any foreplay. It's as if the erotica, whether I am reading it to myself or retelling it to Greg, is a substitute for foreplay and succeeds in turning me on just as well.

The next night, I actually make up my own erotica. I call it *literotica*, and share it with Greg. We have sex again—that's two days in a row! I realize weaving my own story is even more of a turn-on than retelling someone else's erotica because I am in complete control of the images. I can use the words of my choosing (for instance "mons," "pussy," and "clit" are words that do not appear in my stories; "front fanny" is also not used), and I direct what's going on. It's like getting to have sex exactly the way you want it.

Who would've predicted that porn could cure my recurrent SADD? Someone should tell those Pfizer scientists that they can stop spending billions creating female Viagra. I've found it and it's name is erotic literature.

In the last week I have had more sex with Greg than we have had in the last six months. Greg, of course, is thrilled and assigns the vast improvements in our sex life to something *he* is doing, even though he is actually doing *less* (hard to imagine) than he has ever done before. Even at the beginning of our relationship, foreplay to Greg consisted of turning on a red lava lamp and stripping down to his plaid boxers and dress socks. As I write out my tasks for tomorrow, I find myself excited, not at all reluctant now, about tackling the next item on my Porn-to-Do list.

NINE MILLION
BRITISH MEN
–ALMOST 40 PER CENT OF
THE MALE POPULATION –
USED PORNOGRAPHIC
WEBSITES LAST YEAR,
COMPARED WITH AN
ESTIMATED TWO MILLION
IN 2000

Source: Nielsen NetRatings for the Independent on Sunday

Chapter Three
An Anthro*porn*ologist on Mars

Anthropornologist: *n. one who studies the culture of human beings in relation to porn*

Once Greg hears that strip clubs are next on my Porn-to-Do list, he suddenly becomes supportive of my writing and research. He even selflessly offers to escort me on all research trips to strip clubs! Not that he isn't ordinarily well meaning, it's just that his new attitude is ironic because when I was trying to review kitchen appliances for *Ladies' Home Journal*, he made it very clear that he shouldn't interfere with my work.

So, we decide that after our obligatory monthly dinner with my mother, we'll check out a few strip clubs (sans mother).

Having dinner with Mom nowadays means visiting her at Tomiko, the restaurant she owns and manages, which happens to be one of the largest and most popular sushi bars and Japanese fusion restaurants in San Diego. Mom, who opened the restaurant when she was fifty-five—when most women are contemplating retirement—was supposed to open a small, quaint café that seated maybe ten people. This would fulfill her love of cooking and her entrepreneurial drive and not be too taxing on her or the family. But, no, my mom goes for the restaurant that seats 110. It also would have been a more natural choice for Mom to open a Chinese restaurant, but as she put it, "Mark up on Toro better than mark up on chow mein." To customers, she is the charming, graceful, Asian lady; her restaurant is a beautiful serene place that overlooks the Pacific Ocean and caters to celebrity actors and athletes who visit the nearby La Costa Resort & Spa for a relaxing weekend or a professional tennis or golf tournament. Anna Kournikova, Tiger Woods, and Geena Davis have all eaten there recently. What Anna, Tiger, Geena, and others do not know is that behind the scenes, Mom is like a hummingbird on crack. If you were to look up the word *micromanage* in the dictionary, there very well may be a picture of Mom there. On any given night, Mom, who is all of five feet tall and ninety-eight pounds, has been known to serve as hostess (because she doesn't like how the hired hostess is greeting people), cook (because one of the chefs is not julienn'ing the carrots at precisely the right angle), and bus tables (because the busboys are not working fast enough) all in one night.

Not helping matters is the fact that Japanese male sushi chefs (she employs six of them) have a few issues with taking orders from a woman, especially a Chinese woman. Waiters have been caught stealing sake glasses and frequently don't show up when the waves are good. Most of the kitchen chefs and maintenance workers are Hispanic, and, like Mom, English is their second language, so a lot gets lost in translation. For example, last week Mom told Armando, who was a little behind on cleaning the restaurant before the doors opened, that she was going to help him by doing the vacuuming. Only when Armando's face turned beet red did she realize he probably did not understand her. It turns out that when Mom (who tends to leave the last consonant off of hard-to-pronounce words and gets her f's and v's mixed up) said, "I am going to vacuum," Armando thought she said, "I am going to fuck you."

As if all of that is not enough to drive anyone insane, Mom has also chosen to make the business a family affair—a dysfunctional family affair. My younger brother (who has quit, quite dramatically, three times this year) and cousin work (okay, argue is more like it) as managers, my uncle and aunt prep food in the kitchen, and my sister gets sucked in on weekends to fill in for whoever calls in sick. Okay, I get sucked in too, but because I live two hours away, I don't get sucked in as often.

Needless to say, for me personally, having dinner at Tomiko is about as relaxing as sitting through a tax audit in front of a live audience. But the food is always fantastic. On this paticular night Mom insists on making us a multi-course authentic Chinese dinner—did I mention that food equals affection when you are Chinese?

As we eat dinner in a corner table that is shielded from the rest of the restaurant with *shoji* screens, Mom, who just seated a couple before returning to us, sits down and starts rolling spring rolls. As she wraps rice paper around a spoonful of shrimp and vegetable filling, she smiles as she watches Greg, who is eating much faster than usual. The fact that she is smiling would not be strange, except for the fact that my mom does not really like Greg. She "cannot trust him" she has said, because he can't tolerate spicy food; everyone in our family prefers food so spicy it makes you sweat, and we are known to eat hot peppers whole, yet we are surprised each time one of us is diagnosed with acid reflux. Greg also embarrasses Mom when we go to Chinese restaurants with her, and he orders spicy Kung Pao chicken, but asks the chef to make it mild and without the peanuts, which, as Mom puts it, is like ordering a pepperoni pizza then asking them to leave off the pepperoni. But she gets back at him in her own way: Whenever he asks a waitress if the food is MSG-free, Mom tells them in Chinese to just lie to him if they do use it. You see, she is a traditionalist when it comes to Chinese food—if a restaurant tells her they do not use MSG, she just rolls her eyes. According to Mom, when we were growing up, she used MSG in every meal she ever made us and we turned out all right. Well, except for that ADD thing.

Although Mom takes it as a sign that he is enjoying her food, I happen to know that Greg's faster-than-usual consumption of his food tonight is not because he is enjoying the Kung Pao-less chicken, moo shu (heavy on the MSG), and hot pepper (as in you'll be sorry tomorrow) pork Mom has prepared for us; more likely is that it has something to do with where we are going after dinner. Ordinarily, I would be annoyed by his rushing, but tonight I am okay with it because I am not exactly in the mood to talk to Mom about what I am up to lately—*oh, just reading a little porn, masturbating here and there . . . and you, Mom?* Fortunately, I don't have to worry about her asking me what I am currently writing about because she never does that. I count on both of my parents being uninterested in the specifics of my life. They just want to know that I am writing and—this is the important part—getting paid for it. For once, this lack of interest on their part is especially welcome. That way, I do not have to confess to them that their first-born daughter is doing things like scouring Internet porn and trying to get an appointment at a brothel just so that she can write about it for her porn-curious girlfriends.

"So, what are you writing about now?" Mom asks, awkwardly.

I almost choke on my vegetable moo shu. *She is picking* now *to turn over a new leaf?* This new behavior must be a result of the divorce. Her relationship with Dad is being redefined, and I guess I should not be surprised that our relationship will be redefined, too. I mean, I appreciate that she has always shown me a lot of love and support (food, money, food) in her own way, but her showing an interest in what I actually write and do is something I am not prepared for.

For a second, I fool myself into thinking I can make the project sound scholarly, worthy of two masters' degrees and a nightmarish student loan debt to Harvard, by calling myself an anthro*porno*logist. Instead I dance around the subject, which only makes me feel guilty and immature.

I briefly contemplate inviting Mom to go with us to a strip club. After all, she obviously needs her libido stimulated. After thirty-five years of marriage that has ended in divorce, she has, in essence, declared that she doesn't need sex (and she means for the rest of her life). Some porn might be just what she needs. I try to imagine what our excursion might be like. A sort of *Joy Luck Club* meets *Girls Gone Wild* experience? Maybe Mom will let loose, jump on stage, and twirl around the pole proudly exposing her post-post-menopausal boobs, singing, "I'm your freak," except it will sound like "I'm your *fweak*."

On second thought, maybe not. I tell Mom that I am writing about men and relationships, which is not entirely untrue.

During the car ride to the cheapest strip club we can find, I become a total chatterbox, which is extremely unlike me. Probably because I feel like I am about to be de-virginized, and I am half-curious, half-frightened about seeing actual live people do pornographic things. Reading porn is one thing—some people even consider erotica an art form—but seeing live people in live pornographic acts is another. It's as if the *pornophobic* part of me believes that there is no going back to being a respectable feminist after this.

We end up at a low-end topless club known as The Purple Church. (The building was actually used as a church before its present incarnation.) Since it is designated as a topless club, strippers must keep their bottoms on at all times and patrons must be twenty-one or older because alcohol is served on the premises.

As soon as we enter The Purple Church, the ex-Catholic in me is tempted to dip my hand into someone's abandoned martini glass and make the sign of the cross. The place is nothing like the strip clubs you see in the movies. There is no laughing, whooping, or cheering. It is actually kinda quiet, kinda dark, and kinda creepy.

I start to think that maybe men are not merely alien to us women, but they actually are aliens (as in literally from Mars), which would be a great explanation as to why they are so different from us in large and meaningful ways. To begin with, the place is as cold as one would imagine Mars. I find myself wishing I had brought a ski jacket or worn long johns. It's totally obvious that the women who work there are freezing, too. Nipples bursting through T-shirts like polar ice caps are my first clue. However, looking around, I see that most of the men do not seem to notice (that is, they do not seem to notice the extreme cold; the nipples bursting through T-shirts they definitely notice) and that Greg is actually perspiring. When Greg suggests that it's better not to blow my journalistic cover by complaining to management, I quickly get that I'm alone in my concern about the temperature.

Feeling a little conspicuous being the only female customer in a room of thirty or so men, I lead Greg to a seat behind the other patrons just as the main event is about to start. "I'm too Sexy for my Shirt," blares over cheap speakers, and two strippers, China and Asia, billed as identical twins, strut on stage wearing only G-strings and bikini tops (four sizes too small for their balloon-like breasts, I might add). First observation: The twins look nothing alike. Second observation: They both have visible cellulite on their thighs. I am very pleased. Funny how little things like this can put a girl at ease. Third observation: Greg does not notice or celebrate cellulite flaws as do I. *Disappointing*.

Two minutes into the show, I am feeling less nervous. It's clear I won't be turned on at all. What is billed as erotic is anything but. Normally, I'd be embarrassed for performers who are *under*-performing, but in this case I get the feeling China and Asia are not all that concerned about their next employee performance review. I've seen better dance moves at bat mitzvahs.

I begin to wonder: Didn't these girls watch Demi Moore in *Striptease*, Jennifer Beals in *Flashdance*, whatshername in *Showgirls*?

"Where's the heart? The creativity?" I lean over and whisper to Greg assuming he must be thinking the same thing.

Without taking his eyes off the stage he whispers back, "Can we not analyze *everything*?"

Well, yeah, I think to myself, except now I really want to analyze what he just meant by that.

I decide to show Greg that I can be "in the moment." I move up so that I am right in front of the stage, so close my knees are practically touching it, with a handful of regulars. Part of me wonders if I just committed a big faux pas. The men all glance my way. The two guys in cheap business suits seem to look at me with suspicion for a minute—*could they be wondering if their wives sent me to spy on them?*—then let it go and turn back to the striptease. The clean-cut frat-looking guys in their twenties barely seem to notice me. And the bespectacled Asian man who looks like he could be my fifty-year-old uncle Yuen Mai takes out a plastic comb and glides it across the eleven or so hairs on his head as he scrutinizes me for a few seconds. The fact that he reminds me of my uncle amuses me, and to help me relax I imagine what uncle Yuen Mai would be doing if he were here. He would pull out a bamboo back scratcher—he's been known to do this at restaurants, funerals, and reportedly during sex with my aunt—and scratch away.

As the song comes to an end, dancers Asia and China, who are now topless, come around to the edge of the stage, bending down so that customers can place folded dollar bills and fives in their G-strings. I turn my back to the stage to pretend that I am talking to Greg, but Greg has turned away to pretend that he is not with me. When I feel a tap on my shoulder I turn back around and all eyes are on me as the stripper, Asia, stares down at me. It turns out that anyone sitting at the front is obligated to tip.

I search for some ones in my purse, but all I find is a twenty. I fold my twenty into her G-string and then take a ten and five ones out of the other side of her G-string. Asia glares at me with eyes like daggers. Okay, making change from a stripper's G-string is apparently a major faux pas, but before I even have a chance to fix the misunderstanding, Greg is leading me out the door, suggesting that it's time to try out the high-end strip club down the street.

We end up at a high-end "gentlemen's club" recommended by Greg, who claims he's never been there but "heard" it was a classy one. Right away, I am impressed that they have a valet parking service.

The cover charge per person is $20, but Greg whips out a coupon (!) he cut out from the back of the local weekly. I stare at him in shock.

"What? It's half-price with this," he says defensively.

This from the person who rolls his eyes every time I whip out my stack of coupons at the grocery store. Stupid me. Apparently the one place in the world where men are not embarrassed to use coupons is strip clubs. I just shake my head and let it go.

This gentlemen's club is called Bare Elegance, and because it is an all-nude strip club, dancers can take off tops *and* bottoms. As soon as we enter, I notice that, again, I am the only female customer, and I feel kind of awkward because many of the "gentlemen" (the porn industry obviously uses the term loosely) are still teenagers. Every time one of the pubescent pimple-faced boys glances back at me, I can't help but think he must feel like his mother just walked in on him jerking off. Suspicious that the boys are under twenty-one, I ask Greg what the age minimum is and he tells me that all-nude clubs (also known as Triple X or XXX) are permitted to allow patrons as young as eighteen to enter. It does not make sense to me that eighteen-year-olds would be turned away from a place where women only take their tops off but welcomed at clubs like this, where women take it all off. Must remember to ask the manager about this.

The place is definitely nicer than the low-end topless club. It is decorated in velvety reds, they have a full dinner menu that includes steak and fish, and there are numerous small stages with poles in the center. After my lesson at The Purple Church, we sit down way in the back.

As the first dancer arrives on stage, I observe that the dancers at the high-end club have a different look than those at the low-end club. No (obvious) boob jobs, a little more classy, i.e. less makeup, less cellulite. I don't know why, but I am deeply satisfied to be bigger busted than more than half of the women who work there.

Within seconds of the first "performance," my mind begins to wander. *Could strip clubs be old hat to me already? Why do the men have such stoic looks on their faces? Are they afraid they'll get hard ons? It's like watching* Spock* *on Strippers . . . I can't believe I made such a big deal about these places . . . Why is there a sixty-inch flat-screen TV broadcasting ESPN on mute behind a stage where a woman is taking off her clothes? Is it possible that men get bored easily, even at strip clubs? Wow, she's not a bad dancer . . . I wonder if she always wanted to be a stripper? I wonder how much weight I would have to lose if I wanted to be a stripper? . . . I bet a stripper would not have eaten that banana cream pie I had at lunch today. At least bananas are nutritious. I could have had the pecan pie, but where's the nutrition in that? I really need to buy that book on how to stay in the moment. Maybe I can rid myself of my irritating list-making tendencies. Maybe tai chi would help . . . Jeez, I really need to learn to relax . . . I should be observing this woman*

*Stoic Vulcan character from *Star Trek* TV series who grapples with his emotional human side.

who is stripping for us, not trying to remember that I should plant some perennials . . . Wait, what are perennials? Okay, plant some annuals . . . Greg is right. I need to get in the moment. STOP! Breathe, Ayn.

Just as I relax and get in the moment, the stripper on stage whips off her thong underwear. Thank God we're at least seven tables back, is all I can think, since I'm not in the mood for a close-up of female genitals. Greg, on the other hand, orders a steak, rare. One more thing I will try not to analyze.

I watch as men lay dollar bills on the chest-level rail in front of them that encircles the stage. Obviously fiscally-minded, the dancer spends more time in front of spots with the most money. Now fully nude, she approaches the tippers and waves *all* parts of her body—I still do not know exactly what a mons is, but I'm pretty sure she's waving hers—just inches from their faces.

After sitting through four dancers in a row, I find myself watching ESPN. I hate ESPN. Greg looks slightly bored, too. I am ready to leave when I notice one of the dancers exit the stage and work the crowd, asking men if they'd like a private lap dance. One guy nods, and the dancer grabs his hand, leading him up the mysterious red staircase to one of the many three-sided, semi-private booths in the mezzanine overhead.

Lap dances are fascinating and totally corroborate my men-are-aliens theory. Or, at the very least, perhaps men have been *inhabited* by aliens whose driving biological mission is to get turned on, but (ironically) not get laid. Men are not permitted to touch the lap dancers. Can this no-touch rule explain why so many men suck at foreplay? After all, aren't strip clubs the sexual training ground for young men in America? Before I can find more evidence to support my men-inhabited-by-aliens theory, I feel

Greg's arm around my shoulder and find him grinning cheekily as a dancer whispers into his ear.

"Would it help your research if I got a lap dance?" he asks me. *What a trooper.*

As the dancer leads Greg up the staircase, another dancer approaches *me* and asks if I'd like a lap dance, too. *What the hell?* In a rare throw-caution-to-the-wind moment, I decide that if I can't beat 'em, join 'em.

I am led to a booth next door to one in which Greg is already sitting, half-lying really, with his hands gripping the bars that are mounted on either side of the booth while a busty lap dancer straddles him and begins to writhe on top of him to a two-minute-long song, touching him with every part of herself but her hands. I lift my head and peek over the railing to discover that I've never seen him look so happy.

After I get in the same position, my dancer, who is not nearly as pretty up close as I thought she was, starts to do the same thing to me so that, basically, Greg and I are getting simultaneous lap dances. I absolutely hate it. If I ever wondered whether I could be a lesbian, I now have confirmation that I have no tendencies in that direction whatsoever. It is the longest two minutes of my life. Longer even than dancing to a cheesy song at your cousin's cheesy wedding with someone like your pervie uncle Marvin.

I want to just push her off and run away, but the good girl in me knows that that would be impolite, if not outright rude. As the song goes on and on, I notice my lap dancer zoning out every now and then. Could she be making a mental grocery list, too? Just when I think it would be impossible to be more uncomfortable physically or mentally, she breaks the no-touch rule and nips at my left breast with her teeth, causing me to wince and practically yell, "Ouch." *My God! Is that supposed to be sexy?* I lift myself up with a contorted back bend kind of move that makes me look like a mentally challenged gymnast and peek over the divider at Greg while my dancer still straddles me.

"Uh, I'm ready to go," I say, signaling him with my eyes to let him know that I am very uncomfortable. It's the same look I cast at him whenever we are at dinner with his very elderly mother and she starts talking about how all the "brown people" have ruined everything in California. She doesn't think this insults me because she considers me more Chinese than Mexican and, as she puts it, "Those Chinese are very smart people." Greg just gives me a dismissive "yeah, just a sec," wave of his hand without even looking at me. I stare at the smile on his face and realize that while I am in agony, he is in ecstasy.

At last, the song ends. After tipping the dancer to leave me alone in my booth, I pull myself together and spend the rest of the time observing Greg receive numerous additional lap dances, noting that men at strip clubs part with their money with ease. Especially when lap dancers pretend to *really* like them.

Can excessive lap dances be considered cheating? Why is Greg's enjoyment making me feel inadequate? Or am I jealous? She's definitely thinner, but not that much prettier than me; her dark roots are showing, and her makeup, especially the sky-blue eye shadow, is a little heavy handed... Who is this person that is getting off on a complete stranger writhing on top of him as his supposed significant other watches on? Wait... I am watching a complete stranger, who is half-naked, writing on top of my significant other. Who am I?

I continue to watch in wonder as Greg shells out $30 for each lap dance and slips numerous dollar bills to the lap dancer gyrating on top of him. I can't help but recall all of the times I had to guilt him into buying tickets to something like Cirque du Soleil or chipping in for new shams to match my duvet after he ruined my old shams. Not to mention the year it took him to finally comprehend what shams and duvets were and that shams are, yes, like pillowcases, but at $80 to $150 dollars a pop, they are pillowcases just for *looks* and are *not* to be slept or drooled on!

After watching Greg—whom frankly I, as well as The Naughty Knitters, have been having doubts about—buy three lap dances and tip the dancer the customary forty percent gratuity, I decide I could use a drink and time to ponder why the hell I am with a man who would spend good sham money so frivolously on a woman he's not even dating. Unfortunately, I am shocked to learn that the club does not serve alcohol. I am forced to buy a pineapple juice for the price of a piña colada.

I learn that in most states, all-nude strip clubs (as opposed to only topless) are not permitted to serve alcohol, which is one reason why they are permitted to allow eighteen-year-olds to patronize their establishments. This absence of alcohol is just one more thing that corroborates my theories about men and their alien origins. Why else would horny, testosterone-driven single guys put up with no drinking on a Saturday night? Maybe Alcoholics Anonymous should add strip clubs to their list of resources or, at the very least, make them the thirteenth step.

On the car ride home, there is not a word between us for the first twenty minutes, yet the whole time I am hoping Greg wants to know what I think about our porn field trip. But his silence tells me he is, as usual, not interested in what I think.

As usual, I tell him anyway.

"Well, an all-nude strip club's a great place for alcoholics to avoid falling off the wagon, but I thought the turn-on factor was kind of low ..."

"Of course you did," he replies.

I think his comment is kind of snide, but I try to give him the benefit of the doubt. "Unlike reading erotic literature, watching women strip is not interactive, but passive; it doesn't leave much to the imagination," is all I say.

"I think that's why I like it," he says. "Speaking for the male species, watching someone dance in a sweat suit, although it would leave much to my imagination, does not sound like a turn on."

If anyone else said this it might be funny. But he says it in such a way that it is patronizing to me and so clear that he wishes we did not even have to talk about it.

"You're not actually mad at me because I didn't enjoy the strip clubs?" I ask in astonishment.

"You might have enjoyed them if you weren't so frigid," he mumbles almost inaudibly.

"Frigid?" I practically yell. "I just got a freaking lap dance!"

"Yeah," he responds, "but you didn't like it."

"And that's my fault?" I do yell this time.

All he says is, "Forget it."

As if that's ever possible. And that's when it hits me: The Naughty Knitters are right. After more than two years with Greg, I am living off yesterday's orgasms. Not only does Greg lack imagination (otherwise he could muster a better argument every now and then than "forget it"), but he lacks commitment. He can't commit to a good argument, or foreplay for that matter, because he can't commit to this relationship.

"It's interesting how doing just two tasks on my Porn-to-Do list has made me realize that sex is important to me and talking about it, something you never do, turns me on," I admit. "I don't think SADD is my problem. The problem is I need to be with someone who is willing to open up and talk to me about these things."

"Are you saying I don't turn you on?" he asks, defensive.

"Not even if I were a light switch," I whisper to myself. Loud enough to hear, I tell him, "I think the issue is not that you don't turn me on, it's that you don't *try* to turn me on."

"God, it's just like you to overcomplicate this."

The rest of the ride we are silent. I can only wonder if he is thinking the same thing I am thinking: Why did we get together in the first place? I remember I was drawn to him because he said interesting things, which to me meant he thought interesting things. Only later did I realize that the two are not necessarily connected. The first night I met him, he said, "You know, if you replace the word 'God' with the word 'Truth' in the Bible it makes more sense." He would say things like that all the time. Things that were clever and really made me think. Only after we moved in together did I discover he had a little black book with lots of cool things to say in it. I could probably live with someone who had a book of cool things to say, if, unlike Greg, they actually came up with the cool things to say. In Greg's case, he just wrote down things he heard or read that other people said, and then used them like they were his own words. And, I can't deny that even before the Porn War, there were signs that we are not in love. During the first few months of dating, he would slow dance with me to Mazzy Star or Etta James right in our living room. I love dancing. Now, I am hard-pressed to get him to dance at a wedding with me. He hates The Naughty Knitters—that alone is cause for breaking up—whom he recently started referring to as The Snotty Bitters. Probably because he knows they don't think he is good enough for me. Turns out they are right.

Once we get home I can't resist asking him what he was thinking about during the car ride home. He answers, "Nothing."

Sadly, I believe him.

"What were you thinking?" he asks me.

"That it's over between us."

"What do you mean it's over?" Suddenly he wants to talk about relationship stuff.

"I'd explain, but I don't want to overcomplicate anything" is what I am tempted to say, but I really am a good girl. I sit him down on the sofa and explain that in some weird way, my exploration into porn has not only made me realize that the SADD during sex is a symptom of a bigger problem in our relationship, this porn-fueled journey has also made me realize that there may be things out there that I don't even know that I need. Before my Porn-to-Do list, I was just too inexperienced when it came to life, relationships, and sex to know otherwise. Greg is—was—my starter relationship. And, in some kooky way, looking into porn helped me see that before I invested too much of myself. In essence this porn adventure seems to be guiding me toward some self-understanding that I didn't know I was lacking.

Later, even though I know deep down that this is one of our last nights together, I do not cry into my pillow, I do not search the house for one of the secret chocolate stashes, I don't even call an emergency session of The Naughty Knitters to cry on their shoulders. As Greg, now not-so-significant other, snores on the sofa in the living room with his Xbox control still in his grip, all I feel is relief that my shams will forever be safe from his drool.

THE
FASTEST
GROWING
SEGMENT
OF
THE PORN-BUYING
AUDIENCE:
WOMEN

Source: Talk of The Nation, National Public Radio

Chapter Four

Got Porn?

A.W.O.L. (Absent Without a Life): *adj.* post-breakup stage when one shuns all social commitment and life seemingly has no meaning

It has now been a month since my breakup with Greg and, after two disastrous attempts at rebound dating, I call an emergency meeting of The Naughty Knitters to inform them that I am officially entering the post-breakup phase known as Third Wheel*. Their reaction is to Dr. Phil** me.

However, after a one-hour pep talk, they fail to convince me that being single is a powerful state of existence and that I should embrace the chance to date again. Well, everyone pep talks me except for Paige, who has set up her laptop and shamelessly grills us every few minutes for feedback on the screenplay and novel she is writing.

"What about that guy you were talking to at Monroe's last night?" asks Steve, one of my best friends from high school, who has joined us because his orgasmically-challenged girlfriend of ten years recently left him with no explanation. Steve has always been

---

*Post-breakup stage in which one is reduced to hanging out with happily bonded couples.

**v. to motivate a person by stating the ridiculously obvious in spiritual terms.

way better at stereotypical girl things such as knitting than I am, and knits circles around the rest of The Naughty Knitters, too. Ironically, in high school he was the captain of the football team. We never told anybody, but on a number of occasions he did my home ec homework (macramé plant hangers, sew aprons, bake a pie, etc.) in exchange for me doing his shop homework (build a spice rack, weld a metal photo frame, etc.). The Knitters love Steve because it is great to have a male perspective around when we are stitching and bitching about men.

"That guy was cute," Tricia declares with enthusiasm, then, after a pause, she adds, "which probably means he is stuck up."

"I don't know what happened. We were having a great conversation, I mentioned something about Harvard, and he just started looking at me like I was speaking in iambic pentameter," I tell them.

"You have been known to do that," Steve jokes.

"Only when drunk—or inspired," I reply. "Anyway, he pretty much ditched me. I saw him talking to a shiny blonde a few minutes later."

"Duh," declares Vee.

"Someone want to tell me why Vee is *duh*ing me?"

"The H Bomb," says Vee, like I should have a clue what she is talking about.

"Harvard's new on-campus porn magazine?" I read about it in the midst of my porn research. Vassar has one, too.

Tricia proceeds to explain. "She's talking about a piece they did on National Public Radio. Researchers had attractive women go to a bar and flirt with guys. Once the guys seemed really interested in the women, they instructed the women to drop the 'H bomb.' In other words, the women were told to mention to the men that they graduated from Harvard. When the women did that, within two minutes the guy would find an excuse to exit the conversation."

"Wham, bam, *no* thank you, ma'am," laughs Steve.

"When the same women did *not* drop the 'H bomb,' they usually got asked out," adds Tricia.

"God, that's depressing," I admit.

"Not if you went to State." Vee high-fives thin air.

Paige chimes in, oblivious to what we've been talking about. "Hey, what do you think about me writing a cute children's book? They're hot right now."

"Great, except you're the person who thinks, and I quote, 'All children should be incarcerated until they're old enough to vote and be useful members of society,'" I remind her.

"Oh, right." She turns back to her laptop and deletes the idea.

"I don't know why you're complaining anyway," Vee tells me. "You should've called Kale back after he took you out." Kale is the twenty-year-old friend of the nineteen-year-old Vee is currently dating. "He's really into you."

"Do you mean like he's really into paintball or like he's really into Mischa Barton from *The O.C.*?" I ask.

"Isn't Kale the guy who picked you up for a date on his skateboard?" snickers Steve.

Vee points one of her needles at me. "You said you wanted to meet someone into the environment—you don't get greener than a skateboard."

She has a point. "Look, he was really nice," I admit. "And I'm sure that in ten or so years he will be quite a catch, especially if that adolescent acne clears up, but don't you get tired of having to explain things to these guys, like Kiefer Sutherland's dad is an actor, too?"

"Kiefer Sutherland's dad is an actor?" she says with a confused look.

"Forget it, Vee."

Paige's cell rings, interrupting our conversation. It is her agent. We know this because we hear her phone so much that we all recognize the designated rings for her contact list. Her agent's ring is the theme from *Jaws*. My ring on her phone is "How Do You Solve a Problem like Maria?" from *The Sound of Music*, and her mother's ring is the scary *eeek . . . eeek . . . eeek* sound effect from *Psycho*. We are eavesdropping on her conversation when she looks up at us and asks, "Am I available this Thursday at 3 p.m.?" I grab her BlackBerry and scroll through her calendar.

"You already have lunch with your manager at two, and a story meeting with Goldie Hawn at three-thirty," I inform her.

"No problem," Paige tells her agent and then inputs it into her BlackBerry. When she's done with the call she turns to all of us, as if she has been part of our conversation all along.

"I have the perfect guy to save you from Third Wheel hell," Paige declares. I can't believe she can work, take calls, keep track of our conversation, and set me up on a date. "His name is Phil."

We all groan in unison.

"I appreciate the thought," I say, "but you already set me up with Phil once."

"Wait a minute. Are you talking about your friend Phil Johnson?" asks Maya.

"Don't feel bad. She set me up with him twice," Tricia informs Maya.

"Didn't you set him up with Bob Goodman?" Steve says.

We look at Paige for an explanation. "What? I thought maybe that was what Phil needed at that time in his life."

"Hey, what am I, chopped liver? Bob gets to go out with Phil and I don't?" whines Vee.

Paige looks right at Vee. "You were busy taking your boyfriend, DJ Max or whatever his 'street' name is, to his homecoming dance or something." To the rest of us, she says, "And you guys are way too picky. Phil is a nice guy."

"*Too* nice," Tricia, Maya, and I mumble under our breath.

"FYI, he clipped his toenails in front of me on our first date," I complain.

"So now you're turning down guys because they're into good hygiene?" Paige says, defending Phil.

"We were at a four-star restaurant." Everyone, including Paige, cracks up at this.

"Can we just make a promise that, from this point on, we do not pawn off any of our rejects or leftovers onto each other?"

We all raise our mojitos—the NK drink of the week—and shout, "Promise!"

At home, I end up staring at the box of dirty magazines that Greg left behind. I light a fire in the fireplace and start tossing them one by one into the fire. For some reason I pause on the last three. They are the Unholy Trinity of dirty magazines: *Playboy*, *Hustler*, and *Penthouse*. In a way, dirty magazines are what started me on my porn journey and on my breakup with Greg. I don't know why, but I set them aside. I pull my Porn-to-Do list off my cupboard and prepare to throw it in the fire, but I cannot do it. The reality is that I did not make the list to prove to Greg that I am not pornophobic. I made the list to prove to myself that I am not afraid of porn.

So when my brother's ex-girlfriend—still my good friend—Heather, who is eight months pregnant (Heather is constantly pregnant), asks if she and her husband, Brad, may take me on a post-break-up Pity Lunch (my words, not hers), I suggest instead that they join me on a research trip to a high-end sex store, the newest trend in the sex retail business, so that I can cross another item off my Porn-to-Do list. Heather, who is hornier than usual as a result of the pregnancy, jumps at the chance. Brad, who is not especially horny as a result of Heather's pregnancy, comes along because he is told to.

As Heather, Brad, and I (now officially a third wheel) pull up to the retail sex store known as Hustler Hollywood, I am surprised that it is not the slightest bit sleazy looking. Hustler is an upscale boutique located on a chi-chi section of famous Sunset Boulevard, right around the corner from some of Beverly Hills' toniest mansions.

I am further relieved not to feel like a slut when entering, but I do feel slightly silly being greeted by cemented handprints—at least they are *hand*prints and not other famous body parts—of Hustler founder Larry Flynt, along with Ginger Lynn's and Ron Jeremy's. For those of you new to porn like me, Lynn and Jeremy are not Hustler CEOs but top-grossing hard-core* veteran porn

---

*For video, that means penetration and ejaculation included.

stars. And, according to the friendly clerk, if I'd like to learn more about Jeremy, I can watch him on season two reruns of the TV show *The Surreal Life* and can find a life-size replica of his penis (actually, she says "cock") on a shelf in the back—all $9\frac{3}{4}$ inches, for $39.99.

Before we take on Mr. Jeremy's member in the back of the store, we decide to begin by browsing the section in the front of the store, which displays novelty items to slowly ease good girls like me into the mood. There are kitschy "Larry Flynt for President" bumper stickers and "Foreplay Samplers" that include nifty items such as warming massage lotion, chocolate body topping (yum), feminine climax cream (now we're talking), and erection prolonging cream (unfortunately the package doesn't state *how* long).

Just when I start to feel as comfortable as I do shopping at Bed, Bath & Beyond, Heather, Brad, and I split up.

Once I am alone, I look around to observe the clientele and realize that the entire store consists of couples. Mostly conservative-looking couples, sweetly (gag) holding hands as the guy gently guides his female counterpart around in a slightly patronizing but encouraging manner. *Great. Now I am third wheel to an entire store.* One of the many hip, laid-back female clerks—for the record, there are also a few bitchy-looking clerks who are not helpful—seems to read my mind and informs me that couple-rama is only on the weekends; the store is full of singles Monday through Friday. In fact, I learn that as many women as men shop there, and females make up the fastest growing customer base at Hustler, which would explain the chocolate body cream.

The first item I actually pick up is a two-foot-long furry pink neck pillow displayed on a shelf with cute stuffed animals. I have always thought my neck could be more comfortable during certain sexual positions. However, as I test the pillow in the crook of my neck, I catch my reflection in a mirror and realize that I am snuggling up to a furry stuffed penis—with balls and everything. Furthermore, all of the cute stuffed animals have not-so-cute stuffed hard-ons. I try to put the stuffed penis down discreetly and smile to myself when I see the huge sign in the middle of the store that reads: "Relax. It's Just Sex."

Since Heather and Brad have disappeared to another part of the 5,000-square-foot store, I decide to seek out the store's cute café, because even thinking about sex makes me hungry. (Note: At the Hustler café, Pussy Drip = espresso; and, like some sex acts, the Itty Bitty Minty Titty Ice Cream Oreo Shake with mint Altoids is yummy if you can work up the courage to ask for it.)

Just outside the café, there is a small grocery section with bags of pasta in the shape of boobs or penises, and chocolate body frosting in a heart-shaped bottle that goes for $8.99. This is where I realize that many Hustler products rely more on great packaging than content. After all, you can get the same chocolate frosting sans clever name and package at your local grocery store for $2.99.

And, word to the wise: *Read labels carefully*. I found out a few days later that Brad thought imported gummy butts (candies, in the shape of—yes, you guessed it) were anal suppositories until Heather read the fine print.

The most popular Hustler items seem to be practical things, such as Cum Kleen Personal Wipes, which are "for getting it off after getting it off." And the store sports a huge selection of what would simply be battery-operated massage devices if one were at

Sharper Image, but are actually vibrating dildos—which *Webster's* defines as "a penis substitute for vaginal insertion."

Obviously Webster was not a woman.

I have not gotten around to using a dildo yet (that is next on my Porn-to-Do list), but even vibrator virgins know that the "penis substitute" is ideally for vaginal *pleasure*. That is why, to its credit, Hustler tries to meet the needs of the choosiest of females. The variety of vibrators includes flavored, remote-controlled, water-proof, glow-in-the-dark, with or without suction cup bases, and a super-duper-deluxe size. (Warning: I almost threw my back out lifting the super-duper deluxe size off the shelf!)

In the same section, it is hard to ignore the shelf of celebrity replica cocks: dildos molded in the exact shape, size, and color of real porn stars' penises. I spot Ron Jeremy's but can't help noticing that it is overshadowed by Black Thunder, the apparently famous cock of the eponymous black porn star. For $79.99, you get twelve (ouch!) thick inches, which, in my hands, seems much more like a crude weapon I might keep under my pillow to defend against intruders rather than something I would use to turn myself on.

A drawback to many of the sexual toys and tools is that they do not cater to inexperienced good girls like me. Detailed directions are also hard to come by. Consider the leather Vibro Toy Pleasure Panty, which sounds promising, but the directions merely state: "Place Vibro toy in 'Secret Pocket' before strapping on." I briefly imagine Mom trying to figure out what a "secret pocket" is. *Definitely too much room for interpretation,* I think.

Heather and I track down Brad and find that he is actually shopping. Funny, Heather points out, considering that on ordinary shopping excursions he's one of the men sitting bored by the dressing room, or asking to wait in the car so that he can listen to NPR (translation: Howard Stern). Here Brad is in the video section, which seems to be a Mecca for Hustler's male customers.

Videos are conveniently divided into categories: couples, anal, gonzo (which is not sex with Muppets like I think at first. "Gonzo" refers to sex videos with broad physical comedy), all-girl, classic (I search for *Breakfast at Tiffany's*, but the closest I find is *Orgy at Tiffany's*; there is also *Forest Hump*, *Schindler's Fist*, *Sperms of Endearment*, and *On Golden Blonde*), feature, and DVD. Prices aren't cheap, though. VHS items start at $39.99. DVDs start at almost twice as much, but are highly recommended to avoid "worn tape syndrome" that can occur with repeat pausing and fast-forwarding of VHS tapes.

In the store's fashion and accessories section, I sample cherry-flavored lip-plumping balm, while practical-minded Heather tries on a nippleless vinyl bustier, which will be great for nursing, she exclaims. Pleased with my new Angelina Jolie lips, I skim through more accessories in a back corner. I squirm over leather bindings, spiked dog collars, wood paddles, nipple clamps, and other items reminiscent of Home Depot goods.

I quickly change aisles, and I am relieved and delighted to discover a wide selection of smart, sexy bracelets. They're a little on the small side, but I find a mahogany one that perfectly complements my knock-off Burberry bag and try it on. That is, I am delighted until a store clerk asks if I need help picking out a cock ring. I practically shout "No!" and then try to remove the cock ring from my wrist. Somehow, it will not come off. Panic sets in.

I take a deep breath and pull the ring with all my might. All that happens is that my hand slips off the ring and my arm shoots back like a slingshot, slamming into and knocking over a display of condoms, while simultaneously spilling the contents of my purse onto the floor.

When I bend down to pick up the mess, I meet eyes with a really good-looking guy with a great smile. I instantly love his casually mussed hair, which is a unique, deep reddish-brown color, his blue eyes, and his sort of relaxed sense of fashion. He is wearing a comfortable but cool worn-out tee for the alternative band Ween and a pair of Lucky jeans.

Even more important, he is actually helping me pick up the condoms and the contents of my purse. *Wow, cool-looking and polite!* Just when I am about to thank him, I notice that he is picking up a piece of paper on which I have scrawled a few of the Porn-to-Do items from my master list that I am going to research this week. He grins as he reads it:

Porn-to-Do

1. ~~Visit a strip club~~

2. Watch Porn   *Buy wheat-free waffles*

3. ~~Read erotica~~

4. Throw a sex-toy party

Wouldn't you know, I finally meet potential significant other (PSO) material and I come off as a nymphomaniac obsessed with my weight (a description that is only half true)! Just when I'm sure he's going to make a break for the exit, he speaks instead.

"Pretty busy week you got there," he says as he hands me my list. He has now succeeded in making me laugh, a definite PSO requirement. "Hi, I'm Sam," he adds, holding his hand out to shake mine.

"Eehhu..." I try to tell him my name, but it comes out unintelligibly. He looks at me quizzically. I realize then that my lips feel funny, kind of tingly. I put my hand out anyway to shake his and he pauses on the cock ring still stuck on my wrist.

"Is that a...?"

Before he can finish, Brad shouts from across the store. "Hey, Sam, what are you doing here?" Brad makes his way over to us.

That's a good question. What kind of guy hangs out in a sex store? Is he a nymphomaniac (guys can be, too, right?)? A chronic masturbator? Maybe he is here to rent The Buns of Navarone?

It turns out that Brad and Sam know each other because Sam was the architect (definitely a fabulous career for a PSO) for the addition on Brad and Heather's house. They stand there talking, and I decide I like Sam more and more. It was so closed-minded of me to judge him for being in a sex store, especially since I am in the same sex store. He has a great sense of humor and an infectious, easy laugh.

"Do you know Ayn?" Brad asks.

"I was just hoping to get her number," he tells Brad, and then they both turn to me. Brad stares at me with a horrified look and yells out, "Oh, my God! What the hell is wrong with your lips?"

I look in the mirror and see that I now look like Angelina Jolie—on *steroids*! I pick up the tube of lip balm and read the small print.

"Aaaaahhhh!"

I have mistakenly put erection-prolonging cream ($6.99) on my lips, and they are now so numb and swollen that I can barely excuse myself from Brad and Sam as I flee to the ladies' room.

Ten minutes later, I am still locked in the bathroom waiting for the swelling to go down on my lips when Heather knocks on the door. I let her in. She is carrying a large cup of ice and a shopping bag, which contains one nursing top (i.e., nippleless bustier), gummy butt candies, and a few DVDs for Brad. She looks at my lips and winces at the sight of them as I grab the ice from her and tell her thanks.

"Actually, the ice is from Sam," she informs me.

I run the ice cubes over my swollen lips. *Nice of Sam to try and help. Maybe he doesn't think I'm a freak after all.* "You mean he's still here? I thought for sure I scared him off."

"Well, no, he's not here anymore."

"He thinks I'm a weirdo, doesn't he?"

"I didn't get the he-thinks-you're-a-weirdo vibe. He said he was late for an appointment."

"Yeah, right, an appointment." The gesture of ice was probably just his way of feeling sorry for me. *What kind of girl wears cock rings, plumps her lips with lotion meant for penises, and carries around a tattered list of porn tasks?*

Heather has known me for almost two decades now. She can see the negative thoughts wheel spinning in my head. It's times like these that made us, years ago, establish an intervention

good vibrations

mechanism to stop the other when her negative thoughts spin out of control. She knows it is time to intervene now.

"Bright side?" is all she has to say.

I look in the mirror. Thanks to the ice from Sam, the swelling has gone down and now my lips are twice as big as they normally are, but they are kind of flattering like this. I answer Heather's question. "Bright side: Some women have to pay a lot to get lips like these."

Despite my sex-store shopping fiasco, I look forward to another trip to Hustler or other stores like it, especially if I ever date again (which is looking more and more unlikely.) I think browsing a sex store like Hustler while on a date would be a fun, pressure-free way to learn what a partner might like or not like sexually.

And, if that's not one's thing, at the very least, anyone with a sense of humor can find great gag gifts for bachelorette parties. Most frequently purchased item by women: Inflatable Husband ($39.99). According to the package, an Inflatable Husband is a low-maintenance partner for a stress-free life. As if that's not enough to sell a girl, the manufacturer promises: 1. He doesn't watch football; 2. Your parents and all your friends will not find him annoying; and 3. He never breaks wind.

On the way home from Hustler, with the top down in my pink convertible Rambler and my new Inflatable Husband strapped into the passenger seat beside me, I realize that my porn adventures, debacles included, have left me feeling more empowered, liberated, and oddly confident than I have ever felt before. I call Heather from my cell phone.

"Do you think I could get Sam's number from Brad?"

"Uh, can I call you back? I'm about to put the nippleless bustier to work on Brad and I don't think he can wait."

I wish her luck and hang up smiling. Apparently, Brad's libido spiked during the trip to Hustler.

Five minutes later (Brad's first sex in two trimesters, after all), Heather calls me back with Sam's number. I glance over at Inflatable Husband and find myself wondering if Sam could be "Mr. Right." I have that inexplicable feeling, that gut sensation that tells you a man eats his Kung Pao with peanuts. I vow that if I am ever lucky enough to go out with Sam, I will not let Mom lie to him about the possibility of MSG being in his food.

Somehow, by the time I get home and pick up the phone to call Sam, my courage wanes. Although I've never felt quite so strongly about anyone after just one meeting, I decide I am being naive and wildly optimistic and that I should not call him.

Instead, I wonder if he will call Brad for my number, but I restrict myself to fantasizing about him as nothing more than "Mr. Maybe" to keep my hopes down. After all, would fate really have me meet Mr. Right, or even Mr. Maybe, in a sex store? Still, as I prop up Inflatable Husband in a corner of my bedroom, I can't help wondering if Mr. Maybe breaks wind, watches football, or would impress my friends and parents.

PERCENT OF
FEMALE FANS AT
1998 ADULT
INDUSTRY
TRADE SHOWS:
10
PERCENT OF
FEMALE FANS AT
2004 ADULT
INDUSTRY
TRADE SHOWS:
50

Source: Digital Playground

Chapter Five
This Is Not Your Mother's Tupperware Party

Law of Dating Dynamics: *n. social theory that states when a person is searching for love is when they are least likely to find it*

Who knew the Law of Dating Dynamics also works in reverse? Just when I give up on Sam (it has been two weeks and he has not called), and I stop trying to find the perfect guy—less pressure to do so now that I have a personal library of erotica—I find the perfect guy. His name is Ben, and we meet at a singles event hosted by a network that I am part of—a thousand professional working women, who, by day, are known as Ladies Who Brunch and, by night, are known as Ladies Who Cocktail. For this particular singles event, every woman was asked to bring a single eligible male (whom they had no intention of dating), the plan being that they would leave their single male and possibly take someone else's. Kind of like the penny jar at 7-Eleven, but a lot more interesting.

Ben said he was attracted to me because I was the only girl not trying to get his number that night. He also did not balk when I dropped the H Bomb. I am not surprised that he had girls groveling to get his number. He is really cute. He looks a lot like Anderson Cooper, host of CNN's *360*, but a little taller (good thing) and his hair slightly less gray (good thing, too). He also drives a BMW and has an MBA. Ordinarily the MBA or BMW would make him not my type—I go for creative over corporate—so I am thrilled when he tells me he quit the corporate grind last year to work on his first novel, which is being published in June. *Definitely a step up from testing video games in your garage.* My chances of winning a Pulitzer Prize are looking slimmer and slimmer, but maybe I can date someone who has a shot at one.

I read Ben's novel manuscript. Okay, so he's not David Foster Wallace—his book is essentially "dick-lit"*—but at least he gets paid to write. I, on the other hand, am writing a book that, as far as I know, will interest only The Naughty Knitters and is too perverted to tell my own mother about.

After having a great time at the Getty Museum last week, and a picnic at the beach this week, tonight is my third date with Ben, and I am really excited. Not just because he has made me stop thinking about Sam, and he is treating me to dinner at the chi-chi restaurant Chaya Brasserie—the last dinner Greg treated me to consisted of walking around Costco and tasting free samples—but because this is date three, and even in polite circles it means sex is in the realm of possibility.

Back at my place after dinner, we stumble into the doorway, laughing at one of those unmemorable things one says that is only funny because it is date three. If it were date eighteen, it might illicit a chuckle; on date one hundred and eighteen, it would be lucky to get a nod.

---

*Like chick-lit, but written from a guy's POV.

We collapse on the sofa, and he leans in and kisses me. *Mmm-mmm*. He is a great kisser. Our hands start to wander over each other, and I find that I can barely contain myself. So I don't. I unbutton my shirt and guide his hands to undo my bra strap, which is coincidentally and conveniently a sexy lace, push-up, front-clasping bra for this third date. Suddenly Ben stops and pulls away. I think it's cute that he respects me enough to be chivalrous.

"I have to confess something," he says.

"I know, I know. I want you, too." I reach my hands under his shirt.

He looks me straight in the eye, his hands planted on my naked shoulders. "I think you're amazing." It is so sweet that he thinks he has to say these things to have sex with me. I let him go on. "You're smart, you're beautiful, you're fun. . . . "

"I think you're amazing too." *Now let's do it.*

"I think I might be, uh, falling for you." Wow, he's really going for it. It's working, too. I am this close to jumping him.

"Mmmmm, yes, uh-huh," I mumble as I kiss him some more. In between my kissing him, he keeps trying to talk.

"It's just that I really think we might have something here, and I want to be sure that, deep down, *you* know that I'm not just dating you because I think we will have hot sex together."

Hold on. I never said I *didn't* want anyone wanting me just for sex. After a lifetime of guys being turned on by my brains, I was kind of looking forward to my share of someone wanting me merely for sex, especially if it is hot sex.

Of course I do not tell Ben any of what I am thinking. The good girl in me takes over once again and pretends to agree that he is right: We should take our time when it comes

to sex so that we can establish a more meaningful relationship.
Ugh.

At our next Naughty Knitters session, I contemplate not telling the girls about Ben's idea to hold off on having sex, because I know that Vee will never let me hear the end of it. I try to talk about everything but my lack of sex life.

"Who are we knitting clothes for this month?" I ask.

"How about that charity in Somalia we heard about?" Maya suggests.

"Sounds good," a few of us reply. Of course, none of us realizes that it is currently 98 degrees in Somalia. Nor can we foresee the confused looks on the charity reps when they open up a box full of wool beanies, sweaters, and booties.

"Hey, how's it going with the Anderson Cooper lookalike? Hasn't it been two weeks?" asks Vee.

"Yep. Two weeks. He's great." God, it's hard not to tell them everything.

Tricia looks at me pitifully. "It will probably end in misery and tears, but it is so cool that you're enjoying dating again."

Vee, of course, just demands to know, "What's he like in bed?"

"Well, the thing is . . ."

"The thing? You mean *sex*?"

"Of course I mean sex."

"He's better in bed than Greg, I hope."

"Before you start judging him, let me just explain something first—"

Vee cuts me off. "Oh, my God, you haven't had sex with him?"

Maya tries to get Vee to ease up on me. "Give her a break. It's only been two weeks."

"You *have* kissed, I hope," she says, full of judgment.

"Of course we've kissed."

"I mean French-kissed, not butterfly or Eskimo."

I shoot daggers at her. "Very funny. Of course we've French-kissed. He's also great at just cuddling and talking."

"I'm sorry. Cuddling and talking? I thought we had cats and each other for that?" Damn, Vee. "Are you sure he's not gay?"

"I *said* we French-kissed." I swear, sometimes I could strangle her.

"My friend Mark says a lot of gay guys can still kiss a woman," Maya explains. "What's important is what Ayn thinks. Have you had any doubts?"

"Well, he . . . " I start to say something, then pause mid-sentence.

"Say it," they encourage in unison.

"I'm sure it's nothing."

"Say it."

"Fine. But first let me say that being a minority myself I hate stereotyping. It's just that sometimes there's a reason for stereotypes, right? Not that anyone should use stereotypes to profile or anything like that—"

"Just say it!" they shout.

"He took me shopping at Crate and Barrel yesterday and he said, 'You can never have enough candles.'"

"Cool, a guy who actually likes going on shopping dates," remarks Tricia.

"Definitely *Brokeback*," says Vee.

"He is *not* gay!" I shout.

"Don't listen to her," blurts out Paige, who I forgot was even here, because she is in the corner working on her novel or a script.

"She's just cranky because the batteries in her vibrator went out last night," adds Steve.

Maya, the one true romantic in the group, smiles at me, "I'm just happy one of us is dating."

Vee looks hurt. "Hey, I'm dating—"

"I think what you're doing is actually considered statutory rape," I kid.

"I meant dating someone over eighteen," Maya clarifies.

To head off this discussion with Vee, Steve asks me, "So, what do you like about him?"

"Well, he loves to just hang out. He doesn't have to have ESPN on twenty-four, seven; he's perfectly happy watching HGTV. He's great at relationship stuff."

"Did he say why he doesn't want to have sex yet?" says one-track mind Vee.

"He," I can't help but smile when I say this, "thinks we might have a chance at a real future together."

"But he likes men." I swear, Vee is the human equivalent of a broken record.

I don't want to admit the following, but I want Vee to shut up about the gay thing. "Look, I know Ben's straight because he told me he masturbates to me."

"I masturbate to Viggo Mortensen, but that doesn't mean we have a future together," Vee says matter-of-factly.

I am glad date number four, dinner with Dad, is behind us. Of course, I was planning to convince Ben to have sex at the end of the night, but after Dad's strange reaction to him, I found that I wasn't in the mood. At first I thought Dad's odd behavior was a sign that he missed Greg, but then I remembered that Mom once told me that Dad told her that Greg was not good enough for me. Thankfully, Ben had no way of knowing that Dad was behaving differently since it was the first time he'd met him, but it did not take me long to realize that there was something about Ben that brought out the Mexican in my father. The shift in Dad, who is, at best, Martin Sheen Mexican*, became very apparent when Dad, who ordinarily takes anyone I am dating to his favorite expensive, waspy, white-linen bistro, decided after meeting Ben to take us to El Coyote, a casual Mexican restaurant best known for its margaritas and pork *carnitas*. When we arrived, Dad approached the hostess and, in a voice way louder than necessary, informed her, "Table for three for *Carrrrrr*illo." It was quite possibly the longest "R" roll in the history of man. This from the person, who for various social and professional reasons, did not roll his Rs for the first twenty-five years of my life. Boy was he making up for it.

My suspicions were confirmed when Dad paid the Mariachi band to serenade us and referred to the music they were playing as "my people's music." *My people's music?* Growing up, Dad's eight-track deck played nothing but Ray Charles, Elvis Presley, Patsy Cline, Jerry Lee Lewis, and Loretta Lynn. Ben wasn't helping matters either when he declared that the avocados were spicy. Essentially, Dad's actions made me see Ben in a different light. For

---

*né Ramon Gerardo Antonio Estevez

the first time, I noticed that he is so fair that he should probably wear SPF 40 indoors. I recalled that the one time I saw him salsa dance, it looked like he was trying to put a fire out with his feet, and last week he asked me when Cinco de Mayo is.

Later that night after he dropped me off, I wondered if Ben, with his BMW and Brooks Brothers blazers, might be too different from me to make this relationship work in the end?

It is date number five, and I have forgotten all my differences with Ben. After he brought me a bouquet of French tulips (my favorite flower) and whipped up an amazing *coq au vin* dinner and a lemon soufflé for dessert, I am back to thinking that Ben may still be the perfect guy for me.

After dinner, we cuddle on the sofa, and he turns to me, his eyes alight.

"I have to tell you something, but I'm afraid you'll think it's weird."

I just look at him. I am not exactly in the mood to hear anything weird.

"I think I've transcended sex." He starts talking rapidly, as if he is really excited by this notion.

"Oh, good, you don't think it's weird." He does not even give me enough time to respond as he goes on about it. "It's so liberating. It's like somehow being with you made me have an epiphany—sex is not as important to a relationship as I thought it was."

Whoa. Whoa. Whoa. "Excuse me, did you say you've *transcended* wanting to have sex?" I ask him in a voice one octave higher than my usual voice.

"Yeah, isn't that great?"

As soon as Ben leaves my place, I speed dial Vee and shout into the phone: "Tibetan monks *transcend*. Not single guys in L.A.!"

She calms me down and I tell her everything. She must get the seriousness of the situation because she does not stop to make fun of me.

"Can you believe this?" I moan. "I finally start liberating my libido and I find the one guy who doesn't care."

"Why don't you just dump him?"

"I can't help thinking that there is something there. He thinks I'm great. He's hot. And the shopping thing is really convenient."

"Then you need to test him. He's gone astray. You like him, but obviously you want sex. You are going to have to do something to make him have sex. You're young, you're hot, you're damn smart, and you're sexy. If he doesn't want sex with you, then he's definitely gay."

I hate to admit it, but she is right. If I don't want to dump him, I have to jump him. I need to turn Ben on so much that he forgets about transcending sex. I need to *un*-transcend him.

I remember Heather telling me that, when Brad's libido was a little low before she was even pregnant, she went to someone's in-home sex toy party, which provided her with tips and products that helped her kick things up a notch in the bedroom. That's how she ended up pregnant.

I look up different sex toy party providers. There are three big ones. One, Slumber Parties, stands out. It has been in business since 1993, was started by a single mom, and is now a booming business. Its brochure teases you with its slogan "Feel the fantasy..." and claims that "Slumber Parties is (my) ticket to igniting passion..."

I call my local distributor, a woman named Wendy*, and sign up to host a party two weeks from now.

I'm not sure my friends will be interested in coming to an adult toy party, so I send out an e-mail to everyone I know, hoping to get enough interest to justify throwing this event. Within minutes, I have dozens of e-mails back. Everyone wants to go—some of them are going to shuffle their work schedules, dating schedules, and/or their babysitter schedules—and a few of them really want to bring friends. I guess I'm not the only one who needs to stimulate someone's libido. As suggested by Slumber Parties, I whittle the invitees down to fifteen people. Steve gets whiff of what I am planning and begs me to see if the distributor will break company rules—no men, babies, or children allowed—and let him attend. I call Wendy and argue that Steve is one of the girls, and that I'll never hear the end of it if he is not able to attend. She tells me that Steve can attend as long as I promise to keep it mum.

For some reason I decide not to tell Ben about my slumber party. I think it will be better to just surprise him with whatever I purchase. In the meantime, I try some other tried and true techniques to turn a guy on.

The next night, our Friday-night date night, I dress in the sexiest low-cut blouse and tightest, most flattering skirt I can find and pour him a glass of red wine when he comes over.

"I got something for you." I toss him one of Greg's leftover magazines.

---

*Name changed.

"What is this?"

"It's a *Playboy*."

"Yeah, I know that, but I don't read dirty magazines."

"Oh, why not?" I ask.

"Well, for one thing they are misogynistic and anti-feminist."
He flips through the pages, pulling out the centerfold. I'm thinking, *wow, that girl is really sexy,* when he goes on a rant.

"Look at these air-brushed pictures. It gives guys unrealistic
expectations when it comes to women." He turns to me with a
sympathetic look. "And, God, it must make you women feel
totally inadequate." I couldn't put it better myself. In fact, I put it
exactly that way to Greg months ago.

I find myself rolling my eyes as Ben goes on and on about
porn's negative social impact. *If only Greg could see me now.* I could
argue that the articles are really good, but I pour him another glass
of wine instead.

"Didn't I have two already?" he inquires.

"Nope. Just one," I lie.

Ten minutes later he is still on a diatribe about pornography,
and why it is harmful to the male-female relationship psyche
(whatever that is). *Is this what I sounded like to Greg?*

"Why don't you finish that glass of wine so that you can have
another?" I suggest.

"Oooh, I don't know. Maybe I should eat something first."

I tip his glass forward, practically forcing him to finish it,
accidentally spilling it all over his shirt.

"Oh, crap, I'm so sorry! Let me take your shirt off for you and
rinse it." I push him back on the sofa and start to unbutton his
shirt.

"Hey, if I didn't know better I'd think you were trying to seduce me."

Yes, I am, damn it! "What if I am?" I ask with my smokiest gaze.

He stares back with a smoky gaze. I can see him un-transcending. He gets on top of me and rubs against me. He's as hard as a rock, which turns me on even more and means that he is not irreversibly transcended. As he dry humps me, however, I start to feel like we are in high school.

"Don't you think this would be more fun with our clothes off?" I ask. I make a move to kiss his neck when I have to stop myself. I sniff around. It's something on his neck. "What is that smell?"

"Tag."

"Tag?"

"Body spray for men," he explains.

"It smells like perfume."

"Don't be silly. I'm a guy. I don't wear perfume."

"Ah-*choo*!" He hands me a Kleenex as my nose crinkles up and I "Ah-Ah-*choo*" again.

"I'm allergic to perfume."

"It's not perfume," he repeats.

I start to itch uncontrollably.

"Uh, are you all right? You've got some weird rash on your neck," he says pointing to my neck.

I run to the mirror. The rash is on my neck and creeping up my face. My nose is now running, too.

"Noooooooo!" I scream.

The next morning, after another sexless night, I wake up with a Benadryl-and-red-wine-hangover as Ben bounces into the bed-room wearing my favorite crimson sweatshirt—again.

As he approaches, something on the floor catches my eye.

"Aaaaaaaagggggggh!" I scream and jump out of bed, backing into the corner with the sheet pulled up around me.

"What is it?" He looks around the floor like I've seen a rat.

"Y-y-y-you . . ." I can barely say it.

"Please tell me what it is! Are you hurt?"

I blurt it out. "You're wearing my slippers!" These are not just any slippers, these are fluffy bunny slippers with floppy ears.

He answers so nonchalantly, "Yeah, I found them in the back of your closet. They're *really* comfortable."

Paige and I bought the same pair of slippers together a year ago, and made a pact that no matter how bad our love lives ever suck, we will not become a rom-com cliché. In other words, we will never resort to wearing the fluffy bunny slippers while watching romantic comedies like *Win a Date with Tad Hamilton* and eating Häagen-Dazs straight from the carton. The slippers (when they are in the closet) are empowering proof that I am not a rom-com cliché. But I don't tell Ben any of this.

"Hey, I thought we'd make a pear clafouti for breakfast and do some outlet shopping," he chimes in. "What do you say?"

"Sounds great."

He gives me a peck on the cheek and heads for the kitchen.

While Ben makes the pear clafouti, I hide in the shower stall and call Steve on my cell.

"You absolutely cannot tell Vee any of this," I begin.

"He's gay."

"No, worse."

"I knew it. He's a hermaphrodite."

"Yuck, no! I woke up this morning and it hit me: I'm not just dating an MBA with a BMW; I am dating an MBW."

"You're going to have to explain that."

"After years of begging you men to get in touch with your feminine sides, we have created not monsters, not metrosexuals, but 'Men Behaving like Women.'"

"Is that so bad?"

"He is wearing the bunny slippers."

"Ouch."

"He is also bogarting my favorite sweatshirt because, and I quote, 'The fit is more flattering through the waist than men's sweatshirts.'"

"Really? I'll have to try that."

"Can we please stay focused here? It has gotten so bad that I am now compiling a mental list of his MBW symptoms to cure him of the affliction. Number one: 'Body spray for men' is just another name for perfume."

"Maybe you're taking this too hard. Maybe you should consider the upside to Ben behaving like a woman."

Steve's right. Why am I complaining? It is nice that Ben would rather go to a museum than a strip club, and he confided in me that he is confident enough in his masculinity that with past girlfriends, he (pre-transcendence) has been known to cry after sex.

"You're right. Other than not having sex with me yet, he's pretty perfect," I admit to Steve.

"Oh. My. *God*! You still haven't had sex?" Steve shouts.

* * *

When our mother's generation wanted to spice up their relationships, they would throw Tupperware parties. Because back when Tupperware was created in 1948, the best way to a man's heart was through his stomach. And to get to his stomach, you had to get to the kitchen.

Wow, have things changed since then. Now, the fastest way to a man's heart is through his penis, and the bedroom is where we have to strut our stuff. After all, unlike our moms, most of us have full-time careers that are just as stressful and demanding as our male counterparts'. Our designer kitchens are mostly for hovering in during parties, because the fact is we can buy prepared food at our local grocery store that is better than most of us can cook at home.

And thanks to Starbucks, I can't remember the last time I made my own cup of coffee or tea. In other words, for our generation, a Tupperware party is not as practical as what I jokingly refer to as a Tupper*sex*ware* party.

The day of the party I decide to really get into the mood and theme of the event, and I serve penis-shaped pasta, gummy-butt candies, and margaritas, and offer party favors of flavored lubricant samples. Everyone will also get her choice of sexy temporary tattoos that say things such as "Sex Kitten," "Love Muffin," or "Hottie," and one that reads "Stud Muffin," for Steve.

That night as I run around and light candles, Steve finds me in the bedroom, a strange look on his face.

---

*Author in no way intends to confuse consumers as to the Tupperware brand. Tupperware, unfortunately, does not offer sex toys among their innovative kitchen products. Sorry ladies.

"Uh, Wendy the distributor is here."

"Great."

"She's not quite what we pictured."

What I pictured was a hot blonde with a great smile, clad in some sexy black leather outfit and high heels. And the smile I picture is real, not fake, because she knows what she's talking about—she has used all of the sex toys she peddles. And she is a happy camper because of it.

I excitedly go to meet her. This is the woman who is going to change my sex life and the sex lives of my friends for the better. I can't wait to put my arms around her.

That is, until I see her.

Wendy is standing in the doorway. Actually she is filling the doorway, all 250 pounds of her, and I don't think my arms would fit around her. For a second, I wonder if she's been kicked out of her apartment and is going to ask for a place to live, because she looks kind of distraught and there are five very big suitcases behind her. Then I realize she is maybe just a little exhausted from carrying the five suitcases, which I deduce are filled with sex toys and products.

The fact that she's overweight is not what bothers me. Half the time I have one toe in the plus-size door. And everyone knows that being plump can make you more likable and fun—it can even land you a talk show (Oprah, Rosie, Ricki) if you're confident and have a sense of humor. But Wendy—who is wearing a sleeveless poly-silk tank top, the kind with arm holes so big that you can see her white bra through them—does not seem confident or funny. Worst of all, she seems really nervous. Which makes me nervous.

My tendency is to always think of the worst that could go

wrong, and I need to stop that. After all, Wendy does this for a living; she must be comfortable with it. *She's probably just one of those people who does not light up until she's in front of her audience,* I tell myself.

I help her set up as my girlfriends trickle in and rub on their sexy temporary tattoos and grab their drinks. The girls have their choice of glow-in-the-dark penis straws or sippy dick straws that have a gliding penis on them, so that if you move your hand up and down the straw while drinking it looks like you are giving head. The straws are a hit with the girls and cause a few giggles and chuckles. Only my neighbor Erica, who could barely fit this party in between breastfeeding her six-month-old baby, politely refuses one, while Vee asks if she can take her straw home.

My college buddy and fellow feminist sympathizer Tatiana giggles like a junior high kid as Wendy finishes setting up her wares on my coffee table. There are dildos, vibrators (batteries actually included), creams, lotions, fuzzy handcuffs, instructional books, and quite a few things that I can't identify. It's like my own Hustler home.

The last person to arrive is Yvette, who writes the heady book reviews for and is the managing editor at *Tu Ciudad,* the magazine I frequently write for. She enters and removes her overcoat, revealing that she is wearing a Victoria's Secret black silk Teddy set. She looks around at the rest of us and her face drops.

She takes me aside. "The invite said it was a slumber party."

"You are so literal."

"So, we're not sleeping over?"

"Well, you can, but no one else plans to."

"Margaritas?"

I point her toward the kitchen. "Don't forget to get a sippy dick."

This is not the first time something like this has happened. That's why the company's brochure—which I sent to everyone, and Yvette obviously did not read—states, "Please remind your guests that this is not a sleepover."

Apparently the name Slumber Parties, the slogan "Feel the Fantasy . . . ," and the fact that they provide sex toys, leads some people to show up under the impression that hosts are actually hosting sex parties, as in giant orgies. I guess that's why they are adamant about no men attending. One story has a distributor having to climb out a bathroom window to escape horny guests who were a little too eager to test the "toys." Unfortunately for Wendy, and I do not intend this in a mean way, but as matter of fact, should she need to escape us, she would definitely not fit through my bathroom window.

Wendy starts the party with a cute icebreaker that consists of each of us writing down our most hated household chore and why we can't stand said chore. For example, when it is my turn, I write, "I hate unloading the dishwasher because it's so unnecessary." Wendy then goes around the room and reads what each of us wrote, replacing the chore with the word "sex." So, my statement becomes "I hate *sex* because it's so unnecessary." After the icebreaker, Wendy reaches for the first product, a seven-inch-long, thick jelly dong with suction cup base, called Mr. Dependable ($17.00), which is recommended for bath time. I am excited for her, for me, for the girls. Not because she is waving around Mr. Dependable, but because I know Wendy is going to turn on the salesmanship now. I am convinced that she is going to be the chubby girl who becomes cute and sexy before our eyes because she embraces sex and her right to pleasure no matter what her size is. She will become Fun, Wild Wendy.

Nothing. My hopes are dashed. Wendy holds up the dildo with the same enthusiasm she might have for a flyswatter. And in a monotone voice (think Charlie Brown's teacher), she describes how it works. *Whaah, whaa, whaa.* And something tells us right away that Wildless Wendy has not actually tested most of these products. When she moves on to lotion with glitter (not everything is overtly about sex), she dabs some on her neck and passes it around, telling us, "This stuff is great to wear when you hit the clubs."

I start to panic. *What clubs could Wendy be talking about? Sam's Club? Ralph's Club? A turkey club?* We try to pretend we do not notice, but several of us are distracted by the fact that she is sweating. I ask her if she'd like me to turn on the air-conditioning, but she says, no, she's fine. I have trouble believing that, since there are beads of sweat collecting on her forehead and underarm sweat rings staining her poly-silk blouse.

When she shows the Top It Off body whipped cream ($10.50), she says it is non-dairy.

"Yeah, but is it kosher?" I joke.

I get a few chuckles from the girls, but instead of lobbing back a clever quip or response, Wendy just looks at the can and reads the ingredients, then stares at me. I'm not sure if she's upset that I broke her concentration or if she doesn't get the joke. Or maybe it's both.

I make the mistake of trying to explain. "You know, non-pareve . . ."

Vee taps me on the thigh as my joke falls flat again. "Let it go, Ayn."

good vibrations

I'm not sure why we shouldn't just buy a can of whipped cream for half the cost at the supermarket, and then Yvette explains that real whipped cream melts too fast. She must be onto something, because Wendy does mention that Slumber Parties' version of whipped cream is made with ingredients that will not cause yeast infections and will withstand heat longer. Presumably this will be helpful, because, presumably, when you use these products your bodies will be hot with passion.

She explains that we are going to test some of the products, which is good, I think, because it will be more interactive. But even that she doesn't do with much enthusiasm. Wendy puts lotion on two Q-tips and hands one to Maya, instructing her to go into the bathroom and place the lotion on her you-know-what. *Okay, this could be kind of fun.* That is, until Wendy hands me the second Q-tip. I head to the other bathroom, a strained smile on my face.

In the bathroom, I stare at my reflection in the mirror, a little concerned that I am being so trusting with a stranger, which is out of character for me. *What if Wendy carjacked the real Slumber Parties' representative on her way over here? Maybe that's why she's so nervous. The real Slumber Parties' rep could be stuffed into one of Wendy's humongous suitcases. Who knows what this lotion might really be?* I think back to the erection-prolonging cream I put on my lips not so long ago. *Maybe I should go out and tell my guests my suspicions? Nah.* I apply a little bit of it and walk back out to the party.

"How does it feel?" Wendy asks.

I'm not sure how to answer. I am new to experimenting with sex products in public.

"That's Nympho Niagra, one of our best-sellers," she tells the others.

"It's kind of tingly," I awkwardly admit. I guess that's good because Wendy lets it go at that, then turns her attention to Maya, exiting from the bathroom.

"Well?" asks Wendy.

"It's kind of burning," answers Maya.

"It's not supposed to burn." And again Wendy just leaves it at that and picks up the next product, a flexible double-headed rubber dildo that is about three feet long. The thing is shocking looking. Not quite sure what it is, I keep flashing to scenes from the movie *Anaconda*.

Wendy explains matter-of-factly that it's more of a novelty gift, and it allows women to put one end in themselves and suck on the other end. From the head tilts among the group, I can see that I'm not the only one imagining all the other variations that she is not describing.

Thankfully, despite Wendy's lack of enthusiasm, once I hear the words, "Please pass the penis," the event takes on a life of its own. It's kind of like show-and-tell. The act of passing items around to hold and touch helps the girls—and Steve—get into everything more.

Overall, everyone loves that Steve is there so that they can get his male advice on what their partners might like. Vee's response to almost every item as it is passed to her is, "Tried it," or "Got one."

After a while, we are not just passing the items around. We are tasting, testing, touching, and handling the products. This is the real advantage to having a sex toy party in your home. If you go to most sex stores, you cannot usually touch the products, test them, taste them, or turn them on. Well, you can, but you will either be thrown out or arrested.

It is extremely helpful to feel and hear how loud some of the vibrators are, or know how the lotions actually smell and feel on your skin. Burning—not good. Tingling—good. I have to admit most of the products are intriguing, and I know I am not alone when I start to wonder what these products might do if applied to the right person.

My friend Sacha, who has just moved in with her fiancé and is on the lookout for honeymoon toys, sprays a little of the whipped cream on her finger and tastes it with a mischievous smile. She turns to her friend Jenny, a school teacher, and declares, "I am *so* gonna have sex when I go home."

As a sort of intermission, we play another icebreaker that I requested after Heather recommended it. It involves bananas and Wendy said it would be okay to play if I bought the bananas (I guess she did not want to kick in the extra $1.98). Everyone receives a banana and has five minutes to, using only her teeth, sculpt a penis. Wendy wanted to leave the time open-ended, but I know that with perfectionists in the group such as Steve (he has the upper hand because he has a penis) and Sacha (she makes Martha Stewart look like a slacker), we could end up being here all night.

The girls get really competitive about it. Some actually sculpt theirs with balls; others struggle over sculpting circumcised or uncircumcised. In the end, Tatiana is clearly the winner—not surprising since her husband is a professional sculptor. Her banana penis is shockingly realistic with not just balls and an uncircumcised shaft but also a bulging and protruding vein.

After a fifteen-minute break and more cocktails, we try more products, such as Bosom Buddy ($8.50), a flavored moisturizing balm that tingles when applied to the nipples, causing your nipple to become erect and supposedly enticing your lover to linger longer because it is flavored in orange or raspberry. After reaching under the t-shirt that she has changed into and rubbing Bosom Buddy on herself, Yvette looks very pleased and I see her make a check mark in her ordering book.

Then the *pièce de resistance*: The Rabbit Pearl, the vibrator made famous on an episode of *Sex and the City*, a.k.a., the Rolls Royce of vibrators.

It is an opalescent pink latex-covered vibrator with an added tiny rabbit planted at the base of it in order to externally stimulate the clitoris with its ears. It also has pearl-shaped objects in the shaft that move up and down within the latex to add further variation and pleasure. Everyone is definitely in awe of it and everyone has heard of it, but the Slumber Parties' price—a whopping $120— puts some of us off.

The interesting products continue, with a battery-operated tongue that Wendy calls Mini-Me ($36), which is twice as big as my own tongue and would be more appropriately named Not-So-Mini-Me; and an item called Super Stretch ($30), which lights up Steve when he feels it. It is made of a squishy (my word, not the company's) silicone in the shape of a woman's vagina and is meant for guys to give themselves hand jobs that feel just like having sex with a woman. It also has beads imbedded in it that Steve assures us any guy will appreciate. Half of the women end up ordering this for their significant and not-so-significant others.

As I look around, it dawns on me that I can stop being nervous. The party has definitely picked up steam. I go to the bathroom and when I come out, Sacha—who missed a function with her church group for this—and Yvette are posing for a picture with the double-headed dildo between them, sucking on opposite ends as if it were a string of spaghetti. Tatiana has affixed the wall banger (a rubber penis with suction cup at the base) onto my fireplace for her photo op and is pretending to give it a blow job. Vee is on the sofa showing Erica and Maya how the Mini-Me works, while the others test vibrators (on their hands, not their private parts) with curiosity.

Once it is clear that Wendy has demonstrated all of the products for us, there's a lull in the chatter and I have that awkward feeling I have at those time-share orientations—you know, the ones that lure you with a free trip to Hawaii, a cruise, or a new TV? I'm afraid that everyone, including me, is probably going to leave and not purchase a thing, even though poor Wendy has spent hours nicely selling us on the products after schlepping them here from across town. However, even though I am not offering free televisions or trips to Hawaii, all but two of us line up to order products in the privacy of my bedroom.

According to Tatiana, the party is great because "Who has time in their busy schedule to stop at an actual sex store and buy toys?" It turns out that the girls really appreciated being able to handle and test the things like I thought. They also appreciated me setting it up in a comfortable place and the company's policy of letting them order in private.

After the last person has ordered their goodies, I go in to place my small order. "You have seventy dollars in credit," Wendy informs me.

"Excuse me?"

"Your party earned you seventy dollars of free items," Wendy repeats. I completely forgot that that is how it works. Mom's Tupperware parties worked the same way, but of course she bought burping plastic containers, spatulas, and ice cube trays with her credit. I am buying two Cozy Cuffs (fur-lined handcuffs for $15), a Love Mask blindfold ($13), the non-kosher Top It Off whipped cream ($10.50), Cherry Body Butter lubricant ($8.50) and Coochy Cream ($8.50), a unisex shave cream for all parts of the body, and a few of their other bestselling products. With the exception of the Coochy Cream, which is for me, I figure my purchases will let Ben know that I am looking for him to take charge in the bedroom.

Steve knocks on the door and pokes his head in as I hand Wendy my credit card. "Uh, Ayn, your Mom's here."

I practically sprint to the living room. Mom is trying on the Peter lipstick ($5)—a tube of real lipstick, shaped like a penis—while Tricia and Maya are in the background trying to stuff all the dildos and vibrators into a corner behind Mom's back.

When Mom sees me, she looks at me scornfully. "You didn't tell me you were having a Tupperware party. How come you no invite me?"

"I thought you'd be too busy at the restaurant on a Saturday night."

It turns out Mom is in L.A. because she came up to see her psychic, an Iranian woman who lives in Chinatown and charges superstitious Chinese women like my mom $90 per session to tell them what they should do with their lives.

Mom looks around at the other items left on the table—thankfully it is mostly novelty items—and grabs the ice tray molded with twelve boobs. "I'll take two of these." As usual, she does not have her glasses on and, therefore, cannot really see anything up close very clearly.

"And, ten of those, too." I look at what she is reaching for, half-afraid she has picked up the double-header dong. She is looking at a pack of sippy dick straws.

I quickly grab them out of her grip. "Mom, do you really need straws?"

"I'm going to serve iced tea and cake for mah-jongg." She grabs them back. "I need straws." Of course it comes out as "I need *stlaws*." She also grabs one of the cake pans, not realizing that it is in the shape of a penis. She says what a cute idea it is to make a cake in the shape of a cactus.

Vee, who has been in the bathroom, enters the living room with her *two* bags of goodies and is surprised to see my mother, too.

Mom just looks at her. "What are you doing here? You don't cook."

"Huh?" she asks Mom, confused.

I hug Vee and loudly declare, "Thanks for coming to my *Tupperware* party!" My hug so startles Vee that she drops her goodie bags, and we hear the thud of something falling out and rolling onto my hardwood floor. *Please do not be the double-headed cock!* Everyone tries not to look at whatever it is. It's like a pink elephant in the room, which, in this case, turns out to be a pink Cyclone ($57). Vee has bought it for its twirling orgasmic head and adjustable levels of intensity to add to her vast vibrator collection.

I freeze with fear as Mom bends down to pick it up.

"I can use one of these," she says matter-of-factly.

"You can?" asks Vee.

"Yeah, for when I travel." *Oh, my God, I'm a vibrator virgin, but my mother wants to pack a Cyclone for her frequent weekend trips to Sedona?*

Mom switches the Cyclone on. She tests the vibrating head on the palm of her hand. "Good power," she declares. "Better than most." *Most? She's used more than one?* My mind spins. She turns up the power a notch and shows us how the head twirls. "I like this one because you can stick it in tight places."

Okay, I have to sit down. I feel a little nauseous.

"I wonder why Williams-Sonoma doesn't sell these?"

What is she talking about? "Did you say Williams-Sonoma?" I'm afraid to ask, but must know. "Mom, what are you going to use this for?

"It's a cordless hand mixer, honey. I could use it to make cakes, mash potatoes, cream bisque. This one's probably good for getting all the batter on the sides and bottom."

Whew. Of course mom wasn't talking about sex. I should have known it was all about food . . . because food *is* sex to her.

The next night, I slyly leave my goodies on my bedside stand, hoping Ben, who now sleeps over even when he has no intention of having sex, will get the hint.

Three days later they are still sitting there.

How does a guy not notice a blindfold, fuzzy handcuffs, lubricant, and flavored condoms? I have even left—in plain sight—a pair of edible undies that my sister Fran, who has started a San Diego chapter of The Naughty Knitters, sent me as a gag gift. All this, but no, Ben is riveted to my television, crying three minutes into the midnight rebroadcast of *Oprah*, which is about orphans in Africa.

I appreciate all the good Oprah tries to do in the world, but she is hampering things when it comes to my sex life.

After a week, I check on the girls—and Steve—to see how they are faring post-party. Sacha tried the massage love mitten, but somehow the dye on the mitten ended up bleeding red onto her Ralph Lauren sheets. Steve claims his super stretch masturbating helper is worth every penny. Tatiana raved about the flavored-lubricant party favors, and Tricia has not washed off her sexy tattoo.

As for Mom, she served her mah-jongg club a penis-shaped cake without incident.

Also interesting are some facts that might merit further study: The two oldest women in our group, who were in their forties, were the only ones who resisted buying any products. Women in their late thirties in a relationship were more likely to buy things that their man could use by himself to give them a break in the bedroom. The girls in their twenties mostly bought things they could use with their guys, and single working women in their thirties were the most likely to buy vibrators, yet not find the time to use them.

I ponder the feedback from the party guests and my own situation, including my motivations for throwing a sex toy party. It dons on me that the fact that people, especially women, are reportedly using porn more, even in the mainstream, is not a reflection of us having more sex. It is actually an indication that we are having less sex. We need porn, e.g., sex toys, to help us overcome that fact.

As for Vee, she has not called me back in days, so I know she is enjoying (probably too much) her new mini-tongue vibrator, along with everything else she bought.

I am waiting on the sofa, missing the days when I used to take longer to get ready than my date, when Ben comes out, wearing khakis and—can it be?—my funky charm necklace that I bought in India.

"Are you wearing jewelry?" I ask him.

"Do you like it?"

"Uh, it's very David Beckham."

"Exactly what I was going for." When I am uncharacteristically quiet for too long, he volunteers, "If it's too much, I can take it off."

"Really?" *Great, maybe I won't have to break up with you right this second.*

"Hey, no, I totally understand. I was just trying something. I'm glad you said something." He takes the necklace off.

"Sure you're not mad?" I ask.

"No, I totally get it. Don't sweat it."

Maybe there is hope.

The next day, I am at my friend Robin's office, lying on a table, having been poked full of needles. This is not a bad thing, because Robin is an acupuncturist. She is also the closest thing I have to a therapist. We usually share our latest dating woes as she expertly places her needles in my skin to guide my *chi**, then has me sleep for thirty minutes, after which I wake up feeling like a new person.

On this particular day, I tell her that I am breaking up with Ben. That he just isn't getting the message, and that I am not equipped to date a MBW, especially one who has transcended sex.

---

*The circulating life energy that in traditional Chinese medicine is thought to be inherent in all things, and the balance and flow of which is thought key to good health.

After I get that off my chest, she places a comforting heat lamp at my feet, puts on a hypnotic CD of ancient flute music, and leaves me to relax in the dark.

I take a deep relaxing breath. I wonder if Robin could use her needles to un-transcend Ben . . . I take another deep relaxing breath . . . *Maybe she could re-direct all his chi toward his* . . . I take another deep relaxing breath. Just when my head is clear of any thoughts of Ben, my cell phone rings.

Because I am a tech idiot who cannot get my cell off of driving mode, I am subjected to hearing my phone with its robotic voice announce that it is Ben. I try ignoring it with another deep breath, but he calls back. I reluctantly pick up just in case it is an emergency.

"I found your stash of you-know-what," he tells me excitedly.

"Yay! You found the Oreos I hid from myself last month?"

"Huh?"

He must be talking about something else. I try to recall what else I have been hiding.

"Well, actually, if you were trying to hide these things you didn't do a very good job." The Tupper*sex*ware! *Finally,* he noticed!

"I think we need to use these things right away," he says in a very deep, very sexy, *non*-Man-Behaving-like-a-Woman voice. "Now that I know what you want, it's pretty hard to resist."

"I'll be there in ten minutes."

I am so excited to get home that I grab my purse and run out of Robin's office. I am so excited that I do not want to waste time going to the underground parking lot to retrieve my car, lest Ben change his mind.

I see a cab and I step in front of it, putting my hand out like a human stop sign. It's an odd sight—not because I still have twenty or so needles sticking out of my face, arms, and legs—because no one takes cabs in L.A. I've lived here fifteen years and never been in a one. But now it seems like the fastest way home.

In the taxi, after I pull the needles from my body, I find myself getting really turned on. It's been more than three months since I've had sex, and I can't wait to be blindfolded and handcuffed and rendered helpless. I can't wait to have Ben be in charge. It's like my own erotica story come true.

I enter my apartment. The lights are out, but there are a gazillion candles lit. I don't let that MBW behavior discourage me though. I throw off my jacket and shoes when I see a note from Ben. "Meet me in the bedroom," it reads.

Oh, God, this is going to be hot.

As soon as I set foot in my bedroom, I hear his voice. "Stop," he commands, and my heart starts pounding.

Oooh, commanding is *not* MBW behavior.

"Close your eyes."

I do as he says. He is the boss, and I am loving it.

"Walk toward my voice," he orders.

I can tell he's standing near the bed. I hear the clink of the cozy cuffs. I'm very excited, about-to-peel-my-clothes-off excited. To be handcuffed to the bed and not have to do anything for once is exactly what I need.

"Open your eyes," he demands.

Gladly. I open them and can't believe my eyes.

A naked Ben is lying on his back spread eagle in the middle of my bed, his hands cuffed to the wrought iron headboard with *my* cozy cuffs, his eyes covered with *my* love mask blindfold, wearing *my* edible undies!

Three hours later I am sitting at Urth Caffé, eating a croissant and sipping a latte, still thinking about how things turned out with Ben, when Steve walks in to the shop.

"You know this is a little above and beyond friendship," he tells me.

"Are you backing out?"

"Just give me the keys." I hand him my house key and the keys to the cozy handcuffs.

"Where is he?"

"Where I left him, handcuffed to the bed."

"I can't believe you left him without saying anything. Who knew good girls could be so cruel."

"He took my cozy cuffs."

"Fine. What else?"

"Tell him he can keep the edible undies."

"Eeewww."

As Steve turns to leave I remember one more thing. "Steve, wait. You might as well give him this." I hand him a napkin from the coffee shop.

"You wrote a break-up letter on a coffee shop napkin?"

"It's not a letter. It's a list."

He reads it out loud. " 'How to be a good old-fashioned man's man'?"

"A.k.a., a *retro*sexual."

He reads a few items off the list. "1. Don't be fooled: 'Body Spray for Men' is just another name for perfume. 2. No air-kissing.

3. Every now and then, buy *us* jewelry, don't wear it. 4. Watch ESPN, not HGTV. 5. It's nice to go on shopping dates, but not cool to squeal 'Outlet!' every time you drive by one. 6. Have sex just to have sex. Do not cry afterward." Steve stops on the last one and just looks at me like I am crazy. "You've really got issues."

"Yet you still love me."

Steve exits the coffee shop, shaking his head at what he is about to do for me. When he gets to the curb, he looks back and grins at me through the window. It is pretty damn funny, imagining the look on Ben's face when Steve walks in to my room and sees how he has chained himself to my bed, with nothing on but a blindfold and edible undies. Knowing that Steve is imagining this, too, makes me laugh out loud.

Thank God for old friends, I think, as Steve gives me one giant air-kiss, making it even easier to forget what a big waste of time dating Ben was.

I air-kiss him right back.

NUMBER OF VIBRATORS
SOLD BY BABELAND
IN 1993:
500

NUMBER OF VIBRATORS
SOLD BY BABELAND
IN 2005:
167,250

Source: www.babeland.com

Chapter Six

What's Love Got to Do with It?

Blog·a·mist: *n. Person who posts flirtatiously on more
than one blog*

Now I know why I stayed in a mediocre relationship with Greg for so long: *Dating sucks.* After the fiasco with Ben and the edible undies that didn't get eaten, I half-heartedly get myself back into the proverbial dating saddle only to further find how woefully ill-equipped I really am.

For one thing, it is hard to think of meeting other guys when I cannot get my mind off of Sam. I was hoping he *would* call; actually, I had a strong feeling he would call, despite the fact that I made a fool out of myself when I met him. But he never did, and I found out from my friend Hillary who found out from Tiffany who found out from Tim who found out from Mike H. who found out from Gerry that Sam has been seeing someone. And that he has been seeing this someone since before we met.

It is not helping matters that I have been out of the dating scene for so long, which is probably partially the reason why I didn't realize any sooner that Ben was trouble. To make matters worse, somehow, in just a couple of years, I have become too technically incompetent for today's dating methods, most of which involve a computer. When I met Greg, speed dating was *en vogue.* (Speed dating pro: You can quickly eliminate undesirables. Speed dating con: You may be the undesirable who is quickly eliminated.)

Now, according to friends, if I want to find a Mr. Right who has a creative job such as architect, I should log onto Salon.com (*or patronize sex stores more?*), where the more artsy guys list their profiles. According to the same friends, if I am looking for someone who is well read, there is IvyLeague.com. And, if I am looking for the marrying type, I should join eHarmony.com. When I stop to think about it, I am looking for someone who is artsy, well read, *and* the marrying type.

When I admit to Tricia that I alternate between being overwhelmed and underwhelmed by dating, and that I wish I could just flirt with some guys without commitment, she turns me onto flirting through blogs. I start a flirtatious online relationship by posting my opinions on hamburgers—e.g., "I think White Castle is the white trash of hamburger hamlets," and "McDonald's Big N' Tasty is actually Big N' Nasty"—with a guy who hosts a food blog about the best hamburgers in the United States.

I call it *e-flirting* and, unlike all of the effort that goes into meeting and flirting with guys at bars or parties, I can e-flirt from the comfort of my own home, with my unwashed hair in a ponytail, my favorite ratty sweats on, and not a spot of makeup on my face. It's kind of fun.

At first.

A fortnight later—I could just write "two weeks later," but the Jane Austen in me loves to use this old-fashioned English term whenever possible—Steve, Vee, and I are having drinks and ordering chocolate soufflés for dinner at Sonora Café while we update each other on our relationship woes. I go first.

"He accused me of being a *blogamist*! Can you believe that? How was I supposed to know we were posting exclusively? I saw another blog about vintage L.A. restaurants hosted by this other guy. Okay, he was cute—he posted his picture—but I wasn't really flirting, I just connected with what he had to say about Phillipe's* and Apple Pan.** I guess I could see how my post might be construed as flirtatious, in that it was clever and funny, but is that really considered cheating?"

"Two words for you," says Steve. "Anonymous post."

"Get over him. Anyone who has that kind of blog is addicted to blogging. You'll always come second," Vee predicts.

"What is it with me and men? Greg is looking better and better."

"Your problem is you're too idealistic. You're always looking for Mr. Right."

Maybe Vee is right. I think about the future too much. I need to learn to live in the moment. If I can't have Sam, maybe I should stop trying to find Mr. Right and just accept a Mr. Right Now.

The waiter drops off our soufflés and we dig in. It's true: Chocolate heals. I also believe the study I read years ago that theorized why women—and Steve—are so obsessed with chocolate. According to biofeedback experiments done in the lab, consuming chocolate provokes the same chemical reaction the body experiences when falling in love.

Steve gets a funny look on his face. It's different than

*Original home of the French dip sandwich located in downtown L.A. since 1908.

**Classic West L.A. eatery famous since 1947 for its hickory burgers and apple pie.

the chocolate orgasm expressions on my face and Vee's.

"I have something to tell you," he says in a serious tone.

"Okay," is all we can think to say. We're not sure what to expect. Chocolate has been known to put him in a confessional mood.

Vee and I look at each other, bracing for anything. *Could Steve be gay? Maybe he is going to admit that he has been in love with one of us for years? Or, oh, my God, he's going to tell me that these jeans make my ass look big. I kind of thought that when I was on my way out, but I figured it's just Steve and Vee.*

He takes a deep breath. "I'm a metrosexual."

"Duh," Vee and I mutter.

"What do you mean? How did you know?"

"I think you pretty much came out of that closet when you feng shui'd your closet," I tell him.

"But do you still love me?" he asks.

"The fact that you're a metrosexual is *why* we love you," I tell him.

"Ditto," Vee adds. "Now shut up and buy the next round."

I finish my soufflé and sit back, reveling in the feeling of being in love, chocolate smeared all over my face.

"Maybe I can give up sex and just eat chocolate soufflés every day. Dating sucks."

"Yeah, but celibacy sucks harder," Vee reminds us.

She's right. Sex is part of what keeps pulling me off the bench into the game, despite the losing odds.

"Give me your list," demands Vee.

She is talking about my Porn-to-Do list, which she knows I have been carrying around in my purse.

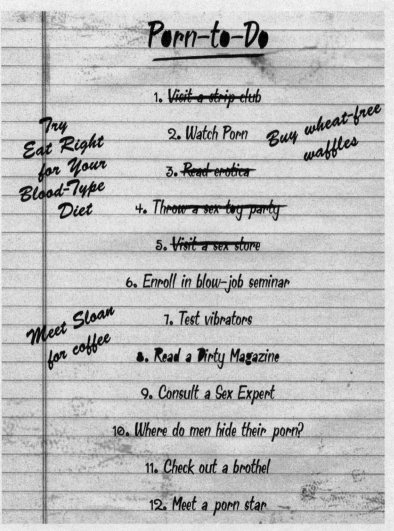

Porn-to-Do

1. ~~Visit a strip club~~
2. Watch Porn
3. ~~Read erotica~~
4. ~~Throw a sex toy party~~
5. ~~Visit a sex store~~
6. Enroll in blow-job seminar
7. Test vibrators
8. Read a Dirty Magazine
9. Consult a Sex Expert
10. Where do men hide their porn?
11. Check out a brothel
12. Meet a porn star

Try Eat Right for Your Blood-Type Diet

Buy wheat-free waffles

Meet Sloan for coffee

She scans my list and then hands it back to me. "Try a vibrator."

"I don't know why I put that on there. I don't think I can do it. It just seems . . . I don't know, off-putting, to stick some plastic thing up there. Besides, until I started reading erotica I could barely masturbate on my own without feeling guilty."

Vee looks at me like I am ridiculous. "Oh, please, if God didn't want us to use vibrators he would not have made them, and if he didn't want us to masturbate he would have made our arms shorter."

"All of a sudden the agnostic has found God?"

"Think about it: Having sex with one's self also satisfies the Pope's rules against sex out of wedlock; it is a natural form of birth control." *This from the person who didn't vote in the last election because it was her time of the month?* "And it's good for world peace."

"If you gave every soldier a vibrator instead of a gun," she goes on, "imagine what would happen."

I do just that. It is not a pretty sight. *Vibrator-toting soldiers attacking each other on dusty battlefields. Ooh, death by masturbation. No, death by vibrator.*

It also gives "friendly fire" a whole new meaning.

I go home and think about Vee's vibrator suggestion. Somehow, Vee says these outlandish things that we always poo-poo when we are with her. But two hours later, sometimes even a week later, you find yourself saying, "Hey, maybe there was something to that."

Like her theory on vibrators promoting world peace. Unlike Vee, I don't believe you can save the world one vibrator at a time, but maybe they can make a difference in my world. I decide I will try one. Plus, it is on my Porn-to-Do list (four items down, eight to go).

Before I go out and purchase one, I decide to do some product research first. I don't buy anything—even toothpaste—without researching brands first. My first question: What is the difference between a vibrator and a dildo?

I call up Babeland, the Seattle-based sex toy store that has just opened two popular retail spots in New York City and a new one in L.A. My research indicates that Babeland is famous—as is Good Vibrations in San Francisco—for catering to female customers. At Babeland, every product has been tested by the female staff, and they dutifully track customer reviews. The sales clerk who answers the phone is relaxed and friendly and doesn't make me feel naïve for asking my question.

"Basically," she explains, "the difference is that dildos are usually shaped like a penis, and are made to be inserted into the vagina or anus, and they don't usually vibrate. On the other hand, vibrators are specifically designed to vibrate and can be shaped like a penis, but they also come in a variety of non-penis shapes and sizes."

I remember the vibrating tube of lipstick, Lifesavers pack, and the mini-tongue we played with at my sexware party. The benefit of the vibrations, she tells me, is that they can be used for stimulation of the clitoris or other sensitive body parts.

At home I do more research. Vibrators come as battery-operated models or models that are plugged into an electrical source. Some even have remote controls, which I will try to avoid because it's just too easy to imagine Dad coming over and trying to turn on DirecTV with the wrong remote.

Vibrators also range in size from mini-vibrators (mini is the new large) that are discreet enough to carry in your purse or, if you are like Vee, on your key chain, to five-inch to nine-inch-size facsimiles of penises. They also range in price widely, from $9.99 to several hundreds of dollars for a "Je Joue," the world's first programmable (Mac or PC) nonpenetrative designer vibrator.

After much thinking, I realize that I do not want to do something so life-altering alone, so I do a shout-out for vibe virgins. Who knew, in a post-*Sex-and-the-City* society with an unfortunate higher ratio of women to men, vibrator virgins are hard to come by. Tricia and I are the only ones in The Naughty Knitters who have not used one, and among the other twenty friends I call, Yumi, who is here on a work visa from Japan, is the only other vibe virgin I can find. They both agree to test vibrators with me.

When I tell Vee about our little experiment, she says, "I'll do it."

I laugh out loud. "You're hardly a vibrator virgin." Vee's earthquake survival kit (all good Californians have one) consists of a Mylar blanket, a flashlight, dehydrated food packets, and a glow-in-the-dark eight-inch rubber deep-stroke vibrator.

"I'll use one I've never used before. That way it will *feel* like I'm a virgin at it."

"Fine."

We go online and look up different vibrators. There is one called the Hitachi Magic Wand that other women and sex experts warn should be used with caution. It is so powerful that women can get addicted to it, and the intense orgasm it produces can make it more difficult for women to orgasm by regular intercourse with a man. After all, what man can compete with 80,000 oscillations per minute?

"I'm getting that!" shouts Vee as she whips out her credit card and starts ordering. We pick the Rabbit Pearl for me, which we find for forty percent less at Babeland.com than what Wendy and Slumber Parties were hawking it for. I have mine shipped to Vee's apartment because I will be out of town—sucked in by Mom to help her cater a wedding—when it arrives. We e-mail Tricia and Yumi and tell them to pick their weapons.

When I return home after a week, I head straight to Vee's. She answers the door, her face all scrunched up. "I have bad news," she says. "Your Rabbit Pearl was stolen."

"How do you know?"

"I called the company. It was delivered two days ago."

"So, one of your neighbors stole my vibrator?"

She nods. "They must have figured out it was from a sex toy company." If they know Vee at all, that would be a good guess.

"You live in a four-plex. It should be pretty easy to figure out who has it."

She gets excited. "Oooh, you're right. I bet it's the comic book geek in the apartment below me."

"You think he's a geek? I think he's kind of cute."

"Oh, shoot," she hits her leg, "I just remembered. He was out of town that day. Maybe it was the lady in 4A?"

"Mrs. O'Halloran? Isn't she seventy-eight?"

"But you can tell she's been around the block a few times."

"Yeah, with her walker. Besides, didn't you tell me she was a nun once?"

"Exactly. She probably got thrown out of the nunnery for using a vibrator." Vee picks up the phone, dials Mrs. O'Halloran's number, and proceeds to leave a message on her answering machine.

"Hi, Mrs. O'Halloran, this is Victoria in apartment 2A, I'm just wondering if you *accidentally*," Vee emphasizes the word like a police interrogator might, "took a package addressed to me?" She hangs up the phone, satisfied with herself.

"You know what," I say, "if Mrs. O'Halloran stole my Rabbit Pearl, she can have it."

Vee is so obsessed with solving the case of my missing vibrator that she is not even listening to me. "Oh, my God, I know who it is! The lesbians who live in the house next door," she says smugly.

"Susan and Alma? They're going at it all the time, why would they need a vibrator? Plus Alma drives a Range Rover. I think they can afford their own vibrators."

"Okay, then maybe—"

I put my hands on her shoulders to calm her down. "Vee, let it go. What would we do anyway if we knew for sure who took it? Knock on their door and say, 'Hey, you took my vibrator, I want it back?' *After* they used it? Yuck, no."

"Fine." We both collapse on her sofa and put our feet up on an oversized ottoman. It's obvious from our silence that we are both still wondering who took my damn vibrator.

After a few minutes, I smack Vee on the shoulder. "Oh, my God, I just figured it out—*you* stole my vibrator."

"I have fourteen of my own. Why would I steal yours?"

Since I do not have a vibrator to vibrate yet, I pass the time doing more research. When were vibrators invented, I want to find out. As far as I can gather, in 1869 and 1872, a man by the name of George Taylor patented what he referred to as the first steam powered "massage and vibratory apparatii," which were initially introduced as medical apparatuses for the treatment of "hysteria" among women. In other words, if the lady of the house was feeling anxious, blue, or depressed, the thinking was that a bit of "uterine manipulation" by a medical doctor would help her stress dissipate through a series of vaginal "muscle spasms." The obvious popularity of this treatment drove the vibrator to become a household appliance by 1905, and it was advertised in women's magazines and catalogs in extremely vague terms that referred to women's health and increased vitality.

The next day, although I could use some stress relief, I find myself relieved that my vibrator was stolen. It must be the universe's way of helping me realize I prefer to stay a vibrator virgin . . .

Before I can finish this thought, Vee drops off my Rabbit Pearl vibrator. It turns out Mrs. O'Halloran accidentally picked up the package thinking it was her cheese-of-the-month-club selection. Thankfully, when she saw Vee's address on it, she realized it was not the aged cheddar wheel from Wisconsin she was looking forward to and did not open it.

I open the box and stare at the vibrator inside. Six inches looks so much bigger when it's bright pink and latex. I take it out and place it on my dresser and stare at it some more. *Why do I feel like my life is about to change? Why do I not want to do this? It's the twenty-first century and I like sex, so what is wrong with me?*

I e-mail Tricia, Yumi, and Vee.

From: Ayn

Subject: Vibrator Virgins United

Date: November 20, 08:48:35 PM PST

To: <Yumi Tsujino>, <Tricia Moore>, <V.Lo Laviña>

Ready, set, VIBRATE!!!

-Ayn

From: Tricia
Subject: V-Day
Date: November 20, 10:50:24 PM PST
To: <Yumi Tsujino>, <Ayn Carrillo>, <V.Lo Laviña>

So, I opened mine last night. I got the AUTHENTIC Rabbit
Pearl, too.
It's very...pink...and rather large. It looks exactly like a
penis–veins and everything, except it has a smiley face on
the underside unlike any penis I've ever seen, and this
crazy rabbit face & big ears camped out on the top of it.
kinda scary looking.

anyway, there's NO directions and NO indication of what
battery size is needed. it's definitely not a C and not AA .
Do ya think I should take it into the drugstore and ask them
what is needed??!!

-t.

p.s. Can you switch to using the above private e-mail add?
last thing I need is my boss reading about this at work.
slightly paranoid, but still.

what's love got to do with it?

From: Yumi
Subject: Vibrator Virgins United
Date: November 20, 11:30:24 PM PST
To: <Tricia Moore>, <Ayn Carrillo>, <V.Lo Laviña>

Hi, Ayn, Tricia, Vee

For my vibrator I used the battery from my Colgate battery
powered toothbrush. Please note: just in case I did not
translate that correctly: I did NOT use the actual toothbrush
as my vibrator.

I got a pink dolphin, but have not tested it yet. Just staring
at it without even touching it...

Yumi

From: Vee
Subject: Vibrator Virgins United
Date: November 21, 9:10:24 PM PST
To: <Tricia Moore >, <Ayn Carrillo>, <Yumi Tsujino>

Stop being wusses.

Ladies: start your vibrators!

From: Ayn
Subject: You know what
Date: November 22, 10:10:14 PM PST
To: <Tricia Moore >, <V.Lo Laviña>, <Yumi Tsujino>

Vee is right.

Report back when (okay, after) it happens,

Ayn

p.s. did a little research. why all the animal faces on the
Japanese-made vibrators we wondered? It dates back to
the Shogun era when craftsman were prohibited from
making sex toys that too closely resembled human male
genitalia. Nowadays the Japanese still honor the rule by
adding the animal faces and making them bright
colors.

From: Vee
Subject: Good Vibrations!
Date: November 26, 10:10:22 AM PST
To: <Tricia Moore >, <Ayn Carrillo>, <Yumi Tsujino>

If the Rabbit Pearl is the Rolls Royce of Vibrators, then my
Hitachi is the Humvee of vibrators. I think I am in love. I'll
never need cock again. Sorry, gals. FYI, if you need to

reach me I will not be at work this week. Taking
personal days to get to know my magic wand.

xoxo

-V

After staring at my vibrator for almost a week straight, I decide maybe it will help if I talk to the girls in person, who, with the exception of Vee, also have not found the time or inclination to test their vibrators.

Three hours later, we are all sitting in a circle, cross-legged on my living room floor with our vibrators in front of us. It looks like our own twisted version of Stonehenge, except instead of worshipping mysterious sandstone monoliths, we are worshipping vibrators.

Actually Vee really is worshipping hers. The rest of us are looking at them half-afraid, half-curious.

"I don't know if I can do it," I admit. "It makes me un-comfortable just looking at it."

"You need to name it," Vee tells me.

"You name yours?"

She starts listing hers, "There's Colin (as in Farrell), Tom and Brad, Javier—"

"Whose Javier?" we want to know.

"The guy who delivers my water bottles. There's Jack Black—"

"Jack Black?" She is talking about the chubby, very hilarious actor who is also front man for the band Tenacious D and sings about things like "cock push-ups" and his own "stinky poo."

"What? I'm not the only one. *Jane* readers voted him 'Boy You Are Strangely Attracted To.'"

"Whatever. I don't think I can name a vibrator. I feel silly."

Vee turns to Tricia and Yumi. "Okay, what about you guys?"

Tricia gives her rabbit an odd little pat on its head and declares it "Mr. Darcy" after the ultimate romantic hero in *Pride & Prejudice.*

Yumi giggles, covering her mouth like a geisha, then blurts out, "Adam." She has had a crush on Adam Sandler since moving to the States.

They all look at me.

Vee acts like a yogi, trying to guide me away from fear. "There is nothing to be afraid of. Just say whatever comes to your mind. Close your eyes and relax. Take deep . . . slow breaths. Just feel the anxiety leaving your body . . . relaxing it. No judgment. You are free to say whatever comes into your head . . . "

"Sam . . . " I say it like a chant.

Vee smacks me on the back with a wide grin. "Aha! I *knew* you still had a thing for that guy."

After they leave, I find myself staring at "Sam," which I have now mounted on my television, while watching the space movie *Solaris.* I was looking for something with absolutely no sex in it because even a little bit might remind me that I may never have it again. I figured minimalist sci-fi was a safe bet. However, the movie is so slow that in the first ten minutes, my mind wanders to sex anyway. *If you have an orgasm in outer space, can anyone hear you? Are female astronauts allowed to bring vibrators on space missions? Those are some long missions, especially for*

the men. Why doesn't NASA develop solar powered sex toys?
I wonder if what happens in space stays in space?

I turn the movie off halfway through and look back up at
"Sam." *What is wrong with me? Why am I such a good girl? Why can't*
I embrace using a vibrator? It's time I explore my fears surrounding
this. I contemplate what has kept me away from the likes of
vibrators. For one thing, I have always been deathly afraid
of electrocution. Not that I've ever heard of anybody getting
electrocuted by double C batteries or death by dildo, but I figure
if it's possible, I would probably be the first.

Also, I seem to be more uncomfortable than most women
inserting anything into myself that is not attached to a man. I did
not start using tampons until college, after my room-mate Jill
convinced me that it would be easy and more convenient than
wearing pads, which always felt way too much like I was walking
with a pillow stuffed between my legs. I am the woman who dreads
the annual Pap smear because the second I see the speculum, my
entire body goes rigid and beads of sweat form on my face. It is
cold, it is hard, it is lifeless. And it is cruel—I don't believe for one
second that we can decode DNA, clone sheep, transplant human
hearts, even faces now, and erect skyscrapers, but we cannot
design a speculum that does not resemble a medieval torture
device (the doctor *cranks* it to stretch your vaginal opening, for
God's sake)!

Another thing that happened a decade ago may be fueling my
apprehension over inserting foreign objects in myself.

My long distance boyfriend Tim and I decided that since we
were having sex so infrequently, it was useless for me to be on the
pill. So I tried the contraceptive sponge for our last night together

before he had to head back to the city. Just insert and have sex. The hard part was after I put Tim on a plane for New York, I was left to remove the sponge, probably no bigger than one inch in diameter.

But the damn thing was slippery and I had to grab onto a very tiny rubber-band handle that was connected to the very small sponge to pull it out. After two hours of trying everything to remove it—including, but not limited to, squatting on the ground, throwing one leg in the air, lying down and trying to relax and meditate it out, and jumping up and down hoping it would fall out—I still could not get a grip on the damn thing. It was like trying to grab a wet bar of soap blindfolded, using only two fingers on the same hand, because your other hand is tied behind you back.

I contemplated going to the ER, but the thought of lying on a gurney as some good-looking ER doctor and his smirking residents extracted a sponge from my vagina appalled me. Besides, I was pretty sure that in Los Angeles, knife wounds, drive-by shooting victims, and celebrity overdoses would have priority over the girl who got a contraceptive sponge stuck up inside her.

Finally, I just went with using the Force. I closed my eyes, tried to relax as much as I could, and squatted on the bathroom floor again with a mirror strategically placed underneath me. I became one with the sponge, stretching my fingers farther than they'd ever stretched before, so that I could desperately get a grip on the microscopic rubber strap. Finally, one finger sprain later, I got the damn thing out.

I call Vee and tell her about my memory.

"Why didn't you just say so? Not all vibrators have to be inserted. You can buy external stimulators. Maybe

142

what you need is a pair of vibrating panties," she suggests.

From:	Tricia
Subject:	More good vibrations
Date:	December 03, 11:10:09 PM PST
To:	<Ayn Carrillo>, <Yumi Tsujino> <V.Lo Laviña>

Well, ladies, I am no longer a vibrator virgin. I'm not sure what to say about the experience. it was...interesting? fun, sort of. doesn't compare to the real thing at all. so far (I've only tried it once) I don't see a huge advantage to masturbating on your own, without a vibrator. but perhaps I'll get better with more practice!

My thing has a weird up and down and all-around motion which does not seem to simulate anything like sex with a guy (or maybe just the guys I know), which seems more in and out to me...the rabbit ears that I earlier dissed, I have to say now, do a very nice job on the clitoris, although I have not mastered the controls enough and ended up doing it at a pace that was a bit frenetic for my tastes.

I hoped using a vibrator would get me more in touch with the elusive "G-spot" but no luck on that yet. like I said, more practice?

okay, now GO girls! join my brave new world. I want reciprocal stories!

-t.

From: Ayn
Subject: You know what
Date: December 04, 12:10:14 PM PST
To: <Tricia Moore >, <V.Lo Laviña>, <Yumi Tsujino>

Tricia's email inspired me to go ahead and buy a pair of vibrating panties ($29.99). No, they do not sell these at Victoria's Secret. They are cute though, and the vibrating device is discreetly tucked away in a pocket on underside. I did not pay the extra $50 to get a remote control since no one is around to use it on me, and felt like it would be kind of silly to use remote on myself and what, surprise me? Thought trying the panties first might help me work my way up to the six-inch. have yet to turn them on, but have worn them to grocery store—I swear the check-out lady knew I was wearing them by the way she looked at me—and to the mall. weird. felt like I was on heat. something about having the vibrator panties (not even vibrating) on made me hyperaware of every male walking by me and it must be my imagination but I noticed more guys than usual checking me out. also got my adrenaline going when I went in to the *Tu Ciudad* magazine offices to get my next assignment and wondered what would happen if the panties went off as I was discussing my next assignment with my editor, Mr. Garza? I guess I could pretend I was sitting on my cell phone.

Vee where are you???

From: Vee

Subject: Vibrator Voyage

Date: December 04, 9:11:14 PM PST

To: <Tricia Moore >, <Ayn Carrillo>, <Yumi Tsujino>

Sorry. been getting to know my Hitachi. Other vibrators are getting jealous. I think this is the start of a very long friendship or whatever that line is from the movie ayn makes us watch every year (*Casablanca*?). It's true what they say; the wand is really powerful. I haven't orgasm'd like this since...Ay, caramba, I've never orgasm'd like this. good thing poor mrs. o'halloran is deaf. did have one unfortunate accident: forgot cleaning lady was coming over and could not hear her over the hitachi's motor. needless to say I need to find a new cleaning lady. any contacts?

If you don't hear from me again, you know why.

Vee.

From: Yumi

Subject: You know what

Date: December 06, 11:34:01 PM PST

To: <Tricia Moore >, <V.Lo Laviña>, <Ayn Carrillo>

Wow. I feel like a real American, yet also proud that these wonderful instruments are made by my own country. I always liked dolphins, but now I love dolphins.

good vibrations

I was finally home on a Friday night and was watching a
sexy movie on HBO, which kind of turned me on, so I lit
candles and took Adam to bed. will it always be as good as
the first time or is it like real sex? I even had the munchies
(is that what you call it when you are hungry in the middle
of night?) afterward and slept better than I have in months.
No one told me vibrators cure insomnia.

best,

Yumi-chan

From: Tricia
Subject: Practice makes perfect
Date: December 07, 11:55:21 PM PST
To: <Yumi Tsujino>, <V.Lo Laviña>, <Ayn Carrillo>

BTW, i have spent a couple more nights (or weekend
mornings!) with Rabbit Pearl and I'm definitely getting
closer to the Big O with the G-spot, but not there yet.
Usually after about 10 minutes of trying, I give in and
succumb to the much more available clitoris orgasm. If I
was more devoted and practiced every night, I could
probably have found nirvana by now! One thing I've gained
from this experience is more sympathy and appreciation
for the opposite sex. How any of them could be expected
to find our G-spots when I can barely find mine with my
finger (let alone the vibrator) is beyond me.

But I'm super-glad I'm not a vibrator virgin any more! I
feel...more sophisticated. And I think Rabbit Pearl makes a
good companion when the real thing is not around.
Available on demand, no questions asked, guaranteed to
be as good as you can make it!

Best,

T

*The things my friends do for me. I am the last man standing. Or, last
woman standing. Or, all right, last uptight chicken-shit virgin standing.*
Except I am not presently standing. I am sitting in my car thinking, stuck in traffic on the 405 freeway with no good music on and
NPR replaying the same story I heard the hour before. I have The
Panties on because I have been trying to work up the courage to
turn them on. *Maybe I should now? No. Why the hell not?*

I look to my left. There is a soccer mom hauling a bunch of
screaming kids in bright-colored uniforms. To my right, there is a
bald guy in a black Porsche swearing into his hands-free phone.
The blonde woman in the Volvo SUV behind me is applying lipstick. The guy in front of me is blasting bassy music in his yellow
Hummer and looking straight ahead while his girlfriend yells at
him. Actually, this is a great place to do it. No one will notice and
there is enough noise to distract me from thinking about it too
much.

I reach down under my skirt and push the button on the
panties and away it goes. In the car it sounds like a cassette tape
rewinding. At first I squirm. The material the panties are made of
is 100 percent polyester and a little scratchy, I now notice. Not

exactly turned on at first. Have to sort of scoot my butt around on the seat to get the vibrator to move into a position that might turn me on. It feels a lot like sitting on a Jacuzzi jet.

After passing a few exits, I'm pretty sure it is not powerful enough to make me orgasm, but I am starting to like it more and more. It is also just turning my mind on to sex by making me hyperaware of this part of my body. I've always thought that because men's sexual organs are external, sex is on their minds more. Throughout any given day, they have to touch, arrange, and feel their penises, whereas women can easily go all day without touching or glimpsing our sexual organs. Having sex on their minds more often would explain a lot of male behavior.

I'm starting to worry a little that the vibrator might chafe me down there, so I sit back a little to take pressure off. I really think that if the material were not so scratchy, like maybe silk instead of glittered polyester, an orgasm might be possible. At the very least I know what I am doing when I get home.

Like Vee said: If God did not want us to masturbate, he would have made our arms shorter.

From: Ayn
Subject: Last woman standing no longer standing
Date: December 08, 10:10:14 PM PST
To: <Tricia Moore>, <V.Lo Laviña>, <Yumi Tsujino>

I am happy to say that there are no more vibrator virgins

left in L.A. Will fill everybody in at Rich and Sacha's
engagement party tomorrow night.

-A

The next day I have a weird dream during my afternoon power
nap. In the dream, I have somehow died. I know this because
Mom and Dad arrive at my place, wearing all black, to retrieve my
last worldly possessions. They weep over my Girl Scout sash that
is covered in badges for things like selling the most Girl Scout
cookies or learning how to start a fire without matches. They put
my Honor Society certificates, my diplomas, my track and basket-
ball medals, and my first communion rosary in a box and weep
over photos of me. Then Mom pulls down a box on the top shelf
of my closet, and *crash*! She is buried in an avalanche of sex toys,
dirty magazines, and dildos.

That night, we are at El Carmen, a kitschy-hip Mexican restaurant,
where Rich and Sacha, one of the few perfect couples that don't
make me puke, are having their engagement party. As guests
huddle around them, Vee, Yumi, Tricia, and I are whispering in a
back corner booth. Earlier, I called all of them about my dream.

"Did everyone bring their keys?" I ask.

Nodding their heads, they each place a key on the table.

Actually, Vee puts two down. "I'm giving the other key to
Steve—just in case the four of us are all killed together in one
freak accident."

The waiter, who thinks he is great at making people laugh
even though we fake laugh at all of his lame attempts at humor,

spots our keys on the table. "Key party?" he asks with a smirk.

"Actually, vibrator search and rescue," I tell him. For once he has no idea what to say. He puts our drinks on the table and rushes away.

We have all agreed that if something terrible, such as death or hospitalization, happens to any of us, one of the remaining three will use our spare key to go into our apartment and get rid of any and all vibrators before our families can find them. Of course in my case they will also have to collect my blow-up doll, Cozy Cuffs, dirty magazines, vibrating panties, Porn-to-Do list, and other *sex*ware.

Boy, has my life changed in a matter of months.

"Mine is in my fireproof safe in my closet with my birth certificate and passport," Tricia confides, handing us each a piece of paper. "Here's the combo."

"In a velvet bag, bottom drawer of my dresser under socks." I tell them. "And I might have a magazine or two under my bed."

Yumi tells us her dolphin is in her bathroom cabinet.

It's Vee's turn, but she doesn't say anything.

"Are you going to tell us where your things are?" I am impatient.

"What? It's not like I hide them."

"They're just everywhere?" I ask her in disbelief.

"Pretty much. My Magic Wand is on my dresser. Lifesaver in my purse unless I've been to the gym. In that case it's probably in my fanny pack. Mini-Me Tongue under my pillow, double dong's usually on my bathtub ledge—"

"Okay, okay, I think we get the picture."

Once we get everything worked out, we split up and mingle

with our friends at the party. Vee leaves suspiciously early, and I make a mental note to call her tomorrow to see what's up. She is usually the last person to leave a party.

I meet a really cool woman named Sabine. She is the type of woman who could make straight girls gay. She has the bone structure of an Italian model, speaks four languages but does not brag about it, has a wit as sharp as Bette Davis', and is so well read that it is clear she is not from L.A. In fact, she is a human rights lawyer from San Francisco. *I wonder if Sabine has ever tried vibrating panties?*

She tells me she came to the party with her ex-boyfriend, who, even though he broke it off with her, has maintained a friendship with her. Just then, Yumi approaches us with Sam. I forgot that Sam knows Rich and Sacha, too. If I had known he would be here, I would have worn heels, not flats. He greets me and we finally shake hands. He looks at the silver band on my wrist and asks, "Is that . . . ?"

I laugh. "No, this is *really* a bracelet."

Sabine smiles at Sam. "Speak of the devil. Your ears must have been burning."

Sam is Sabine's ex? Jesus, if he couldn't be satisfied with her, I don't have a chance!

Yumi gestures to me and excitedly tells Sam, "This is Ayn I was telling you about." She turns to me. "I was just telling him about our vibrator challenge and how we named them."

She turns back to Sam before I can stop her. "Ayn named hers Sam after some guy she met in a sex store."

I practically spit up my drink. There is silence as no one knows quite what to say. That is, except for Yumi.

"Funny, huh?" She looks at me. I am not laughing and I'm

sure I look as pale as a ghost. Sabine is trying to stifle a chuckle, and Sam has a grin on his face.

Yumi is no dummy. "Uh, you're Sam, aren't you?"

He nods.

Yumi and I make up an excuse and leave the party as quickly as humanly possible. "I am so so so sorry," Yumi repeats the whole ride home.

What is it about Sam? Every time I meet him I have to be embarrassed. Yet every time I see him I want to see him more.

I try to call Vee a few times during the next day to tell her about my latest Sam fiasco, but she does not answer. *She must be really enjoying her magic wand.* I hope she doesn't overdo it. *Is there such a thing as vibrator addiction? I would hate to have to organize a vibrator intervention. Who knows? It's L.A.—we probably have Vibrators Anonymous.*

The next day I e-mail Vee and still get no word from her. It is very unlike her to go a day without calling me, and if she were enjoying her Hitachi magic wand that much, she would not be able to resist gloating. I am starting to get worried. I call her from Urth Caffé to see if she wants to split a coconut custard pie with me, and she still does not answer or return my message.

Then everything makes sense as I look out the window.

I see Max, the nineteen-year-old she has been dating; he is riding his board down a handicap ramp and hopping the curb in front of the coffee shop. I get up with the intention of saying hello, when a young girl with long black hair runs up to him and they kiss—for a long time.

I sort of tiptoe backward and quietly disappear.

I go directly to Vee's apartment. She opens the door with a

martini in one hand and the Hitachi vibrator in the other. It's clear she has been crying and has not left the apartment for days.

I grab the vibrator.

"Friends do not let friends drink and vibrate," I console her. We sit on the sofa and even though I want to tell her about Sam, when I see her looking so pitiful I forget all of my own problems. I put my arm around her and ask her to tell me everything.

She admits that she probably made a mistake by whipping out the magic wand on her last date with Max. She thinks it intimidated him because he just stopped calling.

"I told him I'd back off of the vibrators," she tells me.

"Wow." I'm surprised she would go to those lengths for any guy.

She is crying now as she admits, "I wasn't going to really give it up. I just lied. It turns out anyway that he's been interested in someone else for a while now. That's exactly what Andres told me when he left me."

Now she is crying really hard. I give her my sleeve to blow her nose on.

"So I followed him to the video arcade one day and found him with . . . with . . . a younger woman." Her voice breaks when she says the word "younger."

"He dumped me for a younger woman. Her name is Charlie— cute name, huh? Why couldn't our moms give us cute tomboy names? I got dumped for a younger woman again . . ." She is starting to ramble now.

"Wait a minute." I am trying to figure something out. "How old is this girl he's leaving you for?"

"He told me she's twenty-two," she sobs.

"But Max is only nineteen, so actually, he didn't leave you for a younger woman."

Vee's crying subsides for a moment. She looks confused and then tilts her head as she recalculates the data. She looks up at me through her tears. "He didn't dump me for a younger woman; he dumped me for an *older* woman?"

I nod.

A big slow smile creeps over her lips and she busts up laughing. I forget how great her laugh is.

"I guess I can get rid of these." She holds up a pair of knee pads. I had no idea she was that into blowjobs.

She picks up a skateboard helmet, too. "Guess I don't need this anymore either."

I reach into my purse and hold out a bag of Oreos. "Look what I found in my tool box."

She grabs the Oreos and looks at me. "Have I told you recently how much I love you?"

"I love you, too. Now don't bogart the Oreos."

GLOBALLY,
THE TOP
THREE
SEXUAL
ENHANCERS
ARE
PORNOGRAPHY,
MASSAGE OILS,
AND
LUBRICANTS

Source: The Durex Global Sex Survey

Chapter Seven

"L" is For Lube Like You Mean It

Cunnilinguist: *n. a person fluent in oral sex with a*
woman

In some ways, researching porn for the last few months has raised more questions than it has answered, especially when it comes to my own personal sexual performance. How do I know, for instance, how I score in bed? I mean, I think I'm good (especially if I am turned on), but I bet everyone thinks they are good in bed. Maybe what I really want to know is *how good* I am in bed compared to other women. The more I think about this, the more I need to know what someone else thinks.

I decide Greg would be the most qualified person to tell me how good I am in bed. Vee says it's a bad idea to call him, but I figure we've passed that make-or-break two-month mark. If you can get that far without ending up back in each other's arms or killing each other, you are free and clear, so I call him up and he agrees to meet me for coffee.

When Greg sits down in front of me, I'm a little disappointed. He's never looked more handsome or happy. It turns out that after we split up, he started his own company testing and rating video games for advertisers. He tells me he is making six figures for the first time in his entire life, he is dating a twenty-four-year-old from Greece, who just gave up a modeling career to work for

Greenpeace in America, and he finally lost that extra fifteen pounds he was carrying around.

I, on the other hand, look like I gained fifteen pounds since we broke up, he innocently points out. Actually, I gained a mere eleven, but I don't want to argue it and come off as insecure.

He takes a sip of his coffee—he treated both of us, surprise surprise—and sizes me up before telling me, "The Reese's Pieces are in the trunk of your car under the spare. The chocolate bundt cake is in the crock pot that you never use, but it's probably a moldy mess, Ding Dongs are in the attic, leftover Easter candy is in the earthquake kit bag—"

"What are you talking about?"

"Your chocolate stashes. Isn't that why you called me here? You wanted to coax me into revealing where I hid all the goodies."

Wow, does he think I'm that desperate? "Actually, I had a personal question for you," I come back at him.

"Shoot."

"Just one second." I reach for a pen in my purse and write on a scrap of paper "Easter candy in earthquake kit," and then turn back to Greg.

"It's a little awkward." I take another sip of my soy latte followed by a sip of my ice blended—I couldn't decide, so I got both—then just blurt it out. "How good was I in bed?"

He doesn't seem surprised by the question at all. "On a scale of what?"

"How about on a scale of, oh, just tell me if I was good or great."

"When we had sex, you were great."

I grin, feeling cocky. I knew this was going to be his answer; I

don't know why I had to even ask. I guess it just feels good sometimes for someone else to tell you that you're good at something.
Greg noticeably relaxes.

"You look relieved," I laugh.

"For a second there I thought you were going to ask me about
oral sex." After a pause, it looks like what he just said registers
with him; his eyes go wide and his mouth zips shut.

"What do you mean?" I inquire.

He looks at his wrist even though he is not wearing a watch
and pretends he didn't hear my question. "Wow, too bad, I've got
to go. This has been fun. I'm meeting Matina at a fundraiser."

As he rises, I grab his arm and yank him back down. "Now,
tell me how was I at blow jobs." I hear the older gentleman behind
me spit out his coffee.

"Can you keep your voice down a little?" Greg hisses. Then,
in a whisper, he says, "You're not serious?"

"Yes, I am. I need to know."

"Fine. You were great."

Aha, I knew it! But why is he squirming?

"Now, can I go?" he asks.

"*How* was I great? I need details."

"I don't know, it was just good, all of it, well, uh, except for
that thing you did with your teeth." His body shivers uncontrollably as if he is reliving some painful memory. "And I guess
you could have used your hands a little more."

He sees the look of shock on my face. "Hey, it's not that big a
deal. It's like anything else, it takes skill. Some people are born
good at it and others aren't."

"Are you saying I sucked at giving blow jobs?"

"Hey, you know, this is a lot of pressure. It's not like you did it that much anyway." And with that, he makes a hasty exit.

As soon as I get home, I Google "How to Give a Blow Job." I find an article online from *LA Weekly*, one of the city's alternative papers.

According to the article, the nation's reigning expert on blow jobs is a woman named Lou Paget, who has developed an instructional seminar that has been featured on HBO's *Real Sex* and a slew of other talk shows.

I call Lou Paget's office and get an assistant. "Hi, I'd like to write a piece on Lou Paget's blow job seminars," I say, "and was wondering if I could set up a time to talk to her." I figure if they think I'm going to write about them, I won't have to pay the $170 seminar fee.

"How did you hear about Lou?" she asks.

"There was a piece on the *LA Weekly* online."

"Oh, she did not like that article at all," her assistant informs me.

"Really? It sounded like the writer really loved her class."

"Lou takes her work seriously. She doesn't use the term 'blow job.' As Lou puts it, anyone who knows anything about performing oral sex knows there is no blowing involved."

"That's funny. That's exactly the kind of thing I'm hoping to learn." I tell her I am researching things like Lou's class for a project I call *The Good Girl's Guide to Porn*. She takes my number and tells me she'll have Lou give me a call.

"Great. Thank you," I say.

A week goes by. I don't hear from them. I log on to the LouPaget.com website and see that she is conducting a seminar—

it is actually titled "The Ladies' Sexuality Seminar," not "The How to Give a Blow Job Seminar"—in New York City next month for $220, but no L.A. seminar.

Maybe I can score a private lesson, which costs $800, since I am doing research?

I e-mail her a really nice note. This time I do not use the term "blow job," and I downplay that I am investigating porn, just in case that is a problem, too. Part of me doubts it would be, because it would be a tad bit hypocritical for somebody who teaches women how to suck guys' cocks to be too judgmental of anyone else's sexual proclivities.

Two more weeks go by. No e-mail or returned call.

Not only do I possibly suck at giving blow jobs, I think, *but apparently I suck at getting into blow job seminars.*

Another week passes. I get the feeling I've been blown off by the queen of blow jobs. Maybe I've been blacklisted because she is afraid I will write about her oral sex seminars in a sleazy way, too. *I might, if I could get into one.*

I actually consider flying out to New York City just to learn how to give a better blow job. The New York seminar is $220 per person. I can get a red eye flight for $380. I mean, when you think about it, $600 (class fee and airfare) is not a lot of money for a skill that—unlike origami-folding and welding that I learned at a community college last year—you can use for the rest of your life. It's also something you can share with others.

I do what I always do when I want to justify buying something that is obviously outside of the reasonable range of my measly monthly budget: I break it down to cost per day. It's a method I learned from the fundraising campaign drives of various charities and nonprofits. For instance, my local public radio station (KCRW) gets me to donate $100 a year by making me realize that at that rate, it costs me less than 30 cents a day. This is a *lot* less than, let's say, a latte at Starbucks, which I buy almost every day without even thinking, but would give up if forced to make a choice between it and giving up the music and news that KCRW provides me.

So, if I live to be eighty (that's 18,250 more days), the money spent on learning how to give a blow job ($600) would only come to less than 4 cents per day for the rest of my life. *Who can't spare four cents?*

Just when I decide to splurge on myself and sign up for the New York class online, I see that they have added an L.A. class for only $170! I immediately sign up, hoping that if I have been blacklisted, they will let me in before they recognize my name.

As the seminar date approaches, I find myself growing more and more curious, and I am not the only one. My girlfriends and The Naughty Knitters are dying for me to go so that I can bring back information for them. It starts me thinking about oral sex and its relation to actual intercourse. There are definitely some advantages to the former. For one thing, it's a great form of birth control without the bloating, acne, weight gain, or other usual side effects of birth control pills. From all reports, it is also on the rise and increasingly more popular with younger generations. I wonder if the birth control reason explains why.

I discuss it with Steve and Paige over dinner.

"We're a fast food nation." Paige sums up her theory about the increase in oral sex.

"Are you saying that blow jobs are the fast food of sex?" I ask to clarify.

"Exactly. Who has time between work, networking, kabbalah, and Pilates to actually have full-blown sex?"

I think she may have a point. I can't help but wonder if Sam is a fast-food sex sort of guy. *Did he prefer McSex with his ex?*

I have always wondered how Paige squeezes in sex. Everyone I know is busy, but during any given week Paige is doing no less than working on two scripts and a novel; pitching television shows; learning to speak German; having cocktails with agents, managers, and producers; throwing parties for friends; and, of course, experiencing the not-so-occasional nervous breakdown. I am willing to bet she is multitasking even when she's having sex with her husband.

"Blow jobs have saved my marriage—it's either that, or give up sex altogether," explains Paige. "Ten minutes I can fit into my schedule, an hour is really pushing it."

"Look, there is no such thing as a bad blow job." Steve appears to be speaking for all men. "So there's no way to really suck—pun intended—at giving one. If they don't draw blood they're great."

"Yeah, but can man live on blow jobs alone?" I ask.

"If your significant other has a yeast infection, yeah."

On the way over to the seminar, I consider that after earning a bachelor's degree and two masters', I always thought my next educational experience would be a doctorate. But here I am on a Friday night, wondering if I will get a diploma at the end of the evening certifying that I am now proficient in oral sex. *Mom and Dad will be so proud.*

I walk into the Beverly Hills hotel where the seminar is being held, and find that I feel very conspicuous. It's not like I'm Julia Roberts wearing thigh-high boots, a hot pink halter, and a mini skirt, or anything even close to that, but I still feel kind of like a prostitute, albeit a prostitute dressed in Ann Taylor Loft. Must be leftover Catholic guilt. I imagine that the bellman and the concierge and the reservation desk girl are sizing me up when I am not looking. They all know there is a sex seminar going on in their hotel, and they have probably informed the patrons in the piano bar who are staring at me when I walk by. Even the pianist is checking me out. I know what they are all thinking: *What kind of person goes to a blow-job seminar? What kinds of dirty sex secrets will be taught? Will women really practice sucking on dildos?* My mind is spinning with their possible thoughts. *Is she a sexaholic? Is she a slut? A girlfriend desperate to please?* Or worse: *She must suck at sex and therefore has to take this seminar.*

I ask the concierge where "the seminars" are being held. She points to an easel by the elevators and gives me what appears to be a smirk that I graciously ignore. I look at the easel. Thank goodness it says "Frankly Speaking Seminar," not "How to Give a Blow Job Seminar" or what it is really called, "The Ladies' Sexuality Seminar."

Upstairs, I step into a conference room. I was imagining a hundred women, but it is a quiet little room with a conference room table where four other women, who appear to range in age from about twenty to sixty, are already seated. In front of everyone is a place setting that includes a china plate and a white cloth napkin on top of that. Now, I'm really excited, because I am very hungry. In my mad rush to figure out what one wears to learn how to give blow jobs, I did not have time to eat. Food sounds awesome. Maybe that's why the fee is so exorbitant; fancy hors d'oeuvres will be served.

As I unfold my napkin and put it on my lap, I turn to look as the last woman walks in. My jaw drops. It's Vee, who nonchalantly takes the last seat to the right of me.

"What are you doing here?"

"Taking piano lessons," she says sarcastically. "What does it look like?"

"I thought you were great at sex."

"I am. I'm just not as great at blow jobs."

"But why didn't you tell . . ."

As Lou Paget walks in and takes the head of the table, Vee gestures for me to be quiet. I look Lou up and down. So this is the woman who's been ignoring my calls and e-mails. Lou Paget is a stereotypical California-looking woman: tall, blonde, thin, and pretty in a cream-colored designer suit. If she were on a cell phone driving a Range Rover, she'd be the exact kind of woman I love to hate. She introduces herself with a wide smile and starts out the class by telling us a little bit about how she came to teach these seminars.

"I was exiting a relationship," she says. *Let me guess,* I think, *he broke up with you because you never returned his calls or e-mails?*

She adds, "And I decided that in my next relationship, I wanted more information, and I wanted it to be helpful, accurate, and above all I wanted it to work. If I heard one more thing like 'Open a bottle of wine and light a candle' I was going to shriek. I wanted to know where to put my hands and fingers and toes."

She brings up adult videos, which she explains do not help women learn how to be better at sex, because the performers who are having sex are not actually enjoying sex in any given porn video. According to Lou, a famous porn star attending a past seminar stood up and confessed to the other ladies in attendance that when she is shooting a sex scene, she is miserable. "Her eyes are watering, she's gagging, her knees are aching and she is completely disconnected. She may look like she's enjoying it but she is not."

Lou's point is that we should not be in the class because our men want us to be there, especially if they want us to perform like the women they see in adult movies. We should be in the class because *we* want to enjoy and master sex for ourselves. The skills we learn tonight, according to Lou, will translate into confidence in the bedroom and outside of the bedroom. "And confidence is sexy," she tells us. *Easy for her to say. She's tall, blonde, and beautiful.*

"The most important reason to take the class is because sex is one of our most important forms of communication, and we should be proficient in it," she tells us. "After interviewing hundreds of men, and asking them when they knew a relationship was over, the answer they always invariably give is: when the woman expressed that she was no longer interested in sex. Men will be very strategic at that time. They will start putting things into order for their exit. And the woman will not have any idea. She will think things are just fine."

I think of all the women I know, Mom included, to whom this may have happened. "If a man is not acknowledged for who he is as a sexual being," continues Lou, "he will go and get the acknowledgement of that masculine energy elsewhere." This information rivets all of us. It's as if we've all sensed this at times in our lives, but nobody ever said it out loud. Okay, I hate to admit it, but she's got us all hooked. As I listen to Paget, I start to wonder if Sam will ever call me. *Will I ever get a chance to acknowledge his masculine energy?*

"We get told from an early age that men use us for sex, that when they have sex it is about them, that that's all they're interested in. What we [women] don't get told is that, when a man is having sex with the woman he wants, at no time does he feel more male, more masculine, or more who he is than at that time, and that it is you, the woman, who is giving him access to that feeling."

I never thought of it that way. Women actually have more power in the bedroom because we control the access. I have never thought about the pressure that must put on men to perform.

She makes it clear that her seminars are not about her; the information in her seminars comes from her friends, acquaintances, and thousands of people she's met through the seminars. Of course there are self-help—a.k.a. *sex-help*—books, but those books tell you how to *fix* something, and Lou never really thought anything was broken, she just wanted more good information without putting her own body at risk to get it. So, she started asking her girlfriends and her male gay friends questions and it kind of just grew from there. Three million copies of her books and thousands of seminar attendees later, here we are.

"Your fears are like bullies, ladies. If you stare them down, they'll disappear."

I love this statement. It is exactly what set me on this path in the first place. I decide I like Lou, lack of personal communication notwithstanding.

"Okay, getting started." She reaches into her bag. "Did anyone pick mulatto for their training tool?" I must have not received the e-mail everyone else did because I am not sure what she's talking about—and isn't "mulatto" un-PC nowadays? *Maybe I should suggest a different term. Wait. What am I talking about? Why do I care about being PC when we are talking about deep-throating a rubber dong?*

Lou whips out a huge life-like rubber penis, and another and another... They are dildos to be exact, with balls and a suction cup at the base of each one. I am shocked. Not because there are dildos before us. Now that I've been around the porn block once or twice, I've seen a dildo, but the size of these things seems, well, rather *large*. I look around. The other women seem uncomfortable, too, so I have to ask.

"Uh, are those the average size of guys in real life? Because those are bigger than anything I've ever seen."

Lou laughs. "These are eight inch. The average size of a man is five and a quarter inches." *Pheew.* Still, they are intimidating. We each pick one. One woman, who looks like Betty Crocker, and is anywhere from forty to sixty (it's really hard to tell when you live in the plastic surgery capital of the world), very clearly states, "I chose mulatto on the phone with your assistant, but if there is a blacker one, I'll take that. I have a mulatto one at home already." She explains to the rest of us that this is her second seminar with Lou. She decided to come back after a few years for a refresher course. The rest of us are left with the white dildos.

As we all fondle our instructional tools, I can't help but wonder how Sam would measure up to these things. Lou places the suction cup side of her dildo down on the china plate before her and tells us to do the same with ours, testicles facing us.

Damn, no hors d'oeuvres. Before we start, just for fun, she shows us what the guys use as their training tool in the men's seminar.

Wow, a sexuality seminar for men that emphasizes oral sex skills? Sounds like a great Valentine's gift for a future significant other, if I ever date again. The instructional tool for the men is a latex mold of a real porn star's vagina. It is pretty detailed and feels lifelike.

"It even has a G-spot," Lou informs us. Everyone's hands, except Vee's, shoot up. We all have the same question: How do you find your G-spot?

According to Lou, the number one reason women can't find their G-spots is because they look for it when they are not stimulated. "You would have to get yourself excited, manually or with a vibrator, squat down and feel up inside the vaginal area. It's the size of a dime or quarter, depending on the woman, above the vaginal wall, on your tummy side." She shows us on the training vagina. "The position of it explains why a lot of women like deep thrusting doggy style for the best G-spot orgasms."

"It also explains why you never get an orgasm inserting a tampon," I whisper to Vee.

We start with an exercise called "The Swirl." It's basic and simple. To awaken a guy's senses before sex, you have him stand against a wall with his back to you and in a swirling motion you lightly scratch up and down his back and arms in an irregular pattern. It won't be what he's expecting, it will feel good, and it will awaken his entire body. She has us practice on each other. I practice on Vee and she practices on me. It is easy and it does feel great. She informs us that we should apply a little more pressure on a man than we would want it done on ourselves, because men have tougher skin because of the effects of testosterone.

I really like Lou by the time she tells us all of this. She makes us comfortable, she keeps it light; she's classy and very articulate. If she had been leading my sex toy party, I have a feeling she could have sold five times as many toys and there would have been a lot more laughs.

Next, we test different lubricants (ones that actually taste great), massage oils, and moisturizing products selected and researched by Lou. No K-Y Jelly here. As she puts it, "Where is the fun factor with that stuff?"

She also imparts interesting facts about common lubricant ingredients, some of which are the same chemical ingredients used to keep fire hoses from drying or cracking. Apparently nonoxynol-9 was originally created as a cleaning detergent for hospitals. She also shares some great products with us such as Sensura, a "massage" oil that comes in some irresistible flavors (I pick watermelon) and reminds us that oral sex is a two-way street. Sensura becomes hot when blown on or rubbed. Guys love the sensation. So do women.

As we test the lubricants, she sprinkles in current information on sexual trends. One new trend in oral sex is felching. It's when a man comes inside a woman and then sucks it out. *No thank you.* We talk about the use of whipped cream (kosher or not kosher), which can lead to irritation or yeast infections when used internally, and she shares an anecdote with us about a seminar student whose lover put potato salad inside her, which led to a trip to the emergency room for systemic infection. *I wonder if Greg ever considered hiding my chocolate stash in my . . . nah, I'd definitely find that.*

After we are all loosened up, we get more into the material and start the manual techniques that we all came here for. This is where I realize Lou is the big sister I've always dreamed of. Someone who tries everything first and then shares the best with you and helps you avoid the worst.

We learn six hand manipulation techniques, including Ode to Bryan (named after her best friend who was gay and responsible for showing her a lot of the techniques that she is passing on to women), the Hand Cross, Basket Weaving, Basket Weaving with Heartbeat of America combo, Pirouette, and Parlour Trick. As we practice the hand moves, Lou weaves in valuable information about men and sex and makes us laugh along the way.

At first, some of the hand techniques are difficult to master. But after a few tries it's like driving a stick shift. You just stop thinking and you feel it. There are also a lot of squishy sounds that sound anything but sexy. When someone points this out, Lou assures us, "Men love squishy sounds." When I get the first hand move, Ode to Bryan, which is basically a unique way of gliding one's hand up and over a man's penis, mastered, I speed it up, which transforms it into what Lou calls "The Penis Samba," and before I know it, I have forgotten where I am. I am just having a good time. It also feels good on my hands. It's like I'm working the dildo, but I am also making the dildo work for me.

We openly discuss how oral sex is such hard work for some women, and many of us agree that many times, it is more a labor of love than a turn-on.

"A secret you should take away from this class," Lou advises, "is that going down on your lovers will be a lot more fun if you don't have to work so hard." For instance, she adds, "You can control the pace and the position in which his penis enters your mouth, so there is very little chance of gagging, something many women state as their top reason for not wanting to perform oral sex."

Out of the corner of my eye, I see Vee scribble something in her notepad. I am starting to wonder now if Vee is not the skilled mistress of sex we have all assumed she is. She was married for a decade. Now that I think about it, her skills might be a little out-dated, especially to the teenagers she is dating. *Could the cache of vibrators be covering up lack of skill in the bedroom?*

As we continue the hand moves, I wonder why there is so much emphasis on them when most of us are there to learn *oral* sex techniques. "The manual hand moves are foreplay to actual oral sex," Lou explains as if she read my mind, "and should not be under-emphasized. The time one spends on the hand movements translates into less time your mouth actually has to be on his penis. Not that this is the goal, but it makes oral sex a lot easier if it's not a marathon." I couldn't agree more.

She makes us so comfortable that we all start asking questions as we practice the different moves. "What is the guy's most sensitive spot?" asks the youngest of the bunch.

"Typically the frenulum, that quarter-size 'V' shaped area on the underside of his shaft just below the head. For some men who are circumcised, it's the circumcision scar site, and for others it's the glans (top of penis). Next in sensitivity is the scrotum and the perineal area (the area under the scrotum before the anus)." She shows us all of these spots on our training tools as she explains them.

"What percentage of women really swallow?" asks the fifty-eight-year-old grandmother of two, who told us earlier that she is taking the class because she is heading back into the dating scene for the first time in thirty-five years.

"Twenty to twenty-five percent," Lou tells us. We look visibly relieved.

Another woman asks, "I hate it when he grabs my head. How can I prevent that?"

"Tell him it breaks your concentration," advises Lou. *Geez, she's smart. What a great answer.*

As we move onto a more complex hand move, I sense Vee watching me like she used to do in college when she would copy off my exams. I look over at her. Her practice penis is flopping all over the place and she has a very confused look on her face.

"Wow, you suck at hand jobs," I tell her. I turn to Lou. "Excuse me, Lou, I think Victoria could use a hand with her hand job."

Lou patiently watches Vee attempt the Penis Samba. It is ironic because on the dance floor, Vee is the Samba queen, but on her practice penis, she tries four or five times and still can't get it. I want to giggle, but I see the frustrated look on Vee's face and stifle it.

"It feels really awkward," Vee informs Lou.

"Do you have carpal tunnel syndrome?" Lou asks her.

"Sometimes. I do a lot of typing." *Yeah, right. More likely it's from abusing her vibrators.*

"Let's try the Basket Weave. I developed this move for a woman who was suffering from multiple sclerosis. It is less tiring on the wrists." *Wow, Lou even cares about the handicapped. Okay, she's awesome.*

We follow Lou's lead and moisten the lubricant already on our hands with some water—not more lubricant. This is not one of the highlighted tips, but it's one of the coolest I will bring home. A couple drops of water reconstitutes the lubricant so that it has that perfect gliding capability again. "Too much lubricant is possible," informs Lou. I flash to all of the times I've had to re-apply lubricant, only for it to get so sticky it's like giving a hand job with peanut butter, making sex more uncomfortable than it would have been without the lubricant. The stuff is also not cheap.

And back to Basket Weaving: "Clasp your hands together, interlacing fingers, relaxing thumbs in order to make a hole. Lower your clasped hands onto his penis with the thumbs facing you, the fit should be tight." In essence we are creating an impostor vagina. "Move your hands, still clasped, up and down." Then, as she does with all the moves, she adds some variation. "Now, twist your clasped hands slowly as they go up and down the shaft, much like the movement inside a washing machine."

She looks over at Vee, who is making a quick swishing back and forth motion—kind of like a washing machine when you've put too many things in it and it starts to go berserk. Finally, I get up, stand behind Vee, and with my arms around her, I put my hands over hers to show how it is done. I am the Patrick Swayze to her Demi Moore in *Ghost*.

The maneuver helps. Vee finally does the move correctly. She beams and looks up at me. "Thanks, Ayn." She says it with such real sincerity that I'm almost taken aback. I am seeing a whole new side of Vee. I take my seat again, marveling at how a good hand job can bring people together.

After we've all mastered the hand techniques, we move on to the oral techniques. Again, our questions guide Lou's instruction.

"How much suction?" the woman next to me asks.

"Ask him to suck on your fingers or your tongue to show you. Obviously that direction can work in reverse, too." I love these simple ideas. I take a moment to imagine how they would make the act of oral sex with Sam (if he ever calls) more interactive, communicative, and sensual.

She takes us through the basic oral steps, which she calls "Mouth Yoga Rules," such as that your tongue is always in motion, and your hands and mouth work in concert. She also has a bunch of specific techniques that will excite any guy, like strumming his frenulum, massaging the male prostate (*his* G-spot), and stroking his scrotum ("Treat them like breakable eggs," she advises). She also advises that if we are using mints—*you can use mints?*—make sure to chew and swallow them first, and be careful about using strong mints. Apparently Lou's clients have shared with her in the past that using certain mints and breath fresheners, such as Listerine strips, during oral sex have sent guys running and screaming from a bedroom. I love these stories because I can see those things happening to me, but now I will be able to avoid situations like burning some guy's member with super-strength Altoids—it gives their slogan "Curiously Strong" a whole new meaning—in the future. I am also pleased to learn that I have very good hand-mouth coordination compared to the others, including Vee.

Next, Lou demonstrates how to use certain novelty products. Who knew a woman can give a guy a pearl necklace, too? High quality pearls strung on nylon without a metal clasp work best to excite a man, Lou tells us. Basically, after wearing the pearls around your neck when you are out for the night, you take them off at home and surprise him, by loosely wrapping them around his shaft to tease him and then performing one of the manual moves with the pearls between your hand and his shaft.

Shaft sleeves, which look like one-inch tubular rigatoni, made of silicone, not semolina, can be slipped over his shaft to give him a great sensation or they can be slipped on the guy's finger for a great sensation for you. Lou also explains how cock rings can be used to enhance the oral sex experiment by restricting the flow of blood in a man's shaft so that there is a buildup, which helps him maintain an erection longer and possibly experience a more intense orgasm.

She continues by pulling out a series of vibrators that she and her seminar attendees have come to trust over the years. She sells the Rabbit Pearl (the real one) for much less than Slumber Parties was selling it for. She also has something called a Tongue Joy for all of those women who don't want to pierce their tongue to offer up better oral sex, but do want to provide the same unique sensation to their guy. It is basically a mini vibrator connected to a rubber band that you wear around your tongue.

"I am so getting that." Vee announces excitedly.

"Women should use this with discretion," Lou warns about the Hitachi Magic Wand that Vee used for the vibrator experiment. Vee and I exchange a knowing glance.

Before the class wraps up, we put all of the hand and mouth moves together. It's a lot of fun and I feel like I do in step aerobics class when the class is in unison, like we are all part of some well-choreographed Broadway dance number, in the moment, just having fun and strutting our stuff.

As Vee and I leave, with our bags of devices and flavored lubricants and an autographed copy of Lou's book, *How to Be a*

Great Lover, I feel transformed. I see the concierge who earlier was judging me, but now I feel that she is not judging me so much as *envying* me. I am confident about oral sex, and she is not. Funny how this new confidence is already coming in handy outside of the bedroom, too, just like Lou said it would. The same men who were eyeing me in the piano bar and the bellman I thought was probably wondering if I suck at oral sex are now looking at me differently, too. *Or, are they?* Maybe it's like Lou said in class: "Your fears are like bullies. Stare them down, and they will disappear."

Postscript: Lou Paget did graciously return my calls and e-mails the following week. She wasn't blowing me off, just inundated with press calls.

ONE IN THREE

VISITORS

TO ALL ADULT

WEB SITES

IS A

WOMAN.

Source: Internet Filter Review

Chapter Eight

Here Comes the SeXXXpert

Immaculate ejaculation: *n. occurs when a person ejaculates without being touched*

Maya has assembled The Naughty Knitters at her place for our new favorite pastime, which we fondly refer to as "More Swag from the Bitch Boss." Maya's job with Mr. X ended when the movie he was working on ended a month ago. Now, she is assistant to Mrs. X, who is not related to Mr. X, but rather a Hollywood actress whose mother was also famous although a more respected actor than she is. Unfortunately for Maya, Mrs. X has a blame problem. When anything goes wrong—her son gets a C on his report card, she is late to a meeting, she does not get invited to an A-list party, or she cannot fit into the new Chanel suit she bought herself—she blames Maya and throws a tantrum, sometimes even in public.

Maya recently discovered that Mrs. X has done this with all of her assistants—and that she went through *three* assistants in five months on the last movie she shot. Fortunately for us, Mrs. X also experiences guilt, so after each maniacal outburst she showers Maya with fabulous expensive gifts and merchandise (a.k.a. swag) from award show goody bags to make up for being a bitch boss.

However, Maya hates the woman so much she cannot stand to enjoy the goodies herself. She hands me a pair of Prada sunglasses. Paige gets a suede Dooney & Bourke purse, Steve gets a leather Coach planner, Tricia gets a pair of topaz drop earrings, and Vee gets a red silk Hermès scarf.

When I see the scarf, I look at Maya with sympathy. "That must have been a bad one."

"It was. She forgot to get an anniversary gift for her husband, which was my fault apparently for not writing the date down in her calendar. She chewed me out in Neiman Marcus and told her husband that I lost her gift to him."

Steve ties Vee's Hermès scarf around his neck. "Let's knit for Eli today," he suggests, keeping us on track while we talk. Eli is Heather's adorable new baby boy.

We all start knitting except for Paige, who is jotting down ideas for her novel on a notepad.

"Most unromantic romantic comedy lines," Steve calls out. This is a frequent game we play.

"Sometimes it's hard to see the forest through the sleaze," says Vee.

"*Hitch*," Tricia declares correctly.

"There are no happy endings. Just unfinished stories," Maya quotes.

"*All About Eve*," guesses Vee.

Steve makes a buzzer sound. "Not even close. *Mr. and Mrs. Smith*," he answers.

"Life sucks, then gets worse from there," Paige quotes.

"It's a lot more fun, Paige, if the quote is from a produced movie, not one of your works in progress," Tricia reminds her.

"If you start out depressed, everything's kind of a pleasant surprise," quotes Steve.

"*Say Anything*. You always quote that movie," Maya points out.

"A female ferret will die if it goes into heat and cannot find a mate," I quote.

"Eeeew . . ." Vee gives Steve a sideways glance.

They are all stumped.

"Uh, what movie is that from, Ayn?" asks Maya.

"It's not a movie. I read it. It really resonated with me."

"Okay, you really need to get laid," announces Vee.

"I second that emotion," says Steve.

I narrow my eyes at them. "You know, sex is not the answer to everything."

Steve puts my new Prada sunglasses on me. "To cut the glare."

"What is wrong with you?" asks Vee. "You've been moping all morning."

"I heard Sam got back together with Sabine the super girlfriend. Can you blame him?"

"Have you tried Sudoku? It really distracts you from your troubles," Tricia advises.

"I don't know, the last time you sent me on that Krav Maga retreat I practically dislocated my shoulder," I tell her.

Steve grabs my knitting project, a long tube of brightly colored yellow yarn that is now about nine inches long, and stares at it. "What are you knitting?"

"A sock."

"For what? It looks like a cozy for the training dong you got at that seminar."

"Would you get your mind out of the gutter for one second?" I demand.

"Speaking of the gutter, how's *The Good Girl's Guide to Porn* going?" asks Vee.

I pull my Porn-to-Do list out of my purse. (It looks like it's been in a gutter. It is wrinkled and tattered now, splattered with coffee stains, and it is missing a little corner.)

"What's left?" someone inquires.

"Watch porn. Check out a brothel. Meet a porn star. Consult a sex expert." I pause for a second thinking about whom I would even consult, then turn to my friends and ask, "Who is our generation's Dr. Ruth?"

They look at me, blankly. I rephrase the question. "When you want to learn more about sex, who do you turn to?" I look at Vee. "Other than Nikki Tyler and Jenna Jameson."

"HBO documentaries," declares Paige.

"*Esquire*," Steve reveals. "Okay, and sometimes I sneak a look at my girlfriend's *Jane* and *Cosmo*.

"*Sex and the City* DVDs," says Tricia.

"*Loveline*," Maya admits. "And that little gray-haired old lady on Oxygen."

"Sue Johansen?" I completely forgot about her. "Don't you think there is something odd about her?" I ask.

Maya looks wounded. "What are you talking about? I love her; it's like my grandma explaining how things like dildos and mutual masturbation work."

"Exactly. *Eeewww*. And what is she scribbling on that little pad of paper all the time?"

"Dirty doodles. You know, like a younger big-bosomed version of herself riding some giant cartoon cock like it's a rocket to the moon," Steve jokes, making us all laugh out loud.

"Come on, does anyone actually believe for a second that she has sex? Maybe she's a psychic who channels the dead, which would explain the scribbling. But in Johansen's case she channels them to advise her on things like how to use a cock ring or have multiple orgasms." They nod their heads like I might be on to something.

After we knit in silence for a minute—that's about the maximum we can go without gossiping or talking about men, sex, or relationships—Tricia throws out, "How about that sex expert that Brian Price was talking about at Sacha's engagement party?"

"Dr. Suzy Block," Steve reminds us.

"Who is that?" I recall that Greg had *The Dr. Block Show* book-marked on his computer.

"You don't know who Dr. Block is?" asks Vee.

"Brian did say she is the only sex expert he can imagine actually having sex," Paige recalls.

I look up Dr. Block's number and give her office a call. I explain to her assistant that I am thinking of writing a piece on relationships for *Tu Ciudad* magazine (not completely untrue) and that I'd like to get her take on a few things. Her assistant asks me to wait a second; she is going to get Dr. Block and put her on the phone with me—right then. Refreshing.

Surprisingly, I am not nervous about asking a complete stranger about sex over the phone. Knowing that Dr. Block advises people over the phone/radio about sex for a living makes me not sweat it. I didn't even need to come up with my own questions. The Naughty Knitters were so excited that I was going to call her that they each gave me questions they would love for her to answer.

She takes less than a minute to get to my call and introduces herself with a friendly but authoritative-sounding voice. I have not had time to actually see her show because I have yet to load the correct program onto my computer to watch it streaming live. But I do not tell her this, and she is too polite to ask what I think of her show. I start by asking, "Can you describe your show for me in your own words?"

"It's an extremely intimate, sometimes shocking, educational, and always entertaining show about the many splendored aspects of human sexuality, revealing a side of humanity that is rarely seen on television."

Wow. That's quite a description. It makes me think I should try harder to see her show. I learn that she conducts private relationship sex therapy, which is her bread and butter, but her show, which airs on cable television (it is even translated in Hebrew, Arabic, and French) and radio, and the live Internet broadcast, is what makes her popular. Her website receives 50,000 hits *a day,* and, as for paid subscribers—she can't reveal the actual number of people who pay to see her show live on the Internet—she informs me that twenty-five percent of her subscribers live outside of the United States and thirty percent are women. I guess I am not the only woman out there who has a few questions about sex, porn, and relationships.

Dr. Block is so knowledgeable, frank, and articulate that we have a really fun, easy conversation. It turns out she graduated magna cum laude from Yale with a doctorate in philosophy and an emphasis in psychology. Her doctoral thesis was on the four aspects of womanhood, as defined by Carl Jung's disciple and lover Toni Wolf: the mother, the madonna, the amazon, and the courtesan. I love this. I have not had a good intellectual discussion in a while, especially while investigating porn.

When I ask her how she got her start, she tells me she wrote a book *Advertising For Love* in 1984 about a new dating trend that she thought was unique and hip. The dating trend was something called "personal ads." Hard to believe there was a time when there weren't personal ads. She laughs at the fact that she had the foresight to be one of the first people to think personal ads would explode.

"I even had a small chapter on using this new thing on the computer called 'The Internet' to post personal ads," she tells me. That led to *LA Weekly*, L.A.'s most popular alternative weekly paper, to sponsor her first radio show: She helped callers write personal ads over the air. That grew to her giving relationship advice over the air, and that grew to giving sex advice.

I explain to her what I've been doing with my Porn-to-Do list and that, in the process, a lot of questions about sex have come up. I start with something Tricia and I pondered recently.

"Relationships seem to be failing at a faster rate than ever before. In your professional opinion, what's wrong with relationships nowadays?" I ask her.

"I believe there's great pressure nowadays to be perfect in an idealized, unrealistic way. It comes from a lot of different areas of society. Lately, religions are bearing down on people in a way I didn't see when I was a teenager. The new pope is more conservative than the last, especially about sex. Our American president is also sending a strong anti-sex, anti-female message." She has obviously thought about this before.

"Ironically, sex mixed with violence or violence made to look sexy is more accepted than sex in a positive healthy relationship," she goes on. "For example, you see a lot of people in movies looking sexy then doing something violent. You rarely get to see two people having great consensual sex . . . and an image of a female *nipple,*"—she is referring to Janet Jackson's "wardrobe malfunction" at the Super Bowl, a.k.a. NippleGate—"one that actually was covered by a pasty, is cried about and screamed about, fined, and censored. This sends a message that makes us feel like our breasts, a sexual and nurturing part of us, are bad."

"You are so right," I tell her. She has a way of getting you worked up about an issue. Always trying to see both sides, I ask, "Is there anything better or right about relationships nowadays?"

"We are becoming more aware and more open about sex even though the people in power try to constantly control and censor it. Couples are becoming more egalitarian around the world, there is more openness, more opportunity to learn. The Internet is a revolution in sexuality."

I think about my blow job seminar and the sex toy party. I'm a great example of openness and learning lately.

"Is there anything easy"—I don't tell her, but I'm tired of the hard things—"couples can do to improve their sex lives?"

"Get in bed," she says, "and talk about your first time together." I assume she means the first time you had sex together. "It brings a lot of people back to that more spontaneous, passionate energy they had about sex when they first met." I can see this working for a lot of people, but not with Greg, which is probably why we were not meant to be together. The first time we had sex together—he spent more time putting the condom on inside out than he did on foreplay—is the last thing I want to remember.

Thinking about Greg makes me ask, "What if someone you know has what I call sexual attention deficit disorder? My friend has it," I lie. "She'll be in bed having sex with her boyfriend, and her mind will start wandering to everything but sex. You know, the phone call she forgot to return, whether she remembered to pay the gas bill, the dust gathering on the bedside table."

"Ah, I see." Dr. Block pauses to really think about it, before giving her answer. "Talk while you are having sex."

Again with the talking. She says it like it's so easy. Actually, it does sound easy.

"Talk romantic, or dirty, or fantasize—*out loud.* People's minds wander when they are *not* talking. Talking will engage you in whatever act you are doing. I don't always like my husband's fantasies, but they keep us engaged. Build a verbal rapport with your lover. Humans are verbal creatures."

Will I ever get to talk in bed with Sam? Or, perhaps I won't need to talk in bed with Sam because he will be so good at sex that he will cure me of SADD.

"Another thing you can do is focus on your breathing," Dr. Block tells me. "A lot of times when we are tense, we hold our breath. People do it a lot during sex. Focused breathing will help on a mental and physical level."

"So if I feel like I'm not into sex or my mind is wandering I just breathe?"

"Yes, right into your pelvis."

"Sounds kind of tantric."

"It is. It will also relax your pelvis so that you are more likely to orgasm." *Definitely putting that on my list of things to try.*

We talk about relationships and sex for an entire hour, and I love that most of her recommendations are simple and easy to try and do not involve anything you have to buy or read. In fact, I could continue asking her questions for another hour, but I realize I should at least pretend like I have a life. I thank her for her time and tell her that I can't wait to see her show again.

Thanks to my talk with Dr. Block and the things on my Porn-to-Do list, I feel much better equipped now to be in a relationship. The toys I have purchased cannot hurt either. I look at Mr. Maybe, my inflatable husband, in the corner, who is starting to lose some air, and can't help but daydream about Sam.

At first I just wonder what our first date would have been like, what we would have talked about, the things that would have made us laugh. But when I start to fantasize about Sam breaking it off with Sabine (again) and running through the streets of L.A. in the pouring rain to find me, it is just too pitiful and unrealistic. I mean, it never rains in L.A. I stop the fantasy streaming in my head. I pick up the phone and call Steve to distract myself. I hear a voice on the other end as I dial.

It is Steve trying to call me.

"I was just going to call you," I tell him.

"I just ran into your brother, Peter." Steve sounds a little worked up. "He said he thinks your mother didn't come to my Thanksgiving party because she's uncomfortable knowing that I have sex on subways. *I have sex on subways?* What is she talking about?"

I groan. "I told her you were a *metro*sexual. She must think that means you like to have sex on subways. I'll straighten it all out next time I see her. I'm calling to see if you want to come over. I TiVo'd *Ellen* and *Eddie Izzard in Concert*."

"Can't. Paige's here. She wants me to read something."

"Her novel or the screenplay?"

I hear him shout across his apartment. "Paige, what am I read-ing of yours?"

"TV script!" Paige yells back. "Tell Ayn I think that Sam dude likes her."

"Paige says Sam likes you."

"Ask Paige what she's talking about!"

"What are you talking about?" he yells at the top of his lungs.

Paige yells back loud enough for me to hear, "Heather said that Brad said . . . " Suddenly all I hear is what I surmise must be a tin can being ripped to shreds by a garbage disposal.

"Jesus, what is that?" I yell.

"We're making pomegranate margaritas." I hear the screech-ing sound again mixed with Paige trying to scream something over the phone to me.

"Steve, *put Paige on the phone!*" I wait on the phone, impatient and excited to hear confirmation that Sam might be as interested in me as I am in him. *Maybe he's off again with Super Sabine?*

As I wait on pins and needles for Paige, I hear them pouring and tasting their margaritas. Are they that insensitive or just oblivious to the fact that I am dying to know what Sam said about me? Finally, Paige picks up the phone.

"Who told you that Sam likes me?" I demand to know.

"Heather said Sam told Brad he'd love to hang out with you sometime. Guess he thinks—" She just breaks her own train of thought and throws out, "Hey, can you read the first draft of my novel?"

I really don't want to because her novel is about three

hundred pages longer than the TV script Steve has volunteered to read, but I don't want to waste one more second not hearing what she knows. "Yeah, sure, now back to Sam."

"Oh, shit, now I can't remember. I think he said you were cool. Or was it cruel? You should ask him out if you want to know if he likes you." Easy for her to say; Paige is happily married to the easiest-going guy I know and has not had to deal with dating issues for quite some time.

"Paige, how many margaritas have you had?"

"Two. Of the pomegranate ones. You want to—"

I hang up and call Heather.

"Heather, it's Ayn. What did Sam say?"

"He told Brad he thinks you're smart and pretty and—" I can hear the baby starting to cry in the background just as my call-waiting beeps, interrupting her.

"Hold that thought." I beg her. "Let me get Paige off my call-waiting."

"Guess what!" I tell Paige. "You were right the first time. Sam said he likes me. He thinks I am pretty and smart. Can you believe it?"

"I couldn't have put it better myself," she says in a very deep voice. Either Paige has been smoking Marlboro Reds again or . . . *Oh, my God, it's . . . it can't be. Can it?*

"Uh, just one second." I put "Paige" on hold, calm myself down and then three-way call Steve.

"Steve, where is Paige?"

"Passed out on the terrace. Why?"

I hang up on him and click back to Heather. "Gotta go. Kiss the baby for me." And, back to the mysterious caller on line two.

"Uh, who is this?" I timidly ask.

"Sam. Brad's friend. Hope I'm not calling too late."

If only he could see me smacking myself on the forehead. "I'd say I've never been more embarrassed, but of all people you know that would be a lie."

"You definitely get points for being honest."

There's a pause. I have no idea what to say. I am so excited that he has called yet appalled that I've made a total fool of myself. Again. Thank God he says something to break the silence.

"I wanted to see if you were interested in grabbing a bite to eat, or maybe catching a movie."

"I'd love to!" I catch my reflection in the mirror. I have the phone in one hand and my other is clenched in a fist that I am pumping up and down while mouthing the word *"Yeeesss!"*

"Wait. Shoot, I just remembered I have something I have to go to tonight." After my conversation with Dr. Block I accepted an e-mail invitation to a live taping of her show and after-party.

"Oh." He sounds disappointed. "That's cool. No big—"

"Not with anybody else. I was going solo. It's a taping of a radio show. A radio sex show."

I can practically hear him smiling on the other end. "That definitely sounds more interesting than a movie."

I'm not sure whether I should invite him. I think he senses this.

"Anyway, maybe another time," he says. I should just invite him, but part of me is wondering if it's too forward to invite a guy to a radio sex show.

Before I can stop myself, I forgo being a good girl for the time being. "I can bring a guest if you're interested."

"You sure? I don't want to get in the way of anything."

"No. Come with me. I'd love to see you."

Oh, God, Sam will be here in forty minutes, my hair looks like Richard Simmons', my only pair of body-shaping panties—*what the fuck, they're a girdle*—are nowhere to be found, and the contents of my entire closet are piled onto my bed. And I still can't find anything to wear. I make a quick 911 to stylish Maya and beg her to come over and dress me for my first date with Sam.

Fifteen minutes later, she shows up with Vee and Tricia in tow. I am not upset about this because I am desperate, and can use all the help I can get, and I know that they are excited for me. With curling iron in hand, Vee works on my hair, giving me advice like, "Whatever you do, don't be yourself. If he wants to sleep with you on the first date, that's a good thing."

Maya is handing me things to wear and giving me advice like, "Whatever you do, don't listen to Vee." And Tricia is accessorizing me while giving me advice like, "He's probably not as great as you think, but who knows, give the guy a chance. He might turn out to be Mr. Right." She forgets that at this point in my life, I would be happy with Mr. Right Now.

Twenty minutes later, I look better than I have in ages. Hopefully this new image will erase all memories Sam has of me at Hustler with my super-steroidal lips. When he buzzes from downstairs, I hug the girls goodbye and leave them with a few chocolate stashes as reward for their charitable act (I am the charity case). I would introduce them all to Sam, but I don't want him to get the impression—a correct one, I guess—that it takes an army to make me presentable for dates.

As soon as I step out of my building, I see Sam, dressed perfectly in a faded vintage tee, dark blue designer jeans that are slightly frayed at the bottom, a short boxy black suede jacket with double stitching, and Italian sneakers. His style is a perfect cross between Hugh Grant and Jude Law (oral sex with prostitutes and affairs with your children's nanny aside). I find myself stopped in my tracks at the sight of him. It's uncontrollable. I would move if I could. It's as if everything has paused in time around me. The cars that are usually zipping by, the pedestrians walking their dogs, The Naughty Knitters who I know are spying on me from my window, even the ordinary city sounds, everything is frozen except for Sam, and the smallest of yellow leaves tumbling down the middle of the road. I watch him smile and laugh at something my elderly neighbor, Anne, who stands before him, has just said to him. But Anne is frozen, too, with a wide comfortable smile on her face as she looks up into Sam's affable handsome face. This scene really gets to me because I have a weakness for guys who treat the elderly with respect. I have an even greater weakness for guys who treat them as interesting, wise people who do not deserve to be patronized. Before I can command my body to move, I see Sam spot me out of the corner of his eye. He turns to me, and I'm probably imagining it, but he looks at me like the princes all look at Cinderella in her ball gown in the dozens of movie versions of the classic fairytale. *Could Sam be my prince? Could I be his Cinderella? Are The Naughty Knitters my fairy godmothers?*

We have a quick dinner of sushi, which is relaxing and enjoyable because Sam is a great conversationalist who will answer questions about himself directly, but prefers to talk about others, ideas, and current events. On the car ride to Dr. Block's show—Sam drives—we discover that two of our favorite books are the same: *The Fountainhead* and *A Prayer for Owen Meany*, which is ironic, not so much that we both would have them as favorites, but because they are such completely different novels in their outlooks on life. The themes in Ayn Rand's *The Fountainhead* are based on rational objectivism, and the hero of the story is an atheist. John Irving's *A Prayer for Owen Meany* is sentimental and quirky, and several of the characters, in essence, find faith in God. I see this as a good sign. Sam will understand that I am a Catholic agnostic with Buddhist tendencies. He will understand that I cry when I am really happy. And, most of all, he will appreciate that I am an objectivist when I am not being quirky and sentimental.

By the time we arrive at the downtown warehouse loft where Dr. Block's show is taped, I am in love with Sam. But I tell myself that that is impossible. *How can you love someone after a twenty-minute car ride?* I look for anything to make him less perfect in my eyes. Like that he is a terrible parallel parker, but I have fun giggling when it takes him five tries to fit into a space big enough for an eighteen-wheeler. He laughs at himself, too.

Inside the building, we get into an old freight elevator and find ourselves with a girl in her mid-twenties with sandy blond hair, who is wearing a black leather bustier, ill-fitting black leather skirt, and fishnet stockings. From the neck up, she looks like she is from Idaho. She looks us up and down as the elevator makes its ascent. "Going to the sex party?"

I chuckle. "I'm sorry, I thought you said sex party."

"I did." She doesn't have much of a sense of humor.

Sam looks at me with one eyebrow raised.

"Uh, we're going to the *after*-party," I say as the elevator doors open.

"Whatever," she practically sighs, shaking her head like I'm a big idiot, as she exits the elevator.

We enter a funky loft space that is softly lit and decorated with flowing curtains in vibrant red. There are a lot more people mingling about who are dressed like the girl from Idaho, and there are also a lot of men and women of all ages who are dressed casually.

At the sign-in table, we are let in by a security guard as other people pay $15—not really an admission fee, but an encouraged donation to the bonobos* fund. A sign indicates that Dr. Block is a big supporter of the bonobos.

We pass through a part of the loft that is some kind of gallery of erotic art. There is a strange-looking high-backed wooden chair with shackles attached to it that says "Bad Kitty." Nothing looks as erotic as it does sadomasochistic.

Sam is trying not to laugh now. It makes me kind of want to laugh, too. But I'm too nervous to laugh. I am hoping that the girl from Idaho is confusing our after-party with somebody else's.

I ask someone wearing a headset where the taping will take place and she points us to "the stage."

The stage is a gigantic brass bed surrounded by toys... *Wait a minute.* I look a little closer and realize they are not just any toys,

---

*Bonobos are endangered primates who are genetically more similar to humans than common chimps and gorillas, and who settle conflict with sexual acts and loving gestures.

they are sex toys. On top of the bed are dozens of dildos, vibrators, erotic statuettes, stuffed penises, feather boas, handcuffs, and more.

There is also a blond woman on the bed who looks like she could be in her forties, maybe even fifties, but her body is as hard and lean as a twenty-four-year-old's. I can tell because she is not wearing much to cover it. A red lace bustier, red thigh-high stockings, a red felt hat, and red lace *crotchless* panties. She's like a pornographic version of the Red Hat Society social club that is popular among genteel senior women. She has a headset on and is directing a crew—she must be the stage manager—on how to set up the camera and lights as she arranges a long toy snake on the bed. The snake actually moves like a real—*oh, shit, it is a real snake. A live, slithering, flesh-and-blood snake.*

Now I'm not just wondering if we are in the right place, I am praying that we are not.

I look over at Sam. He looks intrigued.

We take a seat on a sofa about ten feet away from the "stage."

A man's voice booms out, "Ready in ten, nine, eight . . ." but there is no sign of Dr. Block.

I stop a cocktail waitress. "Excuse me, do you know where Dr. Block is?"

"That is Dr. Block." She gestures to the giant brass bed.

"The woman in the red lingerie and crotchless lace panties, handling a snake, on the giant brass bed is the magna cum laude Yale Ph.D.?" I ask.

The waitress just nods.

"I have a feeling she is going to give a whole new meaning to 'cum laude,'" Sam jokes.

We watch as she adjusts her outfit, dabs on a little powder, arranges the snake on her shoulder, does a sound check and then adjusts her bustier to *intentionally* expose one nipple and looks into the camera. All in less than ten seconds.

I turn to Sam and whisper, "Oh, my God, I am so sorry. I had no idea it would be like this."

"What are you talking about?" He doesn't look flustered at all. "You had an idea?"

"Yeah, my old roommate used to watch her on the Internet. She's fascinating."

Well, I thought so too, on the phone. Maybe I need to just relax. Not judge. Have some confidence in other people. *Who says you can't do a smart show from a bed?* Martha Stewart does her show from a kitchen surrounded by pots and pans, why shouldn't a sexologist film her show from a bed surrounded by sex toys? I take a deep breath, careful not to guide it into my pelvis.

" . . . and one," her stage manager—a gruff-looking fifty-year-old man who is behind the audience, and thankfully *not* dressed in crotchless red panties—gives Dr. Block her cue that they are now filming live. She stares right into the camera and starts her opening monologue. I get right away that she is poking fun at fundamentalist preachers as her monologue moves from subjects related to sex to current events to some subjects that just fly right over my head.

She's part philosopher, part Dionysian sex goddess, part porn pundit. She uses metaphors that will take me days to figure out. It is poetic, provocative, and pornographic at the same time. Sam and I exchange a look as if to say, she might be slightly crazy, but *damn* is she smart.

After a few minutes, I slowly start to make out what she is talking about as she starts to pull the focus in on her monologue: "Brothers and sisters, it is not a matter of faith, but of science. We are believers in female G-spot ejaculation."

I try to wrap my head around what that might be, as she goes on. "Throughout history, scientists and philosophers have reported experiencing the forceful release of fluids from the vagina during sex." *They have?* "That great Macedonian know-it-all Aristotle"—*ha, I have never heard Aristotle described that way, but it is appropriate*—"wrote about women's vaginal expulsions, insisting they did not have the appearance of or the aroma of urine and they did not stain a lady's toga."

Sam turns to me and whispers, "I must have been out sick the day they covered that in philosophy 101."

"You and me both."

"The first modern description of female ejaculation occurred in the seventeenth century when Ranier de Graf wrote about the urethra being pierced with many large ducts. In 1950 Dr. Ernest Grafenberg"—I know from my other porn activities that he is the discoverer of the G-spot, which, just like a man, he named after himself—"stated that stimulation of the G-spot could lead to the expulsion of fluids from the vagina."

Why is that word "expulsion" alarming me? "Tonight we have a pioneer on the slippery path of female ejaculation. Deborah Sundahl is the master or mistress. She's a long-distance squirter." Dr. Block says this like squirting is part of the Olympic Games. "She'll explain how female ejaculate works in terms of the mind, the body, and the soul."

The show is about female ejaculation. Sam and I look at each other again and just shrug. Neither of us really knows what that is.

Dr. Block introduces Sundahl, who, with her sandy blond hair in a practical cut, barely any makeup, and a nice smile, reminds me of one of the young nuns who used to teach me catechism, but of course she is not wearing a habit. In fact, like Dr. Block she is hardly wearing anything at all.

As Sundahl gets comfortable on the bed, Dr. Block introduces Leila Swan, Sundahl's friend and star of her video *Female Ejaculation for Couples*. Swan is pretty in a schoolgirl kind of way. She has a very nice body and beautiful long hair, but is wearing bookish glasses that make her approachable. Once she is on the bed, too, Dr. Block advises the audience (there are about fifty of us watching and maybe another thirty or so mingling around the bar and erotic exhibit area, which is adjacent to the taping area) to "sit back and relax."

Dr. Block licks her fingers . . .

Why is she doing that? I wonder.

. . . And sticks them into her own *front fanny* on live television.

"I mean *relax*," she says. *Yeah, kinda hard to do that now.* Dr. Block turns to Swan and asks her if it's true she is a preacher's daughter.

Swan describes her father as "a charismatic Mennonite*." Swan is also charismatic, but obviously no Mennonite. Sundahl and Swan reveal their first experiences with female ejaculation and then turn to Dr. Block and goad her into trying it. They do not have to goad much.

---

*A member of an Anabaptist church characterized particularly by simplicity of life, pacifism, and nonresistance.

"You guys have your Ph.D.'s in this. I don't even have a B.A. I am here to learn," she tells them.

Suddenly, the stage manager announces that Dr. Block has a caller on line one. Apparently, Dr. Block takes callers who are tuning in to her via the Internet, radio, or on their TV.

"Hi, Maria from San Fernando Valley. What can we do for you?"

Dr. Block tries to pay attention to Maria as she talks about her girl-on-girl fantasies and her interest in learning female ejaculation, but it's pretty difficult because Sundahl and Swan are starting to fondle each other's breasts and toes and shoulders. Dr. Block talks the caller through masturbating her G-spot. "Feel my tongue down there, Maria . . . "

Once the caller is on her own, Dr. Block starts pinching her guests' nipples as she talks Maria through a fantasy. Before we know it, Maria comes over the phone and claims that she has squirted.

Oh, my God. What have I brought us to? The preacher's daughter is caressing Dr. Block's breasts. I am afraid to look at Sam. *He must think I am a nymphomaniac for bringing him here. I mean how would I feel if he brought me to a circle jerk on our first date—or any date, for that matter?*

"Hey, should we go?" I ask him.

"Are you kidding? This is interesting."

"Really?" I ask, and he nods.

"We've got a call from Richard, who wants to know how to find his girlfriend's G-spot," Dr. Block announces.

I decide to stick it out, figuring that if Sam and I do have a future together, it can't hurt him to learn this little fact.

All of a sudden it is like junior high sex education class, except it's not sixty-year-old Mr. Stanley running the rickety projector and mumbling female body parts under his breath. "Note, class, that the female *u-re-zvk-thraah,* cough-cough, is located within the walls of the *vuhzsttginpbhha,* cough-cough..."

The doctor pulls out a stuffed vagina, a fake anatomically correct vagina pillow. She shows it to the cameras while pointing out different parts. The pillow makes the vagina seem cute and kind of cuddly as she refers to female body parts I didn't even know I had.

Just like in sex ed., though, my mind starts to wander. I take the opportunity to scan the crowd. A real mix of people. Not all good-looking and sexy like one might imagine. Many of the women look like "before" photos for a hair conditioner ad. There is a dominatrix, who looks like Howard Stern in drag, and most of the guys look like they spend their fair share of time eating nachos while kicking back on the sofa watching *SportsCenter.*

I look back up when I feel Sam shudder. Dr. Block has put the fake vagina—I think she last referred to it as a fake "pussy"—aside and is now instructing the caller on how to find the G-spot using Leila Swan's *actual* vagina, which is maybe three yards away from us, pointing out—no mumbling involved—the urethra, the vagina, the labia, the anus, and more.

"Oh, my..." I practically shriek.

Sam puts his hand on mine to calm me. I want to run out, but I feel like it might be rude to run out on someone while they are exposing their genitals for educational purposes. They might take it personally.

"Richard, do you know where the *vulva* is?" Dr. Block asks the male caller.

There is silence on the other end.

"The vulva is not a car that you drive, Richard. It is a pussy that you drive wild."

Wow, the woman retains her sense of humor while fielding a call and holding open her guest's vaginal lips at the same time. And I thought Paige was good at multitasking.

I turn to the monitors that surround the room, some of them less than four feet away, thinking if I look at what is happening onscreen, it will be less shocking. Little do I know that the monitors are showing XXXtreme close-ups. Sam hears me gasp and looks at what I am looking at.

On the screen closest to us, we are viewing a close-up of a fleshy, raspberry-textured gland, a.k.a. the female prostate, poking from Swan's vagina as Dr. Block touches it and describes it. It is the female G-spot—elusive no more. We are horrified. It's like when you are channel surfing at home, looking for some mindless TV like *Entertainment Tonight* or *Trading Spaces* and suddenly you find yourself staring between a woman's thighs while she is in the middle of a harrowing childbirth. You are repulsed by the reveal of human flesh ordinarily reserved for doctors, but it is hard to tear your eyes away.

Meanwhile, another friend of Sundahl's named Annie Body— a full-bodied redhead—jumps onto the bed. They explain that she is notorious for the amounts of female ejaculate she can squirt.

"Isn't it beautiful?" Body comments as Sundahl and Dr. Block prod Swan's fleshy pink prostate, moving it this way and that as they discuss it. I cannot fathom how Swan is able to lay there smiling and calm as these women prod her. Again, I break out into a cold sweat as soon as my gynecologist pulls the speculum out of its package.

Beautiful is not exactly what I am thinking. I'm thinking I am going to be sick.

Sam sees the look on my face. "Are you thinking what I am thinking?"

"What are you thinking?" I'm afraid to tell him how nauseated I am right now.

"I'm really glad we didn't have the oyster shooters tonight." This is funny and makes me forget the nausea momentarily. I am also relieved that I don't have to pretend that I am into this. Thank God he has limits, too.

"Actually, I don't think I can ever look at raw chicken again," I confess.

I look back at the screen and quickly cover my eyes just as Dr. Block pushes on Swan's prostate enough to make it emit some type of bodily fluid.

I put my hands in front of my face defensively. "Eeeewwww."

"You said that out loud," Sam whispers.

Twenty minutes later, Dr. Block is still using her fingers to pry open Swan's vagina to show the different parts, pinching or stimulating the parts to show how they react. She even lets the audience have what she calls *paparazzi* moments in which men from the audience approach with their personal cameras and take photos of what is taking place on the bed.

"Yeah, that'll look good on the refrigerator," Sam jokes.

Finally, Swan pulls her panties up and it is over. *Phew!*

Just when we relax and are ready to get up and go, Body pulls her panties down and exposes herself. We thought she had a full head of curly red hair on her head. Well, it doesn't stop there, we discover. It looks like someone threw a shag throw rug on her lap.

Maybe it's just me, but if I knew I was going to expose myself to 50,000 possible viewers, I might invest in a bikini wax. But it is clear that Annie does not care about what people think. Apparently, Annie lives to squirt.

She is a lean, mean squirting machine. She pushes her prostate way out, letting the cameras get their close-ups. I look at the monitor again (*damn it!*) and then burrow my head into the side of Sam's shoulder. He laughs. I might laugh, too, if I were not so horrified.

"You've got to stop looking at the monitor," he teases.

"I know, it's like a car wreck."

"Yes, but with a happy ending, if it makes you feel any better," he says. I love that he is funny, but it is hard to enjoy because I cannot get the image of Annie's prostate and urethra out of my head. It is pink and fleshy and makes me want to have sex less than do a lot of other things I've ever seen.

"They should show this to teenagers to promote abstinence." And, just as I say this, out of the corner of my eye, I see a stream of mysterious fluid project from the "stage." Annie has just ejaculated. Well, that's what Dr. Block says, but I am not so convinced—it is so powerful it shoots a foot or two and looks suspiciously like clear urine. Annie does it again. And again. And again. She does it almost a dozen times with less than ten seconds between squirts. At one point I reflexively duck when it looks like her stream of ejaculate might hit me. There is so much ejaculate that the stage crew starts catching it in a bowl.

"Nice arc, that was beautiful," Dr. Block exclaims as if she is describing someone's golf swing and not a woman gushing fluids from her vagina. Annie looks gleeful.

Dr. Block senses that there are skeptics among us, so she takes a sip of Annie's ejaculate.

I turn to Sam. "Please tell me she didn't just drink ejaculate."

"Trippy, huh?" He pauses; his eyes go wide. "Uh-oh."

"What now?" My eyes are locked on Sam because I am afraid to see what they are doing now.

Just when things could not get stranger or more uncomfortable, Dr. Block asks for a champagne glass.

"No! They're not . . . ?"

"Yes, they are," Sam warns me. They start passing Annie's ejaculate around the audience for anyone to taste. It's like when you're at a comedy improv show and the performers come into the audience and you are praying that they do not pull you onto the stage. I am always the one pulled on stage.

But I cannot and will not smell, touch, or taste female ejaculate—even if I disappoint an entire audience or Dr. Block on her live show. I can only be so nice, and drinking female ejaculate is *not* on my Porn-to-Do list. I would be fine going my whole life not knowing the particular fine aroma of . . .

I start to wonder about women and men in other countries stumbling across this show on the Internet or their cable access TV channel. Dr. Block did say it was translated into Hebrew and Arabic. If I am squeamish watching this, what will a woman wearing a *burka* think?

As the audience passes around the "drink," mostly just the crew partakes of it. Swan starts to see what she can do in terms of squirting. From Dr. Block's collection of toys and aids, she pulls out a smooth glass device that looks like a funky, curved gelato ice cream scoop. It is designed that way so that it can better reach the G-spot, we learn. She starts squirting after a few minutes of masturbating herself.

After a few more squirts, Swan's boyfriend, Big D who looks like he may be Samoan and happens to be wearing a kilt, is brought on stage. Dr. Block introduces him, playfully flirting with him and lifting up his kilt to discover why he is called Big D. And *bam,* somehow in the moment it took me to whisper something in Sam's ear to the moment I turn back to the stage, Swan is going down on Big D. I look at Sam, my eyes wide open. I think he can read my mind.

"Line definitely crossed," is all he says.

I totally agree. Nothing educational going on between Swan and Big D. "Take a break?" I ask. We get up and head to the adjacent room, where we wander around looking at the erotic art display. Any comments we have, we whisper. There are a lot of people mingling around. We both see a bowl of peanuts on a food stand and give each other a look.

"If the urine content in peanut bowls in bars is high, what do you think it is here?" I say.

He laughs, which makes me feel good. There are also quite a few dominatrices walking around in black leather, lightly whipping meek-looking men who wear black leather vests and dog collars.

The dominatrices do not look like one might imagine. Personally, I imagined them looking like a leather-clad Halle Berry in the movie *X-Men*. One of them looks much more like my child-hood neighbor, Mrs. Tabor, who was skinny (her kids were so wild she never had time to eat) and had frizzy hair (she never had time to condition either) and poorly applied makeup.

I kind of want to giggle as a tall dominatrix whips her mate, first snapping the whip in the air as if to make a statement. I am fascinated by this. Vee is always telling me what a turn-on spanking is if it's done right. I guess juxtaposed with what we just saw and the fact that we can now hear Swan and Big D actually having sex on the stage, a little S&M seems tame in comparison. And, I have a sneaking suspicion that the whip does not actually hurt.

"I am really curious what that feels like," I confess to Sam. "Is that weird?"

"Considering we just saw someone drink female ejaculate, no, I don't think that's weird at all," answers Sam.

Nearby I hear a woman who sounds like Dr. Block's assistant, the woman I spoke to on the phone. I introduce myself and ask about Swan and Big D.

"Is that legal? They're actually having sex."

"It's legal as long as nobody is paying for sex," she replies. Ah, that must be why the admission is a donation to the bonobos charity. "You're not the only one who has wondered that. We've been raided by the LAPD a couple of times," she adds.

"What happened?"

"Suzy sued them for infringing on her First and Fourth Amendment rights."

"Let me guess, she won a settlement?" I figure a magna cum laude Yale Ph.D. would have a good understanding of her legal rights.

She nods and then turns to talk to someone who is tapping on her shoulder.

As I get in line at the bar for a glass of water, I watch as Sam approaches the frizzy-haired dominatrix. After she is done whipping her mate, I see Sam lean in and introduce himself, then ask her something.

I see the dominatrix smile. *God, he's charming.* I see him pointing at me. I see her nod and then he heads back over to me.

"Are you flirting with a dominatrix?" I ask. He laughs. I realize one reason I am falling for Sam is because he reminds me that I have a good sense of humor (something I lost when I was with Greg).

"I told Debbie you're curious. She said you could feel her whip if you want."

"Oh, you're on a first name basis already?"

Sam introduces me to Debbie and I reach out to feel her whip. It is made of several long pieces of suede, each about six feet long, and the suede is sooo soft. It can't hurt. Most S&M, Debbie tells us, despite what is depicted in the movies, is not about violence; it is about control and letting go.

"Hey, want me to whip you with it?" Sam asks me.

"Uh, sure," I say, surprised that I don't care there are dozens of other people milling around us.

He turns to the dominatrix. "May I, Deb?

She hands him the whip.

He gently smacks the whip on my butt—*I was right, it doesn't hurt at all*—and I ham it up, putting my hand to my mock-shocked face as Debbie the Dominatrix captures the moment with my digital camera.

It actually is a little bit of a fun turn-on. In some way it simply focuses energy to the lower half of my body, which I don't usually think about unless I am having sex. I think Sam likes doing it as much as I like him doing it.

We thank Debbie and look at the photo and laugh out loud.

"Hey, I look kinda sexy," I tease.

Suddenly, he gets serious. "Yeah, you do."

"Okay, your turn." I pull him over to the bad kitty chair.

He sits in it and makes a hilarious cat-clawing gesture toward the camera as I take his photo.

He looks at the photo and grimaces. "Promise me that years from now you will not send this to my mother no matter how mad you might be at me."

This makes me laugh out loud, but deep down inside I am treasuring this little bit that he has revealed. I have been given a glimpse into his psyche, and I see that he thinks there is a possibility that we may be together years from now and that we may be in the kind of relationship in which I might have access to his mother.

I am falling in love with Sam as, a mere twenty feet away, women squirt ejaculate all over a big brass bed that is a stage while two people are screwing each other before a live audience.

It's far from the way I imagined falling in love.

We start walking around and making fun of everything and everyone. We crack ourselves up—we don't even need alcohol—when suddenly, the grunts and groans from the stage get louder and we realize Swan and Big D are about to orgasm together. When they finally do, we bust up laughing harder than we have all night. Fortunately, Dr. Block cannot see us from her stage.

Seconds later, we hear Dr. Block give squirting a go. I peek over and see that she is spread eagle on her "stage"; Swan and

Sundahl are fondling her while instructing her on how to squirt. The monitors are showing a close-up of her genitals. *God, she has guts.* I am fascinated how these two women, the hyper-intellectual academic and the seXXXpert, can live in the same body. She looks a little nervous, but she is really giving it her all.

"She definitely takes Dr. Ruth to another level," I am whispering to Sam when we hear a shout from the stage.

"Here she comes!" And just then we hear Dr. Block squeal in delight over the sound of gushing liquid that we realize can only be female ejaculate.

Sam turns to me and says, "Good for her."

"Yeah, good for her," I agree, surprised that I am no longer repulsed.

On the car ride home, we are silent for the first part of the ride, both quietly reflecting on what we have seen and how the experience has changed the nature of our relationship. I feel closer to him, and I am silently hoping that Sam feels the same about me.

"So, did those triple X extreme close-ups turn you off to sex with women?" I ask him.

"I may not be ordering a shaved pastrami sandwich anytime soon," he replies, "but sex with women will be staying on the menu. What about you? Learn anything?"

"A ton. I'm surprised I didn't feel dirtier, you know, naughty, experiencing that. I think if I just heard about the things we saw, I would assume the people were depraved, but I don't feel that way. Dr. Block and her friends are just more interested in and open to a wider range of sexual experiences than I am. It doesn't mean there is anything wrong with me or them. It's just sex, they are enjoying themselves and they aren't hurting anyone."

"So, they've made a squirter out of you?"

"As for that, I think I would be fine going my whole life without squirting."

He pretends to wipe sweat off his brow. "Phew."

"But if I did do it, I would make you drink it from a glass," I joke.

We both "*eeeeewwww*" simultaneously and then crack up.

Back at my place, Sam and I pause at the door to my apartment building. I so want to kiss him. He is definitely leaning in to make a move, but just as he is about to kiss me on the lips, I accidentally drop my keys and bend down to pick them up, causing Sam to miss my lips and awkwardly kiss my hair.

He senses that I am not ready. I don't know that I even sense that. But I guess dropping my keys and stuttering good night is a good indication. He gives me a hug and kisses me on the cheek before heading back to his car.

6. ~~Enroll in blow-job seminar~~

Meet Sloan for coffee

7. ~~Test vibrators~~

8. Read a Dirty Magazine

9. ~~Consult a Sex Expert~~

10. Where do men hide their porn?

11. Check out a brothel

12. Meet a porn star

As soon as I enter my apartment I smack myself on the forehead. *I should have just gone for it.* What stopped me? Am I afraid of being the rebound date? Could he be too good to be true?

I sit on the sofa and stare at my Porn-to-Do list in my hands. I cross off one more item. I am one step closer to proving that I am not afraid of porn. And, somehow, I feel that I am one step closer to not being afraid of other life matters that I cannot exactly put my finger on. But the most important thing I learned from Dr. Block's sex show? When you are with the right person, you can laugh at anything.

IN 2000,
ADULT DVD COMPANIES
REPORTED THAT

9 PERCENT

OF THEIR VIEWERS
WERE WOMEN.

JUST A
FEW YEARS LATER,
FEMALE VIEWERSHIP HAS
EXPLODED TO

53 PERCENT.

Source: Digital Playground

Chapter Nine
Till Porn Do Us Part

Foreploy: *n. when a guy pretends to like foreplay to get a woman to have sex*

I am telling my sister Fran all about my date with Sam at Dr. Block's squirting salon as we walk through the maternity department at the Gap, when she asks, "When are you going to see him next?"

"He's out of town for a week visiting family, so I don't know."

A squealing two-year-old boy runs over Fran's feet, causing her to stop and look around. She was so engrossed in my account of female ejaculation that she didn't realize where we were. She glances over at a waddling pregnant woman who looks like she is about to pop any second.

"What are we doing here?" she wonders aloud.

"Shopping."

Fran hates shopping. "I know that. I mean what are we doing in the maternity department?"

"I'm going to let you in on a little secret," I tell her.

The pregnant woman waddles by again, and Fran gets an excited look on her face. "Oh, my God, you're pregnant?"

"I'm not pregnant," I whisper.

"Then what are we doing here?"

"Remember those designer jeans of mine you said you had to have?"

"Yeah, the flattering ones with the flap pockets, wide bottom, double stitch."

"I got them here," I tell her.

"At the Gap? Okay, let's check them out." She heads toward the women's section.

I grab her by the arm. "I didn't get them in the women's section."

"*Ohhhh . . .*" she says knowingly. "I get it; you got them in the *guy's* department. That's brilliant. Probably why they fit better through the hips."

"No, I got them *here.*"

She looks around again. There are pregnant and nursing mothers milling about all around us. It dawns on her that I mean "here," as in the maternity department. "Oh, *that's* why they fit better through the hips."

"They're called Transition Wear. You can't tell they're for pregnant women," I explain, "because they're for when you are barely showing. Tell me these don't look like jeans Jennifer Aniston would wear." I pull down a pair and hand them to her. "Feel this. They make them out of this great stretchy material." She nods her head, impressed. "And they're low cut, they ride under the belly. Super comfortable. Especially during your time of the month.

"Pull at it," I tell her. She tugs on the fabric, testing its elasticity. "See? Why don't they make all pants out of this stuff?"

We've been whispering in a corner so that the pregnant women don't hear us. That is why we startle when a perky bottle-blond saleswoman with bright lipstick practically bounces toward us. She is all smiles.

"Hi, can I help you?"

I turn to Fran quickly and whisper, "And the sales people are really nice here."

"They're nice to you because they think you're pregnant," Fran whispers back.

The saleswoman puts a comforting hand on my shoulder. "How far along are you?" she asks sweetly.

I smile back just as sweetly. "Three and a half months." I have chosen this number after much testing and consideration because I like the answer it provokes.

She looks at me, her eyes wide with surprise. "Well, you're not showing at all, lucky you, *and* you are positively glowing."

I pat my tummy. "Thank you." It's nice to be seen as thin, relatively speaking, for a change.

Once the sales lady leaves us, Fran looks at me like I've completely lost it. "Three and a half months?"

"What? I didn't lie. She asked me how far along I was. I am three and a half months into my Porn-to-Do project."

It is my time of the month, I have not heard from Sam yet because he is still out of town, and I have recovered all of the chocolate stashes hidden by Greg—some dating as far back as 2004—which are now surrounding me as I sit cross-legged on my living room floor. I had planned to eliminate one more thing from my Porn-to-Do list ("watch porn"), but I am having a hard time getting in the mood.

Instead, I am watching *Supersize Me*, an acclaimed tongue-in-cheek documentary by Morgan Spurlock, who interviewed dozens of experts, including surgeon generals, gym teachers, cooks, lawmakers, nutritionists, and even kids about our country's growing problem with obesity.

The most interesting part of Spurlock's journey requires him to put his own body on the line, living on nothing but McDonald's fast food for an entire month.

I am entranced as I watch him enter the experiment lightly, then slowly spiral downward, gaining weight, experiencing liver damage and even depression—all from just too many Big Macs and supersized fries. But more importantly, he acquires a unique understanding of the impact of McDonald's not just on America, but also on himself.

When the movie is over I have a trippy thought: *Spurlock is to McDonald's as I am to porn.*

I decide to give my next porn exercise more context a la *Supersize Me*, hoping that it will motivate me and give this entire journey more meaning. Inspired by the straightforwardness of Spurlock's methodology, I call up Steve, who recommended I watch the movie in the first place, and tell him, "I'm going to consume nothing but porn for one month. I'm calling it SuperSEX Me."

"You're joking, right?"

"I'm serious. If Spurlock's film *Supersize Me* is 'A Film of Epic Portions,' then SuperSEX Me will be 'A journey of pornographic portions.'"

"You're going to consume nothing but porn from now until New Year's? That should make for an interesting Christmas Eve with your parents," he says.

He's right. I really want to be done with my Porn-to-Do list by the holidays so that I can avoid a XXXmas.

"Okay, *two weeks*. I'm consuming nothing but porn for two weeks. Starting tomorrow."

"You know that guy in *Supersize Me* got liver disease," he reminds me.

"It's just porn, I'm not actually ingesting it, Steve," I tell him.

DAY ONE

Steve e-mails me a list of the current Top 10 porn DVDs to try and scare me off my experiment. The titles are:

1. Rocco's Nasty Tails

2. Teagan: All American Girl

3. Slut Puppies

4. No Cum Dodging Allowed 5

5. House of Ass

6. Internal Combustion 7

7. Cum Stained Casting Couch 2

8. Feeding Frenzy 7

9. The Lady and Her Tramp 2

10. Bare Legal Innocence 3

Where do they get these titles? *I would love to be a fly on the wall in that focus group: (re:* Slut Puppies, *"The word* 'puppies' *makes me want to see it, but* 'slut' *makes me think it might be about promiscuous dogs, and I'm just not into that kind of thing.*"—Retired Plumber, 60); (re: Cum Stained Casting Couch 2, *"The casting couch sounds like it could be kind of sexy, and it's a sequel so it must be pretty good, but the fact that it is* 'cum-stained' *just reminds me of all the housework I need to do.*"—Housewife, 37); (re: No Cum Dodging Allowed, *"Is dodging cum not cool?"*—College Coed, 20).

It's as if the producers are going for a cringe-and-shudder factor. These titles make me not want to watch the videos, but I will not let Steve intimidate me.

I do a shout out to my (non-metrosexual) male friends for "porn support" and ask them to drop off any videos they would recommend for my two-week experiment.

By the end of the night, I have received more than a hundred videos and DVDs, most appearing in groups of ten or twenty, in grocery bags or cardboard boxes, some in duffel bags, and one collection in a ladies' hat box.

I am excited to start the experiment. I find one of the few DVD covers that looks appealing (Sexy Urban Legends), and I pop it in the player. It's not bad at all. They set up a premise clearly; the production values are nice. The people are attractive.

I especially like a vignette about a guy and girl who, despite urban legends that warn of a killer in the park, end up doing it in a tent in the middle of said park with no harm coming to them. It actually even turns me on a little. And thank God there are no close-ups. The most you see are a girl's

naked breasts. After Dr. Block's squirt salon, I don't think I
could stomach another close-up of genitals, male or female.
I watch another vignette, which reminds me of one of the erotic
stories I read months ago, and I fall to sleep with a smile on
my face.

DAY TWO

The next morning, I wake up and start the day the way I
do every Friday (I give myself Fridays off since I usually end
up writing—not about my porn adventures, but actual paid
freelance assignments—into the wee hours on Sundays): I cook
a French breakfast (today it is crepes and sausage), and I sit
down to enjoy a podcast of NPR's This American Life, which
I have downloaded onto my iPod. Just as I hear host Ira Glass'
distinctive voice introducing this week's three-act theme, the
phone rings.

"What are you doing?" Steve asks.

He knows perfectly well what I do on Friday mornings. "I
am about to listen to This American Life."

"So, you're giving up on your SuperSEXperiment?"

"What are you talking about? I'm only on day two."

"Public Radio is about as far from porn as you can get,
Ayn."

"Okay, well, I want to listen to the radio while I eat my
crepes, which are getting cold as we speak, so what do you
suggest I listen to?"

"Howard Stern."

"Fine. Goodbye, Steve."

I reluctantly turn my radio on to Howard Stern, who is

carrying out his version of a charitable act, a perverted version of Make-a-Wish. Instead of granting sick children their last dying wish, he is granting a female guest the new bigger breasts she is dying for. The catch is the guest must first eat a hotdog stuck in the butthole (disgusting!) of one of the members of Stern's wack-pack (must ask someone what the hell a wack-pack* is).

I immediately throw my uneaten sausage in the trash. This is not funny—this is sick. I turn off the radio.

It seems like as good a time as any to pop in Girls Gone Wild, the incessant ads for which I always see on Comedy Central and E!. Right away, something feels flat—and it's not the girls' chests. It is the absence of sound that is off-putting. In the TV ads, there are always pop-ups and moving titles, plus a fun upbeat soundtrack that resembles a Conga-line, complete with girls flashing their breasts.

In reality it is just a guy with a camera walking up to young women on a beach, asking if they will remove their tops in exchange for a free Girls Gone Wild T-shirt. They all do it with very little coaxing. Over, and over, and over. Yawn city.

Midway, the video does get raunchier as the camera guy follows two female friends—who, by their own admission, "are not lesbians"—into a hotel room, where he coaches them to crawl into bed with each other and fondle each other. Something about having the camera on them, probably

---

*Name given to an odd assortment of Stern's regular guests, who include, but are not limited to, Crackhead Bob, High-Pitch Eric, Dan the Farter, and Wendy the Retard.

consuming more than their fair share of Corona, and the offer of a free T-shirt gets them to do things that my lesbian friends would all agree makes you a lesbian.

The camera guy coaxes them with things like, "Hey, why don't you two kiss. . . . Okay, now take off each other's tops. . . . Wow, you're beautiful . . . You've got a smokin' body . . . Show me that ass again . . . Spank it . . . "

The girls carry out each action, only occasionally pausing to giggle or ask things such as, "This is not a porno, right? (giggle, giggle)." The camera guy reassures them it is not.

"Good, because we don't do porn! (giggle, giggle)." When the girls go so far as to remove their bikini bottoms for the guy and perform oral sex on each other while he continues filming, I want to grab one of them by the shoulders and shout, "Newsflash: You are in a porno, ladies! The only difference between you and a porn 'actress' is you are not getting paid for it!"

My phone rings, and I am so glad. I could use a break from these udderless college coeds and all their bouncy bold boobs.

It is Sam.

Sam is another reason I want to be done with my Porn-to-Do list sooner than later. Although I could enjoy doing anything with Sam—he made a squirt salon fun—I would rather imagine us seeing Gladiator *than* Glad-he-ate-her *(real movie from friend Ray), or* Lord of the Rings, not Lord of the G-strings *(from Steve's collection). And if he doesn't mind watching old movies like me, I would prefer* Chitty-Chitty Bang-Bang *and* A Clockwork Orange to Clitty Clitty

Gang Bang *(from friend Howard)* and A Clockwork Orgy *(thank you, Vee).*

He informs me that he is going to be back early from his trip and wants to know if I want to go out next Thursday.

"Ooooh, mmmmm, yeah, yeah." I look over at the television; the girls are now getting a little wilder in their "this is not porno" porn film.

"Did you just moan?" asks Sam.

"No, no, that's Girls Gone Wild. I have a DVD in."

He laughs. He knows all about my Porn-to-Do list now.

"Yes, I would love to go out Thursday," I tell him.

"Great," he says. "So, what do you think of Girls Gone Wild?"

"I always thought I wanted my own Good Girl Gone Wild moment, but after watching one of the videos, I think maybe I haven't missed so much."

"Trust me, you haven't missed that much. But it's never too late if you change your mind."

DAY THREE

Steve and I are at Hooters because he has convinced me that in the true spirit of social experimentation and Supersize Me, I should only be eating at porn-related food venues, which means we had hot wings and mashed potatoes at an all-you-can-eat lunch buffet at a strip club earlier today and are now dining on hot wings—what is it with guys and hot wings?—at Hooters for dinner.

For the record, Hooters is not such a hoot. The girls and the chicken wings are overrated, although they were smart making the waitresses' short shorts bright orange. Steve and I find ourselves staring at the waitresses' asses every time they walk by.

"How goes pornapalooza?" Steve asks as he bites into another not-so-hot hot wing.

"No big deal," I shrug. "I actually kind of liked Sexy Urban Legends. Girls Gone Wild *got a little repetitive. Okay, a* lot *repetitive. And the worst I can say about Howard Stern is I will never eat a hot dog again, which is not necessarily a bad thing." I push my plate away. Now I think I'll vomit if I ever see another hot wing again. "Surprised I haven't given up?"*

"No, considering you're only watching soft-core. You wouldn't survive hard-core for a day."

"Are you saying I am a wimp when it comes to porn?"

"Hey, you know, it is not an insult for someone to tell you that you don't have the stomach for hard-core porn. You're a good girl. It's okay that you've been a bit sheltered."

Something about the way he says that riles me. "It's not like I have not been around the block a few times when it comes to porn. I know how to squirt, Steve."

"You tried it?"

"Okay, well, not a real hands-on working knowledge, but a theoretical second-hand knowledge."

DAY FOUR

I wake up and listen to Howard Stern. Guess he is not so bad. His news reader, Robin, is an interesting voice of reason.

I select five of the hardest core hard-core videos I can find and start watching them before noon.

Yu-uck! What is wrong with men? *Now, I am not only confronted with extreme close-ups of women's genitals, but I also have to grapple with huge cocks and balls, as well as guys ejaculating on women who deserve an Oscar because most of them really look like they like it as the guy drives into them time after time, ejaculating on their face and hair, or has anal sex with them. To make matters worse, the guys look like Ron Jeremy or, at best, a white trash version of Fabio.*

Granted, these film-makers understand the concept of climax, but they are completely lacking when it comes to other film concepts. Didn't any of them go to film school? Have they ever thought of applying the principles of plot, character arc, leitmotif, deux ex machina, or innuendo?

I feel disgusted. The movies are long. I want to stop, but I said I would do this and I am going to do it; otherwise Steve will bring this up for the rest of our lives. I sink into the couch and keep watching for what feels like an eternity.

DAY FIVE

Made croque monsieur* and listened to Howard Stern. When Stern takes a break from the scatological humor and crude objectification of women, he reveals he has a heart and a quick wit. Love how he self-deprecatingly refers to his penis as a thimble. Watched porn continuously for ten hours.

DAY SIX

Where has all the sunlight gone?

I finally drag myself out of the house. Everywhere I go,

---

*A ham and cheese sandwich served hot on a baguette.

*everyone is naked (my imagination is set on hypersex drive)
and not just naked like everyone was after my erotica binge.
As I run errands, my butcher, who is unwrapping a salami,
becomes the oversexed gigolo jerking off his own salami. The
prim lady drinking her latte in front of Coffee Bean becomes a
"bad girl" with cum dripping down the sides of her mouth. A
manager and two checkout girls at Trader Joe's, who are bent
over cleaning up an aisle spill, become a nasty ménage
a trois. My yoga class becomes an orgy of twisted naked
bodies.*

*This is my brain on porn. It's like I have a sixth sense, but
I don't see people who are dead like the kid in the movie with
that title, I see people who are fucking.*

*Back at home, I try to shake the images away. I feel
like Spurlock in that moment in* Supersize Me *when he
realizes that McDonald's uses ingredients and runs their
business in such a way that customers become addicted to
their product.*

Oh, my God! *Porn is to sex as McDonald's is to a
nutritious meal.* Could I become addicted to porn?

DAY SEVEN

What have I done? *This is the longest week of my life,
and my laundry is piling up. The only item in my underwear
drawer is the vibrating panties. What the hell, I put them on. I
am proud that I can tell Steve that I have given the
XXXperiment my all. Last night I watched fourteen dirty
movies. I am tired of cum shots. Three-ways feel passé. Girls
Gone Wild might as well be* Golden Girls, Howard Stern

might as well be Larry King for all the arousal I feel listening and watching these fine examples of soft-core and hard-core porn.

I wonder if at the end of this experiment I will go through porn withdrawal. Maybe I should wean myself off. What if I get PPSD (post-porn stress disorder)? Where will I go for help? Will my family have to send me away in an unmarked white van? Where do celebrities go when this happens to them? What have I done? Is it normal that I had a dream last night that two giant penises were chasing me? Could I have liver damage? Why am I rambling? Is that a symptom of addiction or PPSD? What is that ringing in my head? Oh, no, it's happening. Hallucinations are probably next. I hear the ringing again. *Wow, I must have it pretty bad. Wait a second ... That ringing in my head sounds like my doorbell. It* is *my doorbell—*

It must be Steve; he is like a vulture just circling until I drop dead.

I press the intercom.

"Hey, Ayn, it's me, Sam. Sorry, I'm late."

Late? He's a week early. Or is he? I replay our last conversation in my head. Oh, crap. He was talking about this Thursday, as in today, not next Thursday.

"Just a minute," I call out.

I look around. My apartment looks like a college frat house. There are dozens of dirty magazines and videos and DVDs everywhere. Leftover Ding Dongs and a container of half-eaten hot wings are on the coffee table. In my porn-induced delirium, I did not even realize that the TV is blasting hard-core gay porn. No wonder my neighbors Harriet and Seymour were banging on the walls. I just figured they were having sex, really loud sex for octogenarians.

I scramble around, trying to make the place look presentable. I stuff videos into my closet, shove some DVDs under the sofa, and even hide a few in my microwave. I spray some Simple Green All-Purpose Cleaner in the air to get rid of the scent of the Hooters hot wings and light a Moroccan vanilla candle left behind by Ben.

"Come on up," I tell him through the intercom as I buzz him in. I try to sound calm as my eyes search the room for the remote so that I can turn off the TV as a guy on screen takes it up the ass ... *Yuuuckk!* Finally, I find the remote in a bag of chips and click off the TV.

I run to open the door when I catch a glimpse of myself in the mirror. *Aaarrrgh!* My porn binge has definitely taken a physical toll on me. There are dark circles under my eyes, I have chapped lips, a pale complexion from the curtains being drawn all of the time, stringy hair, and most likely severe liver damage. I pull my hair into a messy bun, noticing as I do that I could really use a shower. Desperate, I spray more Simple Green in the air—*I really need to get some perfume*—and sashay through it. I pinch my cheeks—*who knows where my make-up bag is*—and I knot the baggy T-shirt I am wearing at my waist to make it look a little more sexy.

I answer the door nonchalantly. "Oh, hey," I say. "Come on in."

He sniffs the air. "Is that Simple Green?"

Since Sam is tired of eating out, I offer to cook him my favorite, penne with prosciutto and peas in a lemon cream sauce. Of course, I have to borrow the prosciutto from my neighbor

231

Maja, the peas and cream from Erica, and I pick the lemons from someone's tree around the corner. I figure if their tree branches are hanging over onto the city sidewalk, then the lemons are public property.

"Where should I put my jacket?" Sam asks as I start preparing dinner in the kitchen.

"There's room in the hallway closet."

A few moments later, I cringe as I hear the unmistakable sound of a box of videos and DVDs falling from the hallway shelf and crashing to the floor.

I run out to the living room, where Sam is grinning and bending down to pick up one of the dozen or so pornos that has fallen around his feet like an avalanche.

"Don't tell me, more Porn-to-Do?" he grins.

After dinner, we sit on the sofa and talk, drink Spanish wine, and listen to my iPod mix of songs from my current favorite artists: Sparkle Horse, Tim Halloran, Air, Tom Waits, and Patsy Cline. He loves all of it, and I can tell he means it. That is important to me. I have always had nightmares about falling in love with a guy who is into N'Sync or Ashlee Simpson. During a particularly sexy Sparkle Horse song, Sam puts his glass down and shifts his position so that he is closer to me. Then he gets an odd look on his face and reaches under his butt to grab my *Sexy Urban Legends* loaner DVD that he has accidentally sat on.

"Are you curious?" I ask. It must be the wine talking because I have never in my life even considered watching porn with a guy, but after bonding over watching women squirt in real life, I doubt this can be that harmful.

As we watch the "movie," the sexual energy between us

becomes even more palpable. I find myself extremely turned on. Partially because Sam's thigh unintentionally brushes my own and partially because the video is heightening my sexual awareness. I do not know if guys watch porn this way, but I am imagining Sam as the male character in *Sexy Urban Legends* and that turns me on even more. I turn to him and kiss him. He kisses back and it's no wishy-washy MBW kiss.

He lifts me from the sofa and we sort of sidestep toward my bedroom as we continue groping each other. I step on a copy of *Hustler* magazine and go sliding, but Sam catches me in his arms. He looks at the floor; dirty magazines are everywhere.

"You've really got a problem," he teases.

"Tell me about it." I kiss him deeply.

"We better stop," he tries to say in between kissing my lips and neck.

"Please tell me you're kidding."

"What if it's just the porn talking?"

"What porn?" I say as I kick *Best American Erotica* out of our path.

"Are you sure you want to do this?" he asks, barely able to hold back.

"I've wanted to do this since we met." Just to emphasize my point, I unknot my T-shirt and lift it over my head.

He looks very pleased, then dejected. "Damn it. I didn't bring a condom." I am relieved that he doesn't carry condoms around, assuming that it means he doesn't always expect to get laid.

"No worries. I have leftover party favors from my *sex*ware party." I go into the bathroom, grab a condom, put some deodorant on, remove my jeans, and come back out in just my bra and underwear.

Before I know it we are on the bed and his hands are gliding over me in all the right places, neither too fast nor too slow. I guide his hand to my thigh to let him know I'm okay with him being a little more aggressive, and he takes it from there until he suddenly jumps back.

"Did you feel that?" he says.

"*Mmmmm, yeah,* felt great . . . " I moan, my eyes still closed. He is talking, but I can still feel his lips on mine, his hands caressing me, then I hear a faint out-of-place sound.

"What is that?" he asks.

I open my eyes. I am surprised to see that his hands are not between my legs because I still feel a tingly sensation there. *Wait. That sound . . . ?* It's so . . . familiar. *The vibrating panties!*

I look at Sam as he also figures out that I have vibrating panties on. "I have a perfectly good explanation," I start to explain, "but it would take a really long time—"

He pulls the panties off and tosses them to the ground where they continue to vibrate, but I do not notice after a while because we are having sex. Actually, it is more than sex. It is fantastic sex.

Actually, it is more than fantastic sex.

We are making love.

We end up talking in bed and laughing about our past run-ins and making out for a couple more hours before we have sex a second time. This time we have time for foreplay. He beats Greg and his lava lamp hands down. It is more amazing than anything I've ever experienced. Those Fabio lookalikes in pornos could definitely learn a thing or two from Sam. I want to ask if he has taken Lou Paget's sex seminar for men, but I don't want to distract him from the fantastic job he is doing.

The next morning I wake from a very deep sleep with a smile on my face. This feels so right. Maybe we will have a nice leisurely breakfast at Le Provence down the street, then hit the museum or the flea market or the beach. Truth is, I don't care what we do as long as I'm doing it with him.

I turn toward his side of the bed and reach out. "*Mmmmm,* good morning."

Sam is sitting on the side of my bed, fully dressed, looking very nervous.

"Everything okay?" I ask.

"Uh, yeah, I just really have to get to work."

Something is definitely wrong. I sit up. "Hey, you sure nothing's wrong?"

"It's nothing, really. I just need to go." And with that, he exits the room.

I knew this was too good to be true. *But what would make him turn so quickly?* I look around my room, trying to think. The vibrating panties on the floor are still going like the Energizer bunny. My blow-up doll is in the corner. The dirty magazines are still scattered on the floor, and the eight-inch instructional tool from my blow job seminar is poking its head out of my sock drawer.

Oh, God, maybe he thinks I'm a pornoholic. If I woke up to this room I wouldn't date me either. But he knows about my porn challenge. He knows it's like the Pepsi challenge but no Pepsi involved, just a lot of porn. He told me he thinks it's funny. Well, he thought it was funny last night. In broad daylight it does look a lot more sordid. I can't believe I fucked this up.

I run to the living room to try and catch him before he leaves.

"Hey, if it's the porn, I can stop anytime . . ."

But he is already gone.

Three days later Sam still has not called. Needless to say I have also not received a bouquet of flowers, a box of Belgian chocolates, a rare book of poetry, or anything else that would prove he is the guy that I thought I fell in love with.

I sit in front of my iMac and Google *"Why does my love life suck?"* and it spits back: "Do you mean: *Why do you suck at your love life?"* or at least that's what I am imagining when the phone rings. I practically dive across my living room to answer it.

"Hey, it's Vee. Are you excited about your date with Prem tonight?"

"What date?"

"You asked me to set you up on a blind date."

"That was a month ago. Besides I'm not in the mood. Sam just dumped me."

"Technically, you and Sam weren't dating yet, so he can't actually dump you."

"Whatever. Just tell your friend Prem that I'm not available. I'm coming off my porn binge, I'm a mess, I look like crap, and I don't have anything to wear."

"First of all, you have to go. Prem's probably already on his way to the restaurant, and if you don't show up, he will be devastated. Second of all, he won't care what you look like. He's blind."

"You are setting me up with a literal blind date?"

Twenty minutes later, I am walking out the door in a Juicy

Couture sweatsuit, hair in a ponytail, and sneakers (not designer sneakers like Donna Karan's, but comfortable worn-to-death running sneakers). Ordinarily, the entire contents of my closet would be on my bed before I found the right first-date outfit, and I would spend a good hour in the bathroom dolling myself up, but I figure if there are advantages to dating a blind guy, not worrying about your looks is high on the list.

At the restaurant, I see Prem sitting at a table wearing the designated burnt orange tie he said he would be wearing—he's actually quite good-looking, and even though he is wearing sunglasses after dark, it does not stand out in L.A. It just makes him look a little Hollywood if anything. I actually start to come out of my funk and consider the possible upsides to Prem.

I know that when Dante, my sister's cat, lost her sight, all of her other senses became heightened. Her blind cat could actually chase and swat a ball of foil through table and chair legs without bumping into a thing. I wonder how that translates to humans in the bedroom? I sit down in front of him with a smile on my face. Instead of smiling back he gets a weird look on his. *Did I forget to put deodorant on?* I quickly do a subtle underarm sniff-check and relax. I am definitely wearing deodorant.

"Hi, I'm Ayn."

There is a long pause as if he is trying to figure something out. He reaches out and feels my face, then my ponytail. I am uncomfortable with it as other diners are staring, but I handle it graciously to accommodate the fact that he is visually challenged. When he's done, he still has a weird look on his face.

I know it's improbable, but I start to wonder if he can tell that I have not washed my hair in three days. He still has not said a word but feels the sleeve of my sweatsuit, and I swear he cringes at the touch of it.

Now I'm kind of nervous and I start tapping my foot on the floor. He tilts his head toward the sound and finally opens his mouth. The first thing he says to me is "Are you wearing *sneakers?*", barely able to conceal his disdain.

An hour later, Maya has come over to my apartment to borrow a pair of shoes. We wear the same size shoes, but have not worn the same size clothes since we were roommates in college. Somehow, over time, Maya has whittled herself down to a size 0, and I, well, let's just say I occasionally wear a size 0, too, but with a 1 in front of it.

Maya is not just thin; she is pretty with blond hair and fair skin from her Danish side, and an hourglass figure from her Italian side. My entire life I have been best friend to pretty girls. For some reason, they are attracted to me. Not in a lesbian way, although that would be flattering. I think they know I don't really give a shit that they are pretty. Whereas other people flock to them for their beauty, they sense I am only interested in being friends with them if they are bright, have original thoughts, and are kind.

Maya is too kind. "I can't believe you just left him in the restaurant," she squeals.

"Hey, being blind does not give him permission to be an asshole. And, for the record, that heightened senses thing really blows."

"I don't feel comfortable leaving you alone tonight. Maybe you should come to the party with me," she suggests. "Vee should be there," she adds, trying to cheer me up.

I know going to a party with Maya will mean being stampeded by guys as they try to hit on Maya. But for once I don't care, because right now I feel like I could go my entire life without ever dating again. As Maya watches me, I stomp over to my inflatable husband and thrust a pair of scissors into him, popping him for good.

Maya looks at me like I'm crazy.

"I'd love to go," is all I say.

As soon as we enter the packed party, I sense all eyes on me for once, but that is only because in this sea of hipsters dressed to the nines, I am still wearing my sweats and sneakers.

"Look at all the shiny people," I mutter.

A tall, rugged-looking guy comes over with his wingman, who, like all good wingmen, is less tall and less good-looking than his friend. As his friend tries to impress Maya by buying her a drink, the wingman makes a poor attempt at striking up a conversation with me. After five minutes of explaining to him how I know Maya, I am fed up.

"Why don't you just admit you're not interested in me," I blurt out. He doesn't say anything back so I keep talking. "You've been staring at the redhead over there with the melon-sized breasts since your buddy forced you to distract me so that he could talk to my prettier, more desirable friend."

"Hey, no, it's not like that—"

"Oh, what's it like then, *wingman?*"

He looks at me, silent and dumbfounded again.

"Exactly. Now be free. I mean it. *Shoo*! Go for the redhead. I know her; she's completely vapid. You're perfect for each other."

He grabs his drink and practically trips over himself to get away from me.

Vee finds me in the crowd. "What do you have to do to get a drink around here? I've been here fifteen minutes." We look over at Maya. Guys are buying her drinks left and right and cocktail waiters are hovered around her.

"Nothing like survival of the prettiest," I say, walking over to Maya where I grab two of her free drinks, one for me and one for Vee.

Back in our guy-free zone, Vee spots the ex-boyfriend of an acquaintance of ours making out with a girl who looks a lot like heirhead Paris Hilton. "Jesus, he's only been broken up with Kira for a week and he has a new girlfriend?" she says, shocked.

"Haven't you heard, there's a McGirlfriend drive-thru on Third and Beverly?" I say sarcastically. "It's quick and easy, but less satisfying."

Maya has escaped a huddle of men and is now walking over with someone we remotely know as Holly. She is definitely one of the shiny people; she even wears lotion with subtle specks of fine glitter. Holly is dressed like Sienna Miller and has put together an outfit that would make me look homeless. The same outfit makes Holly look like a runway model.

"Hey, Ayn, have you met Holly?" Maya asks.

I nod. "Hey, Holly."

After talking to us for only ten minutes, it is clear that Holly is one of those women who has a need to announce to the party, nay the world, that she has a boyfriend. She drops the word "boyfriend" every two minutes.

"Yeah, my *boyfriend* loves Japanese beer . . . oh, you have to meet my *boyfriend*; he's here somewhere . . . Oh my gawd, like, you are so funny, my *boyfriend* would love you!" She especially brings up her *boyfriend* when she is in a group of significantly single women.

In this case that would be me, Vee, and Maya. Vee and I just roll our eyes at each other every time Holly speaks, as Maya tries to smile politely. If she could, I have a feeling Holly would brand our foreheads with a capital L so that everyone would instantly know that, unlike Holly, we are too lame to have boyfriends.

"Hey, look there's Kira." It is the first time Holly has not talked about her boyfriend or herself in twenty minutes, so it sort of jolts me awake.

"I can't believe her boyfriend dumped her," I say, pausing to brush some of Holly's skin glitter off my arm. "She's so sweet," I add about Kira.

"What do you expect when you stop counting your calories?" Holly says matter-of-factly.

I turn to her. "Are you serious? She can't be bigger than a size 6. Besides do you even know her?"

She just looks at the white acrylic tips on her right hand and says, "I'm just saying I doubt *my* boyfriend would go out with her."

That's it. I look directly at Holly. "You know, you can get a T-shirt made that says 'I Have a Boyfriend,' so you don't have to brag about it every five seconds."

Suddenly Maya looks horrified, and Vee looks, well, excited.

Holly gives me a scary sweet smile. Even her teeth are shiny, but I see a few hairs on her head standing on end. "Oh, I'm sorry, Ayn. Am I making you jealous?" she says.

"Jealous of what, Holly? Your fake tits? Your McPersonality? Your McThoughts? Or the fact that your conversation topics are limited to, uh, I don't know, *you?*"

Maya is tugging at my sleeve.

"I'm not done yet," I tell Maya. *I've got a lot more in store for Holly.*

"Uh, Ayn, Sam is here," Maya whispers in a panic.

I look over and see that indeed Sam is heading toward us with a strange look on his face.

Holly sees Sam, too, and lights up. "Here comes my boyfriend now."

My heart sinks to the floor. I am speechless. I am so shocked I can barely move. Maya figures out all of this with one look at me and starts to guide me away from Holly.

As we leave, I hear Holly say to Vee, "What is with your friend?"

I wait out in the hallway as Maya goes back in to get her purse. No easy feat considering the groups of guys that will try one last time to get her number. The shock about Sam and Holly has worn off, and now I feel like I might break down and cry at any moment, when the door to the party opens and I turn toward it, praying that it is Maya so that we can get the hell out of here. It is not Maya. It is Sam. For once, I am not happy to see him and realize that I never will be again.

"Ayn, look, I'm really sorry I haven't called."

"You know what, forget it. I'm not in the mood. What's done is done."

"I just think that maybe our lives might be on different paths."

That's funny, I want to tell him, *because when you had your hands down my pants a few nights ago we seemed to be on the same path, but now you are obviously on the fucking Holly-go-glitter-lightly path.* I somehow refrain from saying any of this, though

242

it is very unlike me not to express my feelings. This scares me.

"I just want you to know it's not you. You're terrific."

You sure have a great way of showing that.

He keeps going. "I just have certain hang-ups about things and I don't think I can handle what you're going through. I don't think I'm ready for that kind of commitment."

And what kind of commitment would that be? The you-don't-treat-the-person-like-shit-after-having-great-sex-with-them kind of commitment?

But all I say is, "Sure, I understand." I have no idea why I am letting him off so easily. I have no idea why I feel bad that he seems to be in pain. I have no idea why I still love him. I remind myself that he has a shiny new McGirlfriend. One he probably had three days ago when we slept together. I mean if he were back with cool Sabine, that would be one thing. That I could understand. But for him to have seemingly meaningful sex with me and then go back to Hollow Holly is unbearable. *Do you know how hard it is to be me?* I want to shout at him. *Even* blind *guys expect me to look good!*

Porn-to-Do

Try
Eat Right
for Your
Blood-Type

1. ~~Visit a strip club~~

2. ~~Watch Porn~~ Buy wheat-free waffles

3. ~~Read erotica~~

At home there is a message from Vee, informing me that I can rest assured that she put Holly in her place after I left, but it brings me no comfort. I cry myself to sleep, right onto my once precious $80 Calvin Klein shams, staining them with mascara tears, Holly's pesky glitter, and my runny nose. Tomorrow I will probably realize that they are ruined, but I doubt I will give a shit.

WOMEN

ARE AMONG THE
FASTEST-GROWING
USERS OF PORNOGRAPHY
ON THE INTERNET,
WITH A 30 PER CENT RISE
FROM JUST OVER ONE
MILLION TO 1.4 MILLION
IN THE PAST 12 MONTHS

Source: Nielsen NetRatings for the Independent on Sunday

Chapter Ten
What Goes Around Cums Around

Porn-partum blues: *n. a form of anxiety caused by separation from porn*

The shock and sadness stage over Sam has worn off, and now I am in the anger stage.

"I just don't understand why men have to lie about things!" I rant to The Naughty Knitters. They are all quiet for once as they let me vent all my feelings (to their credit, they have been doing this for the last forty-five minutes) about what happened with Sam.

Finally, Vee speaks up. "Okay, Sam is an asshole, but you're not going to use that as a reason not to finish your Porn-to-Do list, are you?"

"If it weren't for my list, I never would have met Sam."

"If it weren't for that list you would still be with *Greg*," Vee points out.

"That would be a push in blackjack*," explains Paige.

I look at the list. Weird to think I have been carrying it around for months. Nine items down, three to go. *Wow.*

I read the next item out loud. "Where do men hide their porn?"

---

*A tie between dealer and players.

"That's all you want to know when it comes to guys and porn?" Steve asks. I guess there is a lot more I'm curious about when it comes to what men don't want us women to know.

"I'd love to know how many guys we know have hired a hooker," I add.

"Don't stop there," Steve orders.

"How often do you think they lie to their girlfriends or wives about porn?" asks Maya.

Everyone throws out something they are curious about.

"Hey, is anyone else curious what women think about these things, too?" I ask them.

We all look around at each other. Everyone is pretty much nodding.

Together we come up with a list of fifteen questions for men and fifteen questions for women.

"But how will you get anyone to tell you the truth about this stuff to your face?" asks Tricia.

"I'll rent a lie detector machine," I suggest.

Vee shakes her head. "Too expensive. It's one thousand dollars to rent the polygraph machine and the examiner to test just five people, and you only get to ask four questions. Six questions have to be control questions. Besides, the results can be very skewed. Have you heard of Mystery Question number three?"

We all give her blank looks, partially because we do not know what mystery question number three is, and partially because we can't figure out why Vee knows so much about polygraph machines.

"A subject will fail anything asked as question number three, but if they are asked the same question as number five or eight or ten, they will pass it. A subject can also trick a polygraph by computing math equations or other mental exercises in his head while answering 'yes' or 'no,'" Vee explains with the perfunctory tone of a school marm.

"Stop," I put my hand up in the air. "When did you become an expert on polygraph machines?"

"I was going to use one on Andres before he broke down and confessed he was cheating on me. A couple of shots of tequila was a lot cheaper than a polygraph."

That night, I end up surfing the Web to check out some sites, other than Babeland.com, which keep coming up in my conversations about alternative porn in the mainstream. I check out Suicidegirls.com, the porn site known for nude pictures and profiles of women who are a far cry from the plastic Barbie porn stars at other sites. At Suicide Girls, the women are not porn stars, but real women, many who are goth or punk in style, who like to pose nude. They are more likely to have real breasts, original thoughts, a tattoo, and a vintage record collection.

I also check out Nerve.com, which was recommended by a few women and men I know. It is a cool online magazine that states it exists because sex is "in need of a fearless, intelligent forum for both genders. We believe that women (men too, but especially women) have waited long enough for a smart, honest magazine on sex . . . as well as striking photographs of naked people that capture more than their flesh."

And, if I had more time or made another Porn-to-Do list, I would probably add CakeNYC.com, which I come across and remember my New York friends keep bringing up. Cake is a female-run women's sexuality enterprise. They host events, a website, a newsletter, and a membership program that provides safe and fun environments (alternatives to traditional male-focused nightlife), where women can express their sexuality. Too bad they are not in L.A. yet.

After browsing these alternative sex sites designed by smart women, I end up where I always do when I am surfing the Web: at eBay.

I don't know why, but there is something voyeuristically satisfying about watching people bid on other people's junk. In an unusual move, I actually bid on something myself: a portable lie detector machine advertised as being used by the Israeli army. It is only $59.99. More than a bottle of tequila, but it will probably last a lot longer.

My "Truster" (that's what the portable lie detector is called) arrives in the mail a week later. Made of plastic, it resembles a label maker in size and shape. I want to test it right away. I could call Steve, but that would be too similar to testing a girl, so I call my pal Sloan.

"You want me to what?" Sloan asks as we have coffee at my place.

"I want to ask you some questions about porn so that I can test my new little lie detector machine."

I don't tell Sloan that I picked him because he is one of the few old fashioned guys' guys (a.k.a, a "retrosexual") left in metropolitan L.A.—he is to Men Behaving like Women as Russell Crowe is to Elijah Wood.

"Are you *still* doing the porn thing?" His tone makes it clear he thinks my exploration of porn is ridiculous.

I have a feeling that his retrosexuality makes him a little uncomfortable with the idea of a girl co-opting a heretofore male pastime.

"Let me see that." He grabs my Truster and looks at it. "Are you sure the Israeli army used this? It feels like a toy." He checks out some small print on the back. "Made in Korea?"

I snatch it back. "Why do you always have to be a skeptic?"

"Fine. But for the record, I'm totally against this. Men need to have some areas of life undisturbed by the presence of females. That includes sports bars, forward units of the army, and viewing habits of old-fashioned hetero porn. You don't see us ever trying to join in or ask questions when it comes to Mommy and Me groups, Jazzercise, or quilting bees."

"Understood. Now, first, I need to ask you a few non-porn related questions." I run him through a series of control questions to calibrate the machine, which basically analyzes stress levels in someone's voice to determine truthfulness. When I am satisfied that I have a good baseline for Sloan, I get to the real questions.

The first real question I ask is: "Do you ever masturbate to porn?"

"I stopped doing that in my early twenties," he states.

The Truster beeps, indicating that he is lying. "Fine, *late* twenties," he admits.

The machine beeps again, still indicating that Sloan is lying.

"Wait a second, that's bullshit. I'm actually telling the truth."

I just laugh. "Yeah, sure you are, Sloan." Thank goodness my Truster tells the truth. Maybe if I'd had it to use on Greg, Ben, and Sam, I would not have wasted my time.

"Give me that damn thing." He rips it out of my hands and turns it on me.

"How old were you when you first had anal sex?"

"I've never had anal sex." *Beep!* The Truster goes off, dumbfounding me.

"Oh, God, you were a teenager, weren't you?"

"No!" I protest. *Beep!* The machine beeps like crazy.

Sloan is now in hysterics at the look on my face. He thinks it is hilarious that I paid $59.99 for a piece of crap.

I would think it is funny, too, but can't help wondering if anyone has told the Israeli army that the Truster cannot be trusted.

The next day, I end up just typing up fifteen questions for men and fifteen for women, plus space for comments, and e-mailing them to twenty-five friends who then e-mail them to their friends.

People respond a lot faster to porn surveys than they do to charity requests or even party invitations. Most people take their surveys at work and e-mail them back to me within the hour. I get a lot from my friends, but in total there are about a hundred, most from people I don't know, including a few from Kansas, Germany, and Japan. The respondents range in age from twenty to forty-eight, and the one thing they all have in common is that they are all college-educated and heterosexual. Actually, the survey accidentally gets sent to my gay cousin Paul in Texas, who cannot resist taking it and insists that I forward all his responses to The Naughty Knitters.

(Note: Percentages are of the number of people who answered that question. Not every question was answered by everyone who responded to the survey. The margin of error is more than statistically significant, but The Knitters hardly care.)

SURVEY RESULTS

1. Is getting a lap dance cheating?

MEN:	WOMEN:
No (64%)	No (96%)
Yes (18%)	Yes (0%)
Maybe (18%)	Maybe (4%)

COMMENT: "If Bill Clinton can claim that oral sex is not cheating, then lap dances should be just fine."—*Elizabeth, 32, bartender, San Diego*

PAUL: "Only if it's free."

2. Do you prefer reading *Penthouse* or poetry?

MEN:	WOMEN:
Penthouse (50%)	Penthouse (30%)
Poetry (25%)	Poetry (52%)
Both equally or neither (25%)	Neither (18%)

"I prefer *Penthouse* . . . it's hard to masturbate to poetry."—*J. Abrams, 39, engineer, Lansing, Michigan*

PAUL: "*Playgirl.*"

3. If you had to omit one of the following from your life (forever), which would it be: porn or chocolate?

MEN:	WOMEN:
Chocolate (46%)	Chocolate (17%)
Porn (54%)	Porn (83%)

"I would omit chocolate . . . porn has no calories."—*Anonymous*

PAUL: "Chocolate, but I would give up porn before I would give up key-lime pies."

4. **Have you ever lied to a significant other about using porn, including movies, strip clubs, Internet, etc.?**

MEN:	WOMEN:
No (42%)	No (70%)
Yes (58%)	Yes (30%)

"The closest I've come to that is not telling a date that I took Viagra. It got him really hot (and impressed) when I had about 18 orgasms in a row."—*Jennie, 28, third-grade teacher, Manhattan Beach*

PAUL: "Only when he's daddy and I've been a BAAAAD boy! (Just kidding—obnoxiously blatant—my real answer is 'no.')"

5. **Men: Most interesting place you've ever hidden a dirty magazine or adult video?**
SAMPLE RESPONSES: panel in a drop ceiling, Monopoly game box, in the box that held my wedding video, bottom of laundry basket, tool box in garage

PAUL: "Under shelf liner in my parents' bathroom (because I knew they wouldn't look for it there)."

6. **Women: Where do you keep your vibrator?**
31% of the women responding do not have a vibrator.

99% of the women who report having a vibrator keep it in a drawer (lingerie, sock, or underwear) in their dresser.

"It's not where you keep your vibrators that's important, it's where you keep the fresh batteries that counts."—*Paris, 39, graphic designer and new mom, Los Angeles*

7. **Ever visited a brothel (legal or illegal) or hired a hooker?**
   MEN:
   No (93%)
   Yes (7%)

   PAUL: "Not yet."

8. **Share a story about using porn (including vibrators, strip clubs, magazines, sex toys, etc.).**
   MOST INTERESTING STORY FROM A MAN:
   "Never having any real interest in strip bars, I was quite unsure about going to one of these places as they really didn't suit my personality. So the first time I was at a strip club, it was for a bachelor party for which I had accepted an invitation and felt entirely obligated to attend. I was hanging out with a gregarious buddy of mine. He strikes up a conversation with one of the strippers hanging out on her break, and the three of us sit down at a table. I sat nervously chain-smoking cigarettes and drinking beers with my buddy and this entirely naked woman. All of a sudden, my buddy excuses himself and I am left sitting with this naked stripper whom I suppose expects me to carry on an actual conversation with her. I was flabbergasted that my buddy left me there. So I say to her, 'Why do you do this kind of

work?' She says because she loves the attention she gets that one man couldn't ever give to her, but an entire room of admiring men do. We carry on a conversation for the next five minutes or so, and then it ends with her going back to work.

"I think I felt more naked in that situation than the stripper."—*Michael, 38, self-employed, New York·*

MOST INTERESTING STORY FROM A WOMAN:
"Please know that I have *never* told anyone this . . .

"Around three years ago I had a major break-up. I decided that the best thing that I could do would be to have sex with someone so that I wouldn't be thinking about the last person that I had sex with . . . make sense? I didn't want to do it with anyone that I knew, and I didn't want to have the hassle of going to a bar and 'meeting' new people. I just wanted sex. So, on a referral from a friend, I went to the casual encounters section on Craigslist and put up a post. Basically saying that I was looking for misc. no-strings-attached sex with a man who loved going down on a woman and didn't expect reciprocation. I also wanted them to be over thirty. I mean, it is like a Christmas wish list, right? I can ask for anything that I want.

"You would not believe the response that I received. Five minutes after I posted, my in-box filled with about fifty responses. No lie. In all I think that I received close to a hundred replies. Now, most of those were just cock shots. Nice, but I want to see the face of those cocks. Those were deleted. The others were either kids who were way too young (in their early twenties), married men (I think that's bad karma), or just plain unattractive. I narrowed it down to three people. Then after phone conversations narrowed it down to one.

"I figured a gay bar would be a very incognito place to meet. He was very average and recently separated. I don't know what I was expecting from someone off of the Internet. I had never done it before. We talked. He was normal. I think in the back of my head I was expecting a serial killer. After a few drinks I surprised myself and suggested we go back to my apartment. *Who was I?* He followed me there. My heart was beating really fast, but at the same time it was kind of fun. I felt like I was living out one of those fantasy forums that I used to read in college!

"To make a long story short: he came up to my apartment, led me into the bedroom, pulled my pants down, and gave me one of the best orgasms of my life. And, just like the ad said, he didn't expect anything in return. That's all he did, then he left. I have to say that my mind was blown and at the same time a Pandora's box was opened.

"Since then we have been meeting once a month for the past three years. There are no strings attached and it's just really great sex. We joke that we are the longest relationships we have had in a while. He's my modern-day booty call."— *Marianne, 35, PR executive, Los Angeles*

Paul: "My sister found out I was gay by catching me watching gay porn while in high school. I told her I was doing research for a paper, but she didn't believe me."

9. **What would happen if you told your significant other you like porn?**

Most men reported that their significant others would have no problem with it: "My last girlfriend would have turned on the DVD player and said, 'Let's see what you got!'" "She'd ask to see it to see if she might like it too." "She would say, 'What guy doesn't?'" "She'd say: 'What are you, human?'" "What would happen? Nothing. Geez, I'm not pussified, I run the joint." "I did tell my significant other. She didn't care." "Yeah? So? Yawn."

Women responded with things like: "He'd be thrilled." "He knows and he is *allll* for it." "He would break into double-twisting reverse back flips." "He'd yawn." "My guy knows I love porn—it turns him on." "I think he wouldn't believe me—or he would laugh." "Brava! It's about time!" "He would probably want to watch it together all the time then."

PAUL: "He would say, 'No, you don't, you LOVE porn.'"

10. **How many times a week do you look at Internet porn?**

MEN:

36% of the men reported that they look at Internet porn zero times per week.

The rest reported an average of three to four times per week.

WOMEN:

2% of the women averaged one or more times per week.

MOST INTERESTING STATISTIC: A lot of women said they

avoided Internet porn only because they were afraid of spyware and viruses.

PAUL: "Three times-ish? You do know that any answers you get for this question should be doubled to get the truth."

11. **Men:** Would you date a girl who worked at a legal Nevada brothel? What if she worked as a stripper?
    BROTHEL: No (100%)

    STRIPPER: No (31%); Yes (60%); 9% did not respond.

    PAUL: "Is she rich?"

12. **Women:** Would you date a guy who worked as a male stripper?
    No (65%)   Yes (35%)

    PAUL: "In a heartbeat."

13. **Women:** Would you date a guy who has worked at a stud farm?
    No (91%)   Yes (4%)
    Maybe (5%)

    PAUL: "See answer #12."

14. **Women:** Would you pay for sex at a stud farm?
    No (74%)   Yes (13%)
    Unsure (13%)

    PAUL: "Sure, if they'd let me."

15. **Men:** Would you date a girl who's been to a stud farm or hired a male hooker?

No (55%)   Yes (45%)

PAUL: "Only if she would take me along."

16. Do you think prostitution should be legalized?

MEN:	WOMEN:
No (27%)	No (43%)
Yes (36%)	Yes (48%)
Unsure (37%)	Unsure (9%)

MOST INTERESTING STATISTIC: Women were more likely to assume that legal brothel workers were mistreated and that working conditions would be poor.

PAUL: "Prostitution's not legal?"

17. Men: If you could have sex with one porn star, who would it be?

27% of the men who received this survey stated Jenna Jameson; many of these were by default because she was the only name they could think of; 36% stated they don't know any by name.

PAUL: "Sebastian Bonnet."*

18. Have you had Internet sex?

---

*Popular gay male porn star from Slovakia.

MEN:	WOMEN:
No (92%)	No (64%)
Yes (8%)	Yes (36%)

PAUL: "Do you mean today?"

19. **What are you curious about (but have not tried) when it comes to porn?**

98% of men answered "nothing" or "nothing left to try." A couple of guys mentioned the VIP room at a strip club, swinging, or watching porn with their significant others.

Only 13% of women answered "nothing." In general, women were far more curious and specific with their responses. Some of the more common responses were: attend a live S&M show, watch porn made just for women, have sex and watch porn at the same time, watch someone else have sex, watch porn on a hotel television, attend or watch a masked orgy, and play with food during sex. Several women stated they were curious about a "threesome."

PAUL: "I'd give you the entire list, but I'm afraid if I type it all out I'll get carpal tunnel...then there goes my sex life!!!"

The Naughty Knitters and I had a blast compiling the survey results and reading them aloud to each other. It was a great way to take my mind off of Sam. It was also validation that I am not alone in my curiosity about porn. In fact, we enjoyed the juicy sex confessions from women—many of them fellow good girls—

so much that we decided we need our own website (www.TheNaughtyKnitters.com) where we can receive more enlightening sex stories and good girl sex tips. "Build it and they will come," we laugh.

ANNUAL UK PORN REVENUE

EXCEEDS

THE COMBINED REVENUES OF MANCHESTER UNITED, ARSENAL AND CHELSEA FOOTBALL CLUBS

Source: Deloitte.com

Chapter Eleven
Grandmas Gone Wild

S'morgasm: *n. a point of intense pleasure a person reaches from the consumption of chocolate, marshmallows, and graham crackers*

The next day, I am sitting in front of Joan's, my favorite café on Third Street, eating chocolate cupcakes for my birthday and watching ex-*Friends* stars Courteney Cox and Lisa Kudrow pack up their kids after a hard day of boutique shopping, when my friend Randall shows up to commiserate about our recent break-ups. Randall is technically my oldest friend in the world—our mothers became friends before we were even born, when they used to frequent illegal gambling dens in Taiwan—but because he has such an active social life and travels so much, I rarely get to see him. Randall also happens to be gay, but without any sitcom gay characteristics. If you didn't know him, you would just think he was a polite hetero Asian guy.

I know him, and I know when he is up to something.

He takes a bite of one of my cupcakes and leans in with a mischievous grin.

"Remember when you said the best way for you to stop thinking about that guy Sam and for me to stop thinking about Marco"—Randall broke up with the love of his life three months ago—"was to go out, get wasted, and meet a *shitload* of good-looking single men?" he excitedly reminds me.

It was last night when I called him, buzzed, so I nod, my mouth full of chocolate cupcake. He is obviously pleased with himself as he hands me an envelope.

"Happy Birthday!" he shouts, way too loud. I open the envelope; inside are tickets for a four-day, three-night Royal Caribbean cruise to Baja.

"You're sending me on a cruise?"

"With a *ship*load of men." This makes me smile, and I feel the pressure in my head easing slightly.

"Randall, this is way too generous. I can't take this."

"Take it. I sold the most this month at the agency." Randall is a travel agent. "I got two cabins free. So that's space for four people."

"This is awesome. You are awesome." I give him a hug. "Who should I take?" I wonder out loud. "If I take Vee, we will be competing over the same guys. Paige would do nothing but work. Steve gets seasick. Tricia will be in Ireland on vacation. And Maya is stuck on a movie with Mrs. X and couldn't possibly get away for three days, because that would mean Mrs. X would have to buy her own underwear, pick up her dry cleaning, microwave her Zone diets herself, and drive herself around L.A. for three whole days—"

"Yeah, uh, I thought it would be fun if you brought your mom and I brought mine."

I hear the sound of squealing brakes in my head.

"The Moms? Are you sure?"

Randall's mom, Carolyn, is even crazier than mine and she, too, is going through a divorce. It is her second divorce. But she, unlike my mom, is bitter about hers. The Moms also have this habit of speaking in Chinese to each other when they are in our company. The problem is that Randall and I do not speak a word of Mandarin, and it is obvious that they are complaining about us because our names pop up every few minutes along with a loud sigh, a disapproving shake of the head, or a *tsk, tsk* sound that can only mean "when will they ever learn?"

Randall senses my hesitancy. "Come on, it'll be great. The cruise will be a way for us to reconnect. You know, a bonding adventure. A bon voyage to break-ups."

"So, if Amy Tan were writing a book about us it would be called *The Out-of-Luck Club?*"

"Very funny. You need to lighten up about the Moms. It is the perfect vacation to take them on. The ship has a casino and all-you-can-eat buffets. Think about it, we will never see them, yet it still counts as spending time with them. Besides, I really miss your annual travel journals." Randall is talking about the tongue-in-cheek journals I used to write when I traveled to places like Spain and France and India. I sent them out every year in lieu of a holiday letter. Somehow the tradition got dropped when I met Greg. We really never took vacations unless you count losing a transmission in Bakersfield and having to hole up in a Motel 6 for three days.

Despite my protests, I can see Randall really wants to do this with the Moms, so I give in. "Fine. The Moms can come. But they can only complain about us in English!"

Cruise Journal

DAY ONE

2 P.M.: *I feel like a supermodel. I am now on board Royal Caribbean's Viking Serenade and realize why cruise ships attract high proportions of overweight (being polite here) people. Their rear ends are too big to fit into small seats on airplanes. No choice but to travel by ship. All-you-can-eat buffets may also be a factor.*

As the ship leaves port, I imagine that we are setting sail from some place in the French Riviera for some lovely island destination in the south of Spain. Unfortunately, my overactive imagination is interrupted by a loud middle-aged couple from Texas as they spill a can of Budweiser (smuggled on board) on my new Kate Spade suede slides, reminding me that in actuality, we are setting sail from a rusty San Pedro shipyard near Long Beach and are headed for Baja (strangely not quite California, not quite Mexico), where these Texans and many other passengers apparently can't wait to get their hands on duty-free tequila and black market Viagra.

2:30P.M.: *My cell phone rings. I scramble to find it in my tote bag, but the connection is lost by the time I answer. I spend the next half hour wondering if it could be Sam.*

3 P.M.: *Where are all the single good-looking guys? At this point, I would be happy to sight a good-looking gay one (besides Randall). Most people are traveling in families or, in some cases, hordes.*

Since there may be less flirting and picking up of guys going on on this voyage than I expected, I decide to go to our cabin (which Randall and I are sharing and nicknamed "The Closet" because of its size) and immediately set goals for my mini-vacation:

1. *Expand mind. Brought Pulitzer Prize–winning* Guns, Germs, and Steel *by anthropologist Jared Diamond to read for fun, and our current Book Club selection,* Kafka on The Shore *by Haruki Murakami, and one book of poetry (Bukowski); also:* Vanity Fair *(always travel with) and* Esquire *(have not given up on quest to figure out men).*

2. *Will exercise. Every day. Maybe even twice a day. That way I can eat whatever I want sans guilt.*

3. *Pursue enriching activities. Obviously on this vacation I am limited to on-board activities. According to our perky cruise director (think Julie McCoy from* The Love Boat, *but age fifty), I can earn two "ship-shape" dollars for every ship activity I attend. Dollars are redeemable at the ship's store for nifty merchandise. Goal: Earn twenty ship-shape dollars so that I can buy a visor and souvenirs for The Naughty Knitters.*

5 P.M.: *Bummer. Just missed first chance to earn ship-shape dollars, but when you think about it, napping is probably a more useful skill than napkin folding.*

6 P.M.: *Further disappointed to discover that bingo does not count toward ship-shape dollars. Played bingo anyway. Might as well have just thrown money overboard. Do not understand* *why winning bingo pot is only $300 if one hundred of us each put in $50 to play. (Note to Self: Must start compiling a list of recommendations for ship's captain.)*

7 P.M.: *Randall and I walk the entire Lido deck, cruising the cruise for single eligible men. Just when we are about to give up, we spot a reasonably good-looking guy in the ship's gift shop and make a beeline for him. Just when we are about to flirt with him, a perky brunette bounds up to him and gives him a kiss. Randall and I look at each other and roll our eyes in unison.*

7:15 P.M.: *We end up at the magazine stand, where Randall buys Oprah, People, and Star, and I start reading magazines for free. Behind the counter, I see that they have Playboy, Hustler, and Penthouse. I figure that being trapped on a cruise ship hundreds of miles from shore is a great opportunity to check out the magazines that started me on my porn misadventures in the first place.*

I nudge Randall and whisper, "Here's a twenty. Buy me Hustler, Playboy, and Penthouse."

He doesn't even look up at me. He is busy reading Oprah. God forbid you interrupt Randall when he is in his Oprah zone. "Buy them yourself."

"Remember the time you made me French kiss you in public just so that Gabriel would think you were straight and you wouldn't have to tell him you didn't like him?"

He grabs the twenty from me. "Fine."

7:30 P.M.: *Before dinner, in our cabin, I decide to check out the three magazines, now referred to by us as the Unholy Trinity. I lay them out on the bed and study them for a moment. I am surprised to see that* Penthouse *looks more benign than a lot of the men's magazines you see front and center at the grocery store; the girl on the cover is actually "clothed" in a modest silk bra and panty set. I can't remember the last time a celebrity actually wore clothes on the cover of* Rolling Stone, *and on this month's cover of* Vanity Fair, *although she is strategically covering her nipples with crossed arms, Paris Hilton is topless.*

Playboy *has a cover photo of a naked brunette, but key lower body parts and her backside are shadowed, and the model's arms are discreetly covering her breasts.* Hustler *definitely has the naughtiest vibe of the three with a cover photo of a woman with way too much blue eye shadow on and extraordinarily large round breasts that are visible through sheer lingerie.*

Randall is lying on his bed, reading his magazines, too. I tear the covers off his magazines and tape them onto mine so that Oprah *covers* Playboy, People *covers* Hustler, *and* Star *is now covering* Penthouse.

"What are you doing?"

"This way if one of the Moms or housekeepers enter our room, they will not think I am a pornoholic."

The cover of Playboy *catches Randall's eye.*

"Hey, she kind of looks like your ex neighbor." Randall is looking at the real cover of Playboy *magazine. He is right. The woman on the cover is a pretty brunette with a really*

great smile. She even has a tattoo like my ex neigh—

"Oh, my god, it is my ex neighbor." Her name is Cara *and she is currently starring in a prime-time TV show. "Do you think she knows they're using her photo?"*

"Ayn, she's on the cover of Playboy. *She probably has some idea."* Cara *is friendly, down-to-earth, and the doting mother of an adorable two-year-old girl. The last time I saw her, I bought my dining room table from her at her moving sale, which she manned herself, proving to everyone on our block that she is not a high-maintenance celebrity.*

"Well, are you going to check her out?" Randall is dying to know.

I flip through the magazine until I find her spread and take a peek. I snap the magazine shut, waves of guilt coming over me. Am I invading her privacy? *It takes me a second, then I remember that* Playboy *sells ten million magazines worldwide. That is almost ten times more than the most popular women's magazine. Of course Cara expects to be seen by a few people she knows. I flip the magazine back open.* Wow, she looks really great with her clothes off, too. *I decide if Cara can be courageous and open-minded enough to pose nude for* Playboy, *I can muster the courage to "read" it.*

After perusing the rest of the magazine, I come to the conclusion that Playboy *is not any more risqué than FHM, Stuff, or Maxim, which are popular mainstream magazines with a mostly male audience. There are even cartoons and something they call* Playboy's *party jokes that all read pretty much like this one: "Why do the sperm in a gay relationship get claustrophobic? Because there's no womb to move around* in." *If the party jokes, video game reviews, scatological humor, and cartoons are not proof enough that men refuse to let go of their sophomoric selves, there is the full page ad for gold-banded porcelain* Lord of The Rings *plates described as "a magnificent four-piece collection inscribed in Elvish script with scenes from* The Fellowship of the Ring®, The Two Towers®, *and* Return of the King® *displayed in a gleaming sword of Narsil." Need I say more? Okay, okay, I guess guys could read our magazines and make fun of us, too. Although I've never seen cartoons in* Cosmo, *it's never going to win a Pulitzer Prize for its writing. Whereas* Playboy, *which has softer pieces like a review of flip-flop footwear and celebrity weddings gone bad, also presents deeper-issue articles and stories by heavy-hitter writers.*

8 P.M.: *Missed gym hours because Mom has dragged me to hear cruise director describe tomorrow's land excursion possibilities while we dock for the day in the port city of Ensenada. Basically, she gave us shopping pointers and recommended places to buy silver and leather items (can you say "kickbacks"?). "Never pay full price," she said. "Do not drink the water," and, "Absolutely do not buy Chiclets (tiny tasteless Mexican chewing gum) from street urchins because this encourages kids to beg instead of attending school."*

9 P.M.: *Still have not spotted one unattached man. It's like Noah's Ark and only breeding couples (and the four of us) have been sent out to sea.*

10 P.M.: *Maybe* Hustler *magazine won't be as raunchy as it looks. It starts out with a hilarious "X-mas Wish List" from Larry Flynt,* Hustler's *infamous publisher, listing items he would like Santa to deliver. My favorites are: a hairbrush for Phil Specter, sunglasses for the runaway bride, a liberal for the Supreme Court, an IQ for Paris Hilton, and* Ethics for Dummies *for Tom Delay.*

10:02 P.M.: *Jesus, who reads this stuff? After Larry Flynt's funny X-mas list, I can barely stand to turn the pages. I feel dirty, even somewhat violated. It definitely crosses a line that* Playboy *does not. Nothing gentlemanly about it. The full-page back cover ad on* Playboy *is a sophisticated solicitation for Bombay Sapphire London Dry Gin. The back cover ad on* Hustler *is for a phone sex service 1-800-DARK-TWAT and shows a naked light-skinned African-American woman in five-inch heels spread-eagle on a cheap comforter—you'd think at the rate of $2.98 per minute she could afford an actual duvet. The ad copy reads: "I'm dark, sexy, and ready. Give it to me . . . now!" Inside the magazine, one of the highlights is a section called Beaver Hunt, which consists of photos sent in by women of themselves posing with their legs spread, displaying their "beavers." I don't know what is more vulgar: the way they thrust their privates at the camera or the interior design in the background of some of the photos. I can't remember the last time I saw smoky mirror tiles, wood paneling, and plastic-covered sofas.*

One of the featured pictorial subjects is making her nude modeling debut because, in her own words, "Everyone says I have a kick-ass body; so I figured, hey, I might as well show it off." Who is "everybody"? Everybody at the bowling alley, perhaps? Her way of showing off is pushing her boobs together—as if she needs to make 38Ds look any bigger—while on all fours with her butt in the air toward the camera while reaching back with her hand and spreading her vaginal lips apart. It's like some pornographic down dog yoga move. What is with the prodding open of the vaginal lips? Almost every woman in Hustler *does it. Does this really turn guys on? Now I know that the main difference between* Hustler *and* Playboy *is that* Hustler *is hard-core. There are actually spreads of people having real live sex. Including ejaculation. Ironically, viewing all this sex makes me want to have sex less. In fact, I have also lost my appetite.*

When I tell Randall how grossed out I am, he insists there must be something redeemable about the magazine. I try really hard to get the images of "dark twat" and messy ménages à trois out of my head for one second so that I can consider this. I guess if someone had a gun to my head and made me say one thing I liked about Hustler *other than Larry Flynt's letter, the first thing that would come to mind is that it is exceptionally diverse. In this particular issue, he gives equal space to Asian women, black women, white women, Latina women, unattractive women, pregnant women, overweight women, and white trash. So, kudos to Larry Flynt for being an equal-opportunity porn peddler.*

DAY TWO

11:30 A.M.: *Up early for a Saturday and decide that I will just sun on deck after breakfast instead of going to port. Had enough of Ensenada when I was in college and we would take trips down from L.A. because the drinking age is eighteen, not twenty-one. Mom, on the other hand, is really excited to disembark in Ensenada. She reads me the ship's literature, which refers to it as a beautiful, exotic cultural paradise, and jewel of Mexico. Hmmmm . . . elaborate typo? Or, maybe the brochure writer has never been.*

12:30 P.M.: *Randall and I have just finished breakfast and are getting ready to go up to the sunning deck where I look forward to reading "Oprah" (read: Playboy) to finish a feature article titled "Feeding Our Deepest Fears: How Big Agriculture and the U.S. Government Bungled the Biotech Revolution and Made a Deal with the Devil," by Dan Baum, when my cell rings. Could it be Sam calling again to beg for forgiveness? Nope. It's Mom.*

"Where are you?" she asks me.

"We decided to take it easy and stay on board."

"I just want to let you guys know I borrowed your Oprah and one of your design magazines to read on the bus ride back. Hope you don't mind."

"No problem. Have fun, shopping. And, Mom, don't forget—"

"I know. No Chicrets."

As I pack up my stuff, Randall asks, "Hey, can I borrow one of your dirty magazines?"

I reach into my tote bag to retrieve one when I notice none of them are there. Weird. I remember putting them there last night. Wait a minute . . .

"Are you hung over?" *Randall asks.* "You look really pale."

"Please tell me you have your Oprah *magazine," I beg.*

He sifts through his tote. "Well, yeah, minus its cover thanks to you."

"No, not the real Oprah. The Playboy Oprah."

He looks in his tote again and pulls out one of his cover-less magazines and sifts through it. "Everybody's clothed. I see The 'O' List. And unless Oprah Winfrey is posing for Playboy fully clothed, the odds are this is the real Oprah."

"Shit. Shit. Shit. Mom has my Playboy!" *I calm myself down.* "At least she doesn't have Hustler or Penthouse," *I rationalize.*

"Uh," *Randall pulls out the cover to* Star *magazine that earlier I taped to my* Penthouse.

"I can't believe this." *I call Mom.*

"Mom, what magazines did you say you borrowed?"

"Oprah." *Great, she definitely has Playboy.* "Carolyn has your People." *I put my hand over the phone and whisper to Randall,* "Your mom has Hustler." *His eyes grow like saucers.* "And an interior design magazine," *adds Mom.*

"Which interior design magazine?" *I ask her, pretty sure that I left Elle Décor at home.*

"The one about penthouses. I thought I could get some fancy ideas for my kitchen remodel." *Egad, she has all three.*

Randall is following the conversation in disbelief.

"You know, Mom, Ensenada sounds nice after all . . . Yeah,

I'll bring Randall and we'll meet you for lunch . . . Where are you?"

I hang up and turn to Randall, who scolds me. "You really need to keep better tabs on your porn."

I scowl at him.

"I don't see what the big deal is. So what if your mom finds out you read porn?" says Randall.

"Look, at this point I can handle explaining why I smuggled dirty magazines on board. What I'm more worried about is Mom being traumatized when she opens up Hustler and is confronted with a guy giving it to two girls up the ass while one wears a strap-on. Not to mention the centerfold Amber thrusting her lower half at Mom as she pulls her labia apart for a better view of her you-know-what. I don't know about your mom, but I am quite sure mine has never seen her own vagina—how is she going to react to a stranger's?"

Now Randall gets it. "I'm sure we can find them on the main shopping drag. When we do, I'll distract them."

"Great. Just give me enough time to steal all three magazines back. The code for mission accomplished is 'It's Party Time.'"

1 P.M.: *Randall and I scour the dusty streets of Ensenada for the Moms.*

We finally track down the main shopping area by following the trash left behind by American tourists (fanny packs and cameras around their necks are a dead give-away) who appear to be everywhere. They are mostly making fools of themselves and hoarding tequila, Viagra, Retin-A wrinkle cream, and Cipro*.

We would have gotten there quicker if I didn't have to stop every few minutes to hand out change to women and children begging in front of stores.

Finally, we find Mom and Carolyn, their arms filled with shopping bags. We run over to them, and as Randall distracts them by babbling about tonight's on-board dinner menu, I search their totes until Carolyn digs in her tote bag to find her bifocals so that she can read "People" magazine later. Out of desperation, Randall grabs his mom by the shoulders. "Mom, I have something I have to tell you that you may not like." He takes a deep breath. "I'm g-g—"

Randall is picking now to come out of the closet?

"I'm g—"

"Gonna party!" I shout as I steal the magazines from Mom's tote bag and put them in mine. "I'm gonna party!"

Randall looks at me, unsure. Oops. Wrong code phrase. "It's party time," I shout.

He looks relieved and shouts, "Let's go party!"

We spend the rest of the day with the Moms who have really let loose. We drink margaritas (we figure alcohol will kill all germs in tap water), and the Moms, who are both light-weights at five feet tall and barely a hundred pounds, become drunk before their second margarita. First they talk trash about men, then they flirt with the handsome waiter who is

---

Postscript: Do not take these items simultaneously, especially after a midnight gala buffet.

young enough to be their grandchild, then they get really
rowdy dancing to the jukebox, finally grabbing a college kid's
Von Dutch hat and dancing the Mexican hat dance around it
while shouting "Arriba, Arriba," which comes out as "Alliba,
Alliba!" It is "Grandmas Gone Wild." I start to think this is
more uncomfortable than letting them see a few exposed
vaginas in my dirty magazines. (Reminder to Self: Must
not encourage Moms to drink or get in party mood. They
have now taken to shouting, "Let's go party!" but with
their Chinese accents, the phrase comes out as "Let's go
potty!")

   We tear them away from the bar and spend the rest of the
day shopping to sober them up. Not as easy as it sounds. I
have a feeling that news has spread that I am a generous
Americana, because it seems the city's entire population of
beggars (amputees included) and street urchins have made a
beeline for me and are following me everywhere, like my own
J. Lo entourage. Did see a few things I wanted to buy but
prices were high and identical items are available back home
at Wal-Mart or Pier One for less. Only items purchased:
thirty-two packs of Chiclets.

4 P.M.: Back on board now. Did I mention the ship's
"professional" photographers are everywhere? Cannot get off
or on boat without mandatory photo. Made us wear sombreros
and hold tequila bottle in some photos. The Mexican half of
me is insulted, but the Asian part of me loves that I don't have
to ask a stranger to take our photo.

5 P.M.: *Yes! Actually exercised in ship's gym. Hated every second, but looking forward to extra earned dessert tonight.*

8:30 P.M.: *Our assigned dinner appointment is 8:30. By the time we're served something solid it is . . .*

9:00 P.M.: *Fu**ing starving. Don't these people realize how many calories partying with the Moms and shopping burns? Not to mention having to outrun street urchins and amputees to get back on ship about to sail away without us.*

10:30 P.M.: *Dinner was all right. I think we had something like eighteen waiters serving the six of us. They made a big to-do with presentation of food (thus distracting us from the actual taste). In fact, suspiciously they have encouraged us to eat all day and night at free buffets.*

DAY THREE

NOON TO 3 P.M.: *Yes! Earned four ship-shape dollars. "Line dancing class," and "How to Make Ribbon Roses." Surely both will come in handy on land?*

4 P.M.: *I check my missed cell calls and see that I missed another call, but there was no caller identification. I spend the next five hours wondering if Sam is calling me because he's realized he can't live without me.*

9 P.M.: *Our party was invited by the captain to preview the midnight gala buffet and encouraged to bring our cameras. Did admire a few of the ice sculptures and fruit carved into pretty shapes. Guess butter molded into swans was okay, too. But still couldn't help wondering why would I want to take pictures of food?*

10 P.M.: *The loud music at the on-board night club takes my mind off of Sam. Danced with Mom all night. Jitterbug. Twist. Swing.*

MIDNIGHT: *In bed early. Knee is swollen from jitterbug, twist, swing.*

DAY FOUR (FINAL DAY)

7 A.M.: *Forced by ship's blaring klaxons to startle out of bed.* Why? Why? Why? Why do people get up this early? *Feel like zombie, but less pleasant looking, more grumpy. Shove everything into suitcase unfolded. Panic! Pants that fit three days ago now do not button!*

8 A.M.: *Breakfast. Repulsed by all morning people with their chipper chatter. Must remember to add to recommendations to captain: all friendly Roberto Benigni-type waiters must be shot or not permitted to serve food before noon. Want to take butter knife and cut smile off his face.*

8:30 A.M.: *Obvious that captain and crew who swooned over* *us all weekend (pre-tipping), now (post-tipping) do not care about us at all. Forced to wait in smoke-riddled casino with entire ship full of people (who have consumed too many eggs) in Ellis-island like manner before being permitted to disembark.*

9:30 A.M.: *Have secondhand smoked three packs of cigarettes while waiting to get off f'ing ship. Do not understand why I had to get up at 7 a.m. if I could not get off ship before 9:30! Cruel.*

On the way home, Randall and I decide that cruises are the fast food of traveling. Cheaper, easier, less satisfying. We will remember to advise The Naughty Knitters of the following if they ever want to take a cruise:

1. Ice sculptures do not make food taste better.
2. More is not necessarily better, especially when accompanied by heartburn.
3. Books are heavy. Luggage space would be better utilized by packing anti-puffery eye cream, Visine, and antacids.
4. Some people should not consume tequila. Ever.

MOST IMPORTANT THINGS LEARNED FROM READING POPULAR MEN'S ADULT MAGAZINES:

1. All dirty magazines are not dirty.
2. Men may not be lying when they say they read *Playboy* or *Penthouse* for the articles.

3. Women's vaginas vary a great deal in looks, size, texture, and color.

MY FAVORITE THING ABOUT THE CRUISE: getting the chance to potty with Mom and old friends.

GERMANY, AUSTRALIA,

NEW ZEALAND,

GREECE AND OTHER

COUNTRIES HAVE

LEGALIZED

BROTHELS

AND,

FOR BETTER OR WORSE,

BRITAIN COULD

BE NEXT.

Source: BBC News online

Chapter Twelve

Strip*geez*

Post-relationship stress disorder (PRSD): *n. undesirable*
physical and emotional symptoms following a break-up

When my life is too depressing to think about, I turn to my friends. Not for help with my problems, but to help them with theirs. This distracts me from my own troubles and gives me a chance to feel good about myself in a constructive and charitable way. Today I am channeling all of my negative (*I hate Sam*) and ridiculous (*maybe I can forgive Sam*) thoughts into helping Steve.

I am at my acupuncturist's clinic again, but this time I am sitting in a chair in the corner with the lights dimmed low, as Steve lays on the massage table with twenty tiny needles in his arms, legs, face, and hands, with the heat lamp directed at his feet. He was too chicken to try traditional Chinese medicine by himself, but he was desperate. Psychotherapy, Dr. Phil, Oprah, and a bookstore of self-help books have not cured him of a terrible case of PRSD, complete with hallucinations (he thinks he sees his ex everywhere), feelings of dread (he says every day feels like April 15), and breaking into a cold sweat every time he hears a woman nagging her boyfriend.

He is supposed to be relaxing to the ancient flute music, but he is too uptight for that.

"I am the original forty-year-old virgin," he declares, almost knocking out one of the needles in his chin.

"Except you're not a virgin," I point out. Steve was dumped by his orgasmically-challenged girlfriend of ten years who left him for—not his lawyer because that is such a cliché—but his lawyer's *wife*.

"I might as well be," he says. "Not only did I put up with mediocre sex for ten years, I have now gone ninety-eight days, four hours, twenty-two minutes," he looks at his watch, "and three seconds without any sex at all.

"I need to get laid," he declares.

"Great! Let's go to a bar," I suggest.

"Last time I did that, the woman I picked up wanted to actually date first. She left me nineteen messages before I changed my phone number. And, if I did find someone to sleep with me who wasn't interested in a second date, I would wonder what was wrong with me, especially in bed, that makes them not want to come back for more."

I go home that night and contemplate how I can help Steve find good, commitment-less, pressure-free sex. I pose the question to The Naughty Knitters at our next stitch and bitch session. We decide Steve should help himself by helping me—with an item on my Porn-to-Do list. An item that I never thought I would really do that I can now do vicariously through Steve.

The next day I call him. "Pack your bags, we're going to Vegas."

"I'm already going to Vegas."

"You are?" *He thought of going to a brothel on his own?*

"Yeah, for Rich Radford's bachelor party."

"Oh, right. Well, I'm going with you. I figured out how to get you laid without the pressure of commitment, guilt, or second-guessing your performance."

The thing is that when I go to Vegas, my mom goes to Vegas. Because Mom loves Vegas and she gambles so much (which unfortunately sometimes translates as "loses so much") at the four-star Bellagio casino, that she gets comped rooms and meals (even for guests like me), which beats staying at Excalibur where Steve was going to stay.

Greg treated me to the $29.99 rooms at Excalibur once, and except for being called "M'lady" by hotel workers dressed in cheesy medieval garb, it was not even close to four stars. The wall-paper and linens looked like they hadn't been changed in decades, and the food sucked, unlike the food at the Bellagio, which has an amazing pastry shop, gelateria, and the world's largest chocolate fountain.

Paige, who is writing a novel about a guy addicted to gambling, joins us on our Vegas trip so that she can do hands-on research. We catch a flight from Los Angeles and meet Mom, who catches her own flight from San Diego.

When my mom asks why we wanted to come to Vegas, I can't lie, so I tell her that Steve and I are going to visit a chicken ranch (we plan to visit The Chicken Ranch Brothel) to help him relax.

She gives me a "whatever" look, and says, "If you need me, I relax at Three Card Poker."

Later that night, Steve leaves for the bachelor party, which we are hoping will make him nice and horny for the visit to the brothel the following day. I track Paige down in the casino, where she is getting a little too into her research and playing high stakes poker. I drag her to Coyote Ugly, the bar famous for their female bartenders who look like models and dance on top of the bar.

"Hey, I saw your Mom," Paige says. "She said to tell you she's going to see some man named Brew Gloop. Sounds Korean."

It takes me a second. "She's going to see Blue Man Group," I tell Paige.

Coyote Ugly is really loud. There is hard rock playing, and a young blond host/bartender wearing tight jeans and a halter top is standing on top of the bar with a mike shouting at the audience, while other "bartenders" spray the audience every now and then with what I assume is water. (I doubt they would waste alcohol.) Sounds kind of fun and harmless, unless you're wearing a suede jacket, which, of course, I am.

As Paige and I order drinks, we check out the pseudo-western bar décor with bras hanging from the ceiling. I am really surprised by the makeup of the audience. We expected a bunch of hot guys. There are some, but it is at least sixty percent female. It also feels more like a stage than an actual bar, which could just be the effects of Vegas and its effort to entertain tourists as opposed to locals.

I feel like the whole thing is a show just to get people to drink. Mostly people just stand around and watch girls in tight jeans and belly-baring tees dance to loud rock music. The blond bartender, Jenny McCarthy–like in her enthusiasm, shouts into the mike in an attempt to convince customers to join her on the bar. She also teases the guys in the audience with some very sassy, mean-spirited humor, including implying that some of them cannot get it up or accusing them of having small penises. I'm sure if I tried the same thing with a roomful of guys, I would not get the same reaction. Her, guys love.

Paige nudges me with her elbow. "You should do it. Get up there." She knows that there is a secret part of me that has always wanted to do something crazy and spontaneous. I wasn't joking when I admitted to Sam that deep down I crave a Good Girl Gone Wild moment.

This could be that moment.

I have another drink and recall all those times that Vee and Paige and everyone else went on spring break to Cancun or Lake Havasau, while I was doing charity work in India, interning in France, studying for the GRE, or tutoring rich kids to earn money for grad school. It's about time I do something like this. Maybe doing something so against my nature will be liberating. Maybe it will make me forget Sam once and for all.

Now happily buzzed and feeling kind of bold and sexy, I approach the bar and reach up toward the host.

"All right," she says. "We've got a live one! Come on up!"

I try to hoist myself up on the bar and almost fall backward. Climbing onto a bar is tougher than it looks. I feel like I'm in phys. ed. and everyone is watching me do chin-ups. I finally get on top of the bar, after slipping back down twice, but I lose one of my clogs along the way and end up sort of standing lopsided on the bar top. I should probably just lose the other clog, but I freeze and am not quite sure what to do.

I look over at the hostess, who is making weird motions at me. I realize she wants me to dance. *Of course; that's why I'm up here.* I start to bust a move when the song abruptly ends. I stop mid-move in a kind of robotic manner until the next song comes on, which is one of those classic rock songs that is *impossible* to find the beat to, but I make an attempt anyway.

First, I try snapping my fingers and grooving to the beat. Then, not feeling it, I try to add some Latin twist, a little rumba sort of move. *Still not working.* I try my own version of the cabbage patch,* until I have finally gone through a bizarre medley of dance moves that would look awkward even at a junior high school dance. To top it off, in the middle of all this I have a very sobering thought: *I have not consumed enough alcohol.*

I look for Paige in the crowd. I don't know why, but I'm hoping she can give me some signal of encouragement. She signals me all right. She holds up five fingers as in, "Be right back in five minutes." But I know she is going to play poker and is not coming back!

I can't believe this. I am dancing—well, sort of—on top of a bar in public before 200 total strangers and I have never felt more embarrassed in my life. It's as if the alcohol has been completely sucked out of me. I can see the slightest actions of everyone in the room with more clarity than I've ever had before. I notice a hot girl snickering at me, a fake smile—*is it pity?*—from a sweet-looking brunette, I see a nice-looking guy's eyes get really big when he looks at me, then he stares into his *empty* beer bottle, and pretends to drink from it.

Or is it my imagination? I reach deep inside. It could all be in my mind. I remember a psych study I was an assistant on years ago. Subjects were given a drink concoction that tasted like

---

*Dance routine which involves shoulders and fists (placed together in a manner that looks like you just connected both ends of an extension cord) moving in time with each other in a fluid, circular motion; all the rage in the late '80s and early '90s. The dance owes some of its popularity to San Francisco 49er Jerry Rice, who celebrated touchdowns with the cabbage patch.

alcohol but in fact was not alcohol. Subjects who were told they were drinking alcohol scored lower on all cognitive and motor tests. In other words, if they *believed* they were drunk, they reacted to things like a drunk.

I am desperate; the song is going on for infinity, so I figure it is worth a try. *I am drunk . . . I am drunk. Yay, it seems to be helping.* I close my eyes and sway my hips to the music, feeling a little more into it. I feel kind of sexy. I bet I look pretty good up here.

I slowly open my eyes. *Crap.* Nobody is watching me. I convince myself that I am so drunk that I whip off my shirt and watch as it gets caught on the spinning blade of a ceiling fan above me.

Still, nobody is watching me. How ironic: Part of me has always avoided going topless because my biggest fear was everybody staring at me half naked, but now I realize my biggest fear is *nobody* staring at me half naked!

To complicate matters, the Coyote Uglies are making more weird faces at me. I think they sense that I am losing it up here. As they send a few of their own to dance on the opposite end of the bar to distract everyone from me, the oldest of them, her huge boobs touching my arm, whispers in my ear that everyone on the bar must have shirts on. I try to tell her it's not my fault—"The shirt's hit the fan!"—but she merely scowls at me, impatient. I try jumping up and down to reach my shirt, but I keep missing it as it goes round and round on the blade of the fan.

I decide I will just get down from the bar, but the bar is pretty high up. I could jump, but I will definitely sprain an ankle. I consider doing a "tuck and roll," but I've never done one and have a feeling that, too, may be harder than it looks.

I start to lower myself down, my butt facing the audience,

when, out of the corner of my eye, I see a guy trying not to laugh at me. It must be this unflattering angle. Photographers always say that people look twenty pounds heavier when you shoot them from below. Basically, my ass must look gigantic right now. Someone should slap a sticker on it that says, "Objects may appear larger when descending from a bar." I'm just one big laugh riot now.

"Do you need a hand?"

I turn toward the practically laughing guy's voice, practically falling on my ass, but catching myself at the last minute. *Wow, the guy could be Sam's identical twin.*

"Hey, you finally got your Girl-Gone-Wild moment," he comments, grinning.

Oh, shit, it is Sam.

Duh, he is friends with Rich, thus in Vegas for the same bachelor party that Steve is going to. I glance down and am reminded that I am not wearing a shirt.

I am trying to cover myself up with my hands when he takes his jacket off. "Need this?"

I nod and he helps me put it on as we exit the bar. There are a million questions swimming in my head that I want to ask him—like, *How could I be so wrong about you?*—but I push them all aside. The reality is that there is a very unwise part of me that is elated to see him.

"Here for Rich's bachelor party?" is all I ask him.

"Yeah. What about you?"

His voice gives away that he is conflicted. Maybe being a jerk to a nice girl like me has not been easy for him. I can only hope so.

"I came with Steve," I tell him. It's subtle, but I notice a look of disappointment. *Weird.* This is the guy who had sex with me and then never called, but for some reason I feel compelled to be nice to him, to ease his mind. "I'm just here to get him laid," I explain. He looks disappointed again. "By someone else. Not me." He smiles at me, somewhat sadly, but he looks relieved to know this information.

"So how much of that did you see in there?" I ask him.

"All of it," he freely admits.

"Okay, now I'm *really* embarrassed."

"Don't be. It beats watching twenty drunk guys watch a stripper jump out of a cake."

"Uh, I guess I'll take that as a compliment."

"You want to get a bite to eat?"

I should say no. "Sure. All that dancing really worked up my appetite."

We end up at the all-you-can-eat buffet back at the Bellagio, where I pile my plate with all kinds of food. But when we sit down, I can't eat. I am thinking about shiny Holly. I gather that she must not be in Vegas with Sam. Of course she isn't; he's here for a bachelor party.

Part of me decides I am going to forget for a moment that we ever slept with each other, forget how he once brought up his mother and me and the future in the same thought, forget that I ever thought I was in love with him. *How could I know that anyway after just a few chance encounters? Who would I be hurting—besides myself—by talking to him right now as if there were no Holly?*

I let loose a little and we end up talking and laughing about everything. It's one of those great effortless conversations.

Only when the waiter comes by to refill our water glasses does Sam notice that my plate is still piled high with shrimp cocktail, prime rib, and crab legs.

"You haven't touched your food," he says.

"I know. This is not like me. I actually feel a little queasy."

He gets that nervous look again. He probably thinks I'm one of those girls obsessed with her weight, who will go anorexic just to fit into her favorite pair of tight jeans. Which is only half true.

He puts his hand on mine in my lap and I realize why I am queasy: I have contracted butterflies. I was having too much fun talking to Sam to figure it out, plus I have not had this feeling since I was a freshman in college. When he puts his hand on mine, the sound drops out around us and it feels suddenly like we are alone in the dining room, an electric pulse connecting our bodies.

Damn it. I am still in love with a guy who is unavailable.

He escorts me to my room so that he can get his jacket back once I can grab one of my own shirts. At my door, we pause to say goodbye.

"I'm glad I ran into you," he says like he means it. I should just leave it at that. But curiosity gets the best of me.

"Why?"

He doesn't try to dodge the question, nor does he appear the least bit uncomfortable. "For one thing, I can't stop thinking about you." What a great thing to hear a guy say.

Too bad he has a girlfriend.

Now my feelings are mixed. He is definitely coming on to me, which means Mr. Perfect really is a philanderer and a cheat.

Fuck it.

"What about your McGirlfrien—" My hand clasps over my mouth before I even get it all out. "Did I say that last part out loud?"

He nods.

"I meant Holly. What about *Holly*?"

He laughs out loud.

God, his laugh turns me on.

He pushes away a wisp of hair that has fallen in my eyes. "Holly was a set-up."

"A bad set-up or a good set-up?" I ask.

"Let's just put it this way: I think her IQ was fifty-two."

"Funny, I think that was her bra size, too." I didn't mean to say that out loud either, but he's laughing, so, again, I don't feel too bad. When he stops, there is that surreal soundless pause again, electric with possibility. If he asked me where I am right now, I would not be able to tell him.

"Well, I guess I'll be seeing you," I whisper in a sort of softer, sexier version of my usual voice.

Kiss me, damn it.

I slip out of his jacket as slowly as possible just in case he wants to make a move. When he doesn't make a move, I hand him his jacket, accidentally hitting him in the face with it. He was obviously moving in to kiss me and I fucked it up.

Please try again.

Then, just as I insert my keycard into the door, he kisses me on the back of my neck and we end up stumbling into the room.

"What, no dirty magazines?" he teases between kisses.

"I prefer to travel porn-free." We continue to caress each other as I kick off my shoes and he progresses to kissing the nape of my neck.

I so want to sleep with him again.

Not just because I find him physically attractive, but also because I now realize I am still madly in love with him.

Suddenly, a stray thought pops into my head and I stop him. "I have to know something. If it wasn't because you had a girlfriend, why didn't you call me after we had sex?"

"I was scared and stupid."

That's good enough for me.

I move to rip my shirt off and then realize it is still hanging on the fan at Coyote Ugly. Instead, I fall back onto the bed and pull him on top of me. Suddenly, he leaps off of me with a yelp. He looks scared to death.

"What is it?"

"I don't want to hurt the baby," he says.

I'm guessing he is not completely comfortable with the new term of affection for me and used a definite article instead of a pronoun out of nervousness.

"Do you mean 'I don't want to hurt you, baby'?" I ask him.

"No, your baby," he explains, gesturing to my stomach.

"You think I'm pregnant?"

"Aren't you?"

God, do I need to get on those sit-ups. "Look, I'm really embarrassed—again. I don't know what to say except, I'm not pregnant. My stomach may be a little poofier than usual, no thanks to these all-you-can-eat buffets and avoiding the gym for the last month, plus that damn chocolate fountain downstairs is not helping matters, and I guess I can see that sometimes I act a tad bit hormonally, but—"

He puts his finger on my lips to shush me. "Did you say you're not pregnant?"

"Not pregnant. Never have been."

He pushes me back down on the bed and kisses me hard, our hands wandering everywhere, until he pauses awkwardly on the elastic of my underwear and looks at me questioningly.

I grin. "Don't worry, these don't vibrate."

The next day we sleep in until noon and eat breakfast in front of the window watching the waterworks show that takes place to the tune of "Luck Be a Lady Tonight" in the man-made Bellagio lake. It is perfect. I imagine us years from now, doing the same thing, but at a real Italian villa, the kind with no all-you-can-eat buffets and a real lake made by nature. As he polishes off my continental breakfast—I still have some butterflies—I finally ask him, "What made you think I was pregnant?"

He picks up the pair of jeans I slung over the chair last night. "I saw the label on a pair of jeans like these in your bathroom last time I was at your place." On the pant leg of the pair of jeans he is now holding up is the long manufacturer sticker that reads "Barely Showing—size 8—Gap Maternity."

I don't know what I'm more embarrassed by now. That I wear maternity jeans—*with the sticker still on*, no wonder guys weren't turned on when I was dancing at Coyote Ugly—or that he knows I am a size 8.

I explain that once in a blue moon I wear transitional maternity clothes because they are more comfortable.

He feels the stretchiness of the material. "Too bad they don't make transitional wear for guys," he remarks.

I am seriously in love now. I am about to lean in to kiss him again when someone bangs on the door and shouts from the other side.

"We're going to be late. If we get there after three, it's going to be too crowded. Wake up!"

I open the door. It's Steve. He looks at the glow on my face with suspicion. "I thought you said you left the vibrators at home."

"I did." I open the door wider so that he can see Sam.

"A-*ha*! I knew it!" Then his voice drops to a whisper. "He's not coming to the brothel with us, is he?"

"Yeah, Steve. I have the perfect guy in my clutch, but I'm thinking maybe I'll hook him up with a prostitute. *Are you insane?*"

I look at the clock. We are seriously behind schedule. We had planned to get to the brothel by 2 p.m., right before it starts to get busy—which, according to my research, is after 3—and in time to head back to Vegas before rush-hour traffic.

I quickly get dressed, throw my hair in a ponytail, and turn to Sam. "I'll call you later? I have an appointment at a brothel." He looks taken aback, and slightly confused.

"Not for me. For him." I point to Steve, who is sitting on the bed, eating our chocolate mints from last night's turndown service.

"That's a relief," he says, with that great grin of his, as I grab my purse. At the threshold Sam stops me and kisses me on the lips. I hear a funny swish sound and look down as he swipes the manufacturer's size sticker from my pants.

"You're the best." I kiss him back.

As Steve and I race through the lobby, we run into Mom, who has been up all night gambling with a group of women from mainland China that she met at the Noodle Bar. She waves a stack of hundred dollar bills in the air at me.

"I love the clap," she says excitedly. I'm pretty sure she means "craps." "You guys going to relax at the chicken ranch?" She turns to Steve, who looks slightly pale. "Better than sex on subways."

"Happy gambling, Mom." I pull Steve away before he can freak out. "Where's Paige?" I ask him.

"Where she's been since she left you last night." He gestures to a bank of video poker monitors a few yards away. I spot Paige, huddled over one of the games, eyes bloodshot, passed out with a cigar burning in an ashtray beside her and a scotch on the rocks in her grip. If I didn't know better, I would think she was a seventy-year-old bookie in a Juicy Couture sweatsuit.

"Paige, look at me." I pick her head up in my hands. "When is the last time you ate?" She holds up a pack of Marlboro reds. "I can't believe I have to tell you this again: *Tobacco is not food.*" I turn to Steve. "We can't leave her here."

"I don't see why not. At least if she's passed out, she can't gamble away her life savings."

I give him a look.

"Fine," he says. "You take her legs." He puts his hands under her arms and we drag her to the car, where we throw her in the back seat.

On the car ride to the brothel, the desert scenery has a calming effect on me. It does not have the same effect on Steve. As I stare out the window and daydream about my night with Sam, Steve flips through satellite radio stations like a mad person.

"What if they have diseases?" he asks.

I anticipated him trying to back out, so I did my research and called the madam of the brothel, a woman named Debbie, earlier that week. "You have a better chance of contracting an STD at a sorority house," I report. "At the brothel, the workers have to take an STD test every week and have the results faxed to the local sheriff's department in order to retain their work cards. The women also inspect every customer's genitals for outbreaks or symptoms, *and* they use baby wipes and antibacterial soap to wipe each guy's genital area before having intercourse, which is only permitted with a condom."

"Sounds sexy." He is getting cold feet. "What if I can't afford it?"

I'm ready for this answer, too. "The minimum is $150 for half an hour. That doesn't include intercourse. You'd pay twice that if you took someone to a movie and Matsuhisa for dinner, and you still wouldn't be guaranteed sex."

"I don't know . . . that sounds like a lot for not getting actual sex, and I really should be saving for—"

"Here." I hand him an envelope. He opens it and counts out five hundred-dollar bills.

"What's this?"

"The Naughty Knitters and I chipped in—call it an early birthday present."

"Wow, I must really be annoying lately."

"Let's just say you need to get laid."

He's quiet for a few miles, staring out at the dry landscape peppered with odd-shaped Joshua trees.

"What if I'm not attracted to any of the women?" he finally asks.

I hand him a printout. "I went online. You get to see the

line-up of working girls that are working any given night." The girls are all pretty, most of them with nice smiles, and most are posed in lingerie. There is Carmen, who is described as "young, cute and sassy"; Ashley, who is supposedly "warm and sexy"; Girlie, who is an "insatiable seductress"; Nikki, "The Puerto Rican Rapture"; and the most sexual photo is of Paris, who is African-American and described as a "sex artist." She is posed in the nude with a Mardi Gras mask over her eyes.

Steve studies the pictures.

"Fifty on eleven red!" shouts Paige.

We practically jump out of our seats, and I have to yank the wheel to avoid getting stuck in the gravel ditch on the side of the road.

"Oh, shit, I forgot she was back there," says Steve, turning around to check on Paige, who is talking in her drunken sleep.

"Me, too."

Paige is mumbling incoherently about everything from roulette to screenwriting to some argument that she's had with her husband, Ray. Even when she's drunk, she is multitasking.

"Of course, the turning point of the story is when the girl is hit by the bus . . . no, no, two hundred to win on the five horse. . . *Verlliecht, werde ich es machen wollen* . . . Ray, the dishes will not wash themselves!"

We tune Paige out and continue our conversation. I can tell Steve is surprised that the photos are not pornographic and that the girls, except for Paris, look like girls you might run into at Starbucks. "Wow, they don't look, uh . . . prostitute-ish."

"I think they prefer to be called 'working girls,'" I inform him.

"You're coming in with me, right?"

"Steve, they don't patronize single women." According to the madam, this is because they cannot guarantee that on any given night, there will be enough girls who like sex with women, and they would not want lesbians or straight girls who like girl-on-girl sex—I wondered but didn't ask why the madam thinks there's a difference between the former and the latter—to drive or fly all the way out to their ranch and be disappointed.

"We'll pretend we're a couple."

"Eewwwww." I scrunch up my face.

"What? We played doctor when we were eleven."

"Yeah, exactly my point. *Eeewwww.*"

"Just till I pick a girl, then you can tell them you're chickening out."

I can see he won't do it if I don't agree, and now we've driven an hour on this two-lane highway and I really want to know how the place works. "Fine. I'll do it."

"Consider it payback for that time you made me pierce your ears in college."

"You fainted when my ear bled, and I had to finish it myself," I remind him.

"Exactly my point. Because of you I can't look at a pierced ear now without getting queasy."

As we finally pull into the parking lot, I can't believe I am about to enter a brothel. A whorehouse. A den of iniquity. *What was I thinking? Brothels are to strip clubs as Jenna Jameson is to Pamela Anderson.* I cannot admit to Steve now that I am chicken after spending the last hour and a half convincing him to go through with this. I will also never hear the end of it from The Naughty Knitters, who are dying to know what goes on here. I let the fear pass through me, remind myself that this is perfectly legal, and open the car door.

The place has a cute western theme going on, a façade painted in baby blue and a sign out front that has their famous logo: a cracked egg with a woman's legs playfully kicking out of them. We throw a protein bar and a bottle of water in the backseat for Paige, and we exit the car, both with a deep, strength-building breath.

We ring a bell at the front gate. The plan is that I'll go in as Steve's partner and then back out and hang at the bar while Steve finally gets laid, which I'm guesstimating will not take long, considering how long it has been since he's had good sex.

I guess we don't look drunk or dangerous, because we are buzzed in. We walk up the handicap-accessible ramp to the front door, where we are met by a shift supervisor. I'm expecting Dolly Parton, but this woman is as far from that in appearance as you can imagine. She looks like an older version of our high school gym teacher, after the ravaging effects of forty years of smoking and hard living.

The main room is dark, and it looks like my grandma's parlor room. There are fake floral arrangements, a red velvet curtain covering one wall, and floral brocade sofas facing the curtain with antique-ish coffee tables between the sofa and the curtain. We take a seat on the sofa, facing the curtain. There is a lot of space in front of us, which I am presuming is where the line-up will take place.

There are two other guys on another sofa next to us. They are also not what I would expect. They are the guys you'd want to go out with if you met them at a bar. Clean-cut, good-looking, well-dressed. No sleaze factor or nerd factor at all. They might as well be Sam. On second thought, I doubt Sam would patronize a brothel. *Or would he?*

The shift supervisor invites us in to sit on the sofa and hands us yellow "menus" listing the twenty-eight different services that they offer at the ranch—ranging from acts like "massage" (can include masturbating a customer to climax depending on how much he pays), to "straight lays" (conventional missionary intercourse), to "two-girl shower parties," and a lot more. Meanwhile, another gentleman enters. He looks a little more like I imagined customers looking. He's dressed neatly, but looks a little rough around the edges, like a trucker who stopped off on the interstate and spiffed himself up in a gas station bathroom before coming here.

I put my hand on Steve's leg to stop it from shaking up and down. "Relax. It's just sex." He grabs a mint from a bowl on the coffee table and pops it in his mouth. Then another. And another. I grip his hand to stop him. "You already have two in your mouth."

Suddenly, the two good-looking guys start whispering to each other and stand up as another woman walks into the room. She is not as old as the shift supervisor, but she looks like one of those women who is surprised by nothing. She's seen everything—twice.

She asks the guys if they need help. I recognize her voice from the phone. She is the madam, Debbie. She is also not dressed in anything even remotely sexy. She has glasses on, a pair of mom jeans, and a very conservative blouse. "Uh, we just wanted to get a drink," the guys tell her, obviously needing a little more courage to go through with paying for sex at a brothel.

"Bar's that way." She points them through a door off the parlor room.

Now it's just us and the trucker as seven women stride in one by one and soft lights come up and spotlight them as they stand before us. I can't believe I'm not uncomfortable. I guess the matter-of-fact quality of the women who work there and the very unsexy décor, plus the fact that it has sunk in that this is perfectly legal, has made me realize how practical, not sleazy, all this might be. Or could it be that my previous porn adventures have desensitized me? I will explore this notion later when seven scantily clad prostitutes are not waiting for us to choose one of them.

Most of the girls are wearing lingerie or Spandex shorts and halters. They are all pretty, or cute, but none of them is runway gorgeous. They have sex appeal, but not a lot of style. *If I were Sam and I had to choose one of these women, who would I choose? Oh, that's right, he chose* me!

"Ladies, please introduce yourselves," the shift manager says. As they tell us their names one by one, it reminds me of a weird sort of sorority rush ritual. The trucker guy gestures to the shift manager.

"Hey, can we see—?" Before he can even get the entire sentence out, she presses a button on a remote control, and the velvet curtains behind the girls slides open, revealing a wall-to-wall mirror. Guess they got tired of guys asking for the girls to turn around and show their backsides.

"What about the third woman from the right?" I whisper to Steve, getting excited for him. "She kind of looks like that girl from work you had a crush on a few years ago."

"Wendy? She ended up stealing my job."

"What about her on the far right? She looks like your type."

"What is it about hot pink Spandex and five-inch Lucite heels that reads my type?"

"Okay, but did you ever consider maybe it's time for a *new* type?"

"*Shhhhhhh*. Pretend it's a library, Ayn." He looks at the lineup again and then turns back to me, finally ready to choose, I think.

"I'll be right back; I have to go to the bathroom."

Now it's just me and the trucker. Again, I can't believe I'm not nervous. I watch as the shift manager steps up to him and asks, "Which lady would you like to spend some time with?"

He gestures to a blond woman wearing lace panties and a tank top, who appears to be in her thirties. I recognize her from my online printout as Sugar, a "sweet southern belle."

I lean over to the trucker. "Good choice. She looks really nice."

I guess I broke some kind of fourth wall, because he looks at me like I'm crazy and just says, "Uh, thanks," in a confused tone.

After they exit, it's just me on the sofa, facing a lineup of six working girls. Some of them look like they are trying to figure me out; others are just looking off to nowhere. I think I see the shift manager glance at her watch. After a long—what's the opposite of New York? Idaho?—minute, my cell rings and I pick it up.

It's Steve.

"Where the hell are you?" I ask.

"I'm in the parking lot."

"Why are you in the parking lot?"

"I can't do it."

"I cannot believe you are chickening out."

"Why do you think they call it the Chicken Ranch?"

"They call it the Chicken Ranch because during the 1840s, cash was hard to come by," I tell him. "So they would allow local farmers and ranchers to barter for their services with chickens."

"Whatever. I'm still not doing it," he says.

"But you're our *spy* on this one. The girls are going to be really disappointed. I'm going to be disappointed." Out of the corner of my eye, I see the madam asking the shift manager about me, and then she heads my way with a concerned look on her face. The girls are looking impatient, too.

"I gotta go," and I hang up on him.

Debbie approaches and tells me nicely that they don't service single women at their establishment. I don't know what to do. I am dying to see the rest of the place now. My curiosity is piqued, and I do not want to hear the girls bitch about how Steve and I chickened out, plus I want to cross this off my Porn-to-Do list.

I make a panic decision.

"Actually, I'm here to apply for a job," I lie.

She looks me up and down. "As . . . ?"

"As a, uh, a, what they do." I point to the working girls in the line-up. Debbie gives them a little tilt of her head and they go into the bar. When they open the door to the bar, men are waiting in there. It seems some men like to get to know the girls in a more natural setting—if you can call a bar in a brothel a natural setting—before choosing.

Looking me up and down, Debbie clarifies, "You want to be a working girl?"

"Yeah. Can I get the tour and an application?"

"There is no application."

"Well, I can send in my résumé. Unfortunately, I forgot to bring it with me."

"No résumé either. I usually just talk to the girls and get a sense of what they're looking for. It's mostly based on looks and personality. If they pass the physical exams we give them a shot at working here. Room and board is thirty dollars per day."

"Oh, what does that include?"

"We have a staff of thirteen. We cook for you, provide food and snacks, we clean for you, even do laundry. Some of the girls get spoiled."

We have unofficially started the tour now and are in a dark hallway. I look around at the dark paneling and shag carpet. Hard to imagine me getting spoiled here.

"Have you done this kind of work before?" asks Debbie.

"Not for money, no," I tell her.

She looks confused. "You've worked at a brothel for free?"

"Well, no, I mean I've had sex for free before." Then I lie. "Lots of it."

"I'm not sure you're right for this place," she declares gently.

"Oh, why is that?"

She hedges a little. "Most of the girls are a little thinner. The guys seem to prefer that." *Ouch. Again, I really need to work on those sit-ups.* "You might want to lose a little weight first, and then try back."

"You sure you don't have customers who might appreciate some Latina hips, or I can play up my Asian eyes?" *Who am I?* I'm *groveling* for a job at a brothel that I don't even really want.

She tells me that Asian women, full Asian, do really well. When they get them—which is rare, she admits—they are always picked first in a lineup. "We had a Japanese woman here once," she tells me. "Straight from Japan, with jet black hair down to her waist, very demure. She made bank."

I convince Debbie that my personality can win guys over. I make her laugh, and she likes that. She confesses that she does believe in giving people a chance at the Chicken Ranch. She's let women in their fifties, who look really good, give it a try, but in the end they never got picked enough by the men over the other working girls to justify them rooming and boarding there.

"What other jobs have you held?" she asks.

"Actually, I've only had two." I consider lying, but she is being so nice that I can't bring myself to do it. "Right now I'm a freelance writer. Before this I ran a nonprofit community revitalization program in Los Angeles." Not exactly related to prostitution.

"Where'd you go to school?"

I hedge on this one, remembering the H-bomb theory. "Uh, Harvard."

She doesn't seem surprised. "What's your degree in?"

Damn it. I really don't want to talk about myself. "My bachelor's is in psychology. I also have a masters in education and social policy, and a masters in fine arts."

"You're not really interested in a job here, are you?"

"No, I'm not, Debbie."

"So why are you here?"

I let it all out. "My knitting club, The Naughty Knitters, are really curious about things like this, and I promised them, okay I promised myself, that I would find out what it's like, and so I had this great plan, we'd get my uptight friend Steve—"

"The nervous looking guy in the parking lot?"

I nod. "We thought we'd get him laid so he would stop being so annoying. Then, well, he changed his mind. So there went my spy, and I so badly did not want to come all this way for nothing."

"You should have just said so. I can talk about this place all day. What do you want to know?" She is too cool.

She really opens up as she shows me around the place, which is so quiet that I forget some people are having sex in some of the small rooms, as I just fire off questions.

"What are the women like?"

"Big range. Most of them are here as a way to make some good money so that they can use it to do other things in their lives."

"Like what, if you don't mind my asking?"

"We've had a lot of younger girls use the money they've made here to pay for college, others have used their earnings to build a recording studio, open up a counseling center, record a rock album, start a stock brokerage. One person even used her money to breed emus and ostriches."

Who knew that women who work at brothels would be so entrepreneurial?

"We get a lot of local women who come through here to pay off debt or just get through a divorce. It's not uncommon for us to have married women whose husbands know they are doing this."

Now that's *an open relationship*, I think.

Debbie has a way of making you feel at ease. She is also super-articulate, full of facts, and self-aware about how her profession might be perceived by those who do not patronize their services. I'm surprised to find that I do not feel uncomfortable asking her things like, "Is there anything to the common perception that some of the girls work here because they are sexaholics?"

She says she doesn't find that to be the case. "Most of the women are just really practical people."

"They don't have dreams of marrying one of their rich customers?" I ask. She points out that it's happened only once in the twenty years she's worked at the ranch.

The brothel beyond the parlor room looks like something out of the '70s. Prefab trailers slung together to make a small compound on a barely landscaped property. Guys obviously don't care; they come enough—in more ways than one—so that the place makes enough money (she won't say how much) to have sold for $1.2 million in 1982. The original owner opened it for $60,000 in 1976. And it is now on the market for $6.9 million.

Debbie becomes the best of docents as she shows me around and shares some of the history of the place. The Chicken Ranch is the brothel on which the movie and Broadway play *Best Little Whorehouse in Texas* was based. When it was shut down in Texas in 1973 for political reasons, it moved to Pahrump, Nevada, where it has been ever since.

The Chicken Ranch was so much a part of the history of the southwest that our Texas-born President Lyndon B. Johnson once paid a publicized visit to the Ranch for historic value, a photo op, and reportedly nothing else.

Debbie admits that there are not as many celebrity visitors as some imagine, but that doesn't mean wealthy customers don't come through. It is not uncommon, according to Debbie, for some customers to shell out up to $10,000 to rent their back "bungalow" (also a prefab trailer) for a few nights.

"The minimum for an overnight party in the bungalow is $3,000. Last week we did ten thousand dollars of business in the bungalows alone," she tells me as she opens the bungalow door. It is pretty basic, reminds me of an old timeshare with its small kitchen and living room and three bedrooms and bathrooms shooting off of the living room. "There are multiple rooms, so that a guy can rent the place with two buddies, each with their own girl. For safety reasons we do not allow men to ever outnumber women. There is a big-screen TV to watch sports, a kitchen to make snacks. Some guys might rent the bungalows to have more intimacy."

The word intimacy strikes me as incongruent with the services they offer. I thought it was just about practical sex. It makes me ask, "Have you ever had a problem with a customer stalking a girl or a girl wanting to stalk a customer?" She tells me it's never happened.

In addition to the STD test they conduct when hiring, the girls are also subjected to background checks, which decreases the chances of getting a girl who might be a whack job.

I want to ask her if any of the girls are long-distance squirters, but I don't. Instead I ask, "How do the prices work?"

"Each girl is an independent contractor who sets her own prices, with a $150 minimum. Some girls might make $400 per customer, while others can make a few thousand from a customer for the same thing. It's all about personality and negotiation skills."

I wonder if some of these working girls should apply to be on Donald Trump's *The Apprentice*. Then Debbie tells me how much some of the girls net after giving the house fifty percent of their earnings. Many of them earn more than $200,000 a year. They don't need to be an apprentice.

"How often do most of the girls have to have sex in one day?" I ask.

"It's up to them, but I'd say most average three to four times. Some do it up to ten times a day." I was lucky with Greg to do it ten times a *month*.

She goes on to explain that everyone is required to work a minimum of nine days a month. There are usually thirty working girls, most in their twenties and thirties, on the roster at any given time. They can, of course, work more days if they want. But most like to go back to their families or boyfriends or communities for a break, according to Debbie.

We start discussing the news that Heidi Fleiss is going to attempt to open up a stud farm with male sex workers for female customers in Nevada. Debbie doesn't think it's going to work for the same reason I do: It's easier for women to go to a bar and get a nice-looking guy to have sex with her for free. Of course, a normal bar can't guarantee you that the guy is disease-free like a brothel or stud farm can. Debbie adds that there is another reason a stud farm might have trouble. "A guy can't have sex as frequently as a woman in one day."

Good point.

We head back into the main part of the house, where I meet some of the girls as they exercise in a tiny weight room, eat chips in the kitchen, or hang out in the computer room, which has four PCs.

Debbie explains that this is where the girls spend a lot of their free time, checking e-mails, instant messaging boyfriends, shopping online, and just surfing the Web.

Before the girls begged for the computer room, their favorite pastime was watching videos. They're really not allowed to leave the property on the days they are working. Not that there would be much to tempt them out in Pahrump—it's a one-Starbucks sort of town. It's just that when they are at the brothel, they need to be available for lineups pretty much all day. Because customers are not required to make appointments, business is conducted on demand, seven days a week, twenty-four hours per day, 365 days a year.

It's interesting to meet the girls. They are more average-looking without makeup on and the five-inch Lucite heels. Again, it's like I'm visiting a friend at a sorority house, except they are not quite as chipper, their clothes are a lot tighter, and their shorts are definitely shorter.

Meeting the girls reminds me of the one question The Naughty Knitters said *had* to be answered: Do the women have orgasms?

"No," Debbie reveals, "they pretty much fake it," further explaining that it's not that they don't enjoy the sex, it's just that they are into it in a different way than they would be with someone they know more intimately.

To cap off my tour and introduction to The Chicken Ranch, Debbie loads me up with free T-shirts, "menus," and a warm handshake. She also tells me to come back any time just for a visit ... or with a significant other.

On the drive home, I tell Steve—who is kicking himself for not going through with it—everything and forgive him for chickening out. I feel like a different person driving back to Vegas. I thought it would be sordid and sexually explicit, but it was really just a profitable and practical business. I tell Steve that Debbie said there are a lot of older locals, or regulars in their forties, fifties, and sixties who are sent by their wives. The wives are not interested in sex, but they know their husbands are, and this is a way to keep their men satisfied while enjoying all of the other benefits of their marriage that they do not want to give up. I have a thought: Maybe if brothels were legal everywhere, the divorce rate would be a lot lower.

I definitely see the advantages of prostitution now. Especially if it is legal and as safe as it seems at The Chicken Ranch. As for the actual women who work there, I left a little impressed. Steve, too, was surprised to hear that most of the women have not worked as hookers before. Many of them were nurses or preschool teachers in their prior careers; they've also recruited women from corporate America who were tired of the hassles, the crap, and the lousy pay.

I don't know if charging strangers to have sex with them is the best career move for them, but I can respect their choice. It's just different from mine. The end results may be the same. They are not hurting anyone, and they are treated better on the job than a lot of writers I know. Actually, their *laissez faire* attitudes make a lot of sense in some ways. Now that I've been to a brothel, I can look at what they do from another point of view: There are a lot of people out there who like having sex. Prostitutes are just smart enough to get paid for it.

In the middle of my retelling of my brothel experience to Steve, Paige comes to. She looks around and figures out that we are headed back to Vegas.

"Did you actually do it?" she asks Steve.

He looks at me, unsure what to tell her because he knows

he will be harassed by The Naughty Knitters for wimping out.

"He did it." I say for him. I give him a look to tell him this is a better way to go and it will be our little secret.

"Wow," Paige says. "I really underestimated the size of your balls."

Back at the Bellagio, I find a box of Belgian chocolates *and* a bouquet of fresh tulips waiting for me in my room. Plus a note that reads: "See you in L.A.—Sam."

Before we head home, Steve and I visit the new Bellagio Spa Tower, where we get full body massages and a relaxing warm stone treatment.

In the middle of it, he turns to me, a look of zen on his face. "Okay, this makes up for the ear-piercing trauma," he says with a smile, before falling into a deep sleep on the table.

He hasn't looked this relaxed in years.

1. Bellagio spa treatment for two, courtesy of The Naughty Knitters: $500

2. Curing your friend of his post-relationship stress disorder by taking him to a brothel: Priceless.

50 PER CENT OF
RESPONDENTS FROM THE
UK REPORT THAT THEY
INDULGE IN WATCHING
PORNOGRAPHY WITH
THEIR SEX PARTNER

Source: *bbc.co.uk*

Chapter Thirteen
What's So Funny About Porn, Love, & Understanding?

Pornophobic: *adj. describes a person (usu. female) who has an irrational fear of pornography*

When we are back in Los Angeles, I get a call from Heather. "He really likes you," she says excitedly. She is talking about Sam, and our call is so seventh grade but I love it.

"I can't remember the last time I liked somebody this much. Actually, I've never liked anybody this much," I tell her.

"I think I can actually hear your heart beating," Heather teases.

"I think that's your call waiting," I let her know. "But don't you dare pick it up until you tell me exactly what Sam said," I warn her.

"He thinks you're *The One.*"

"Why does he think I'm The One?"

"Does it really matter why?"

"Yes. If it's for some reason like he thinks I am a nymphomaniac . . ."

"But you're not a nymphomaniac."

"I know, but—"

Suddenly Heather is gone, and I hear Brad's voice on the phone instead. He has obviously grabbed the phone from Heather.

"He said that he loves how you put yourself out there, and do things you know will embarrass you. He also loves your laugh," Brad says matter-of-factly. "Now can I have my wife back?"

Later that week, Sam and I go together to a small rehearsal dinner party for Sacha and Rich. There are two long banquet tables, with twenty of us seated at each one. Old Significant Other Greg, with his new girlfriend, Matina, happens to be right across the table from us.

At the other table I catch a glimpse of Vee, looking more radiant than I have seen her looking since her divorce. She is whispering and laughing with a very handsome older Latin gentleman who has been seated next to her. For once, Vee is having less sex than anyone I know, but she is the happiest I have ever seen her. She had an epiphany after Lou Paget's seminar. According to Vee, she had convinced herself that more orgasms and more sex were better than fewer orgasms and less sex. Furthermore, by relying on an overabundance of vibrators and dating young men at the peak of their horniness, she claims she tricked herself into ignoring the fact that great sex and intimacy is a two-way street, and until Lou's sexuality seminar, she was treating it like a one-way street, one that she was driving down the wrong way.

Not that she's given up all of her sex toys. I happen to know she is hiding her Rabbit and a brand-new Je Joue in her sock drawer, and her earthquake kit is still outfitted with the glow-in-the-dark eight-inch rubber deep-stroke vibrator "for emergencies."

After the food is served and everyone toasts the happy couple, Greg leans across the table to talk to me while Matina and Sam strike up their own conversation.

"Whatever happened to your Porn-to-Do list?" he asks me.

"I finished it," I tell him.

"Are you serious?" he asks in disbelief.

"You can ask The Knitters. I read erotica, went to a strip club, threw a *sexware* party, went to a sex store—that's where I met Sam—tested vibrators, attended a blow job seminar, watched more pornos in a week than you have in your lifetime, went to a taping of Dr. Suzy's squirt salon, and visited a brothel."

"*You* went to a brothel?" he says, slightly blown away.

"Yep, I've got a T-shirt to prove it."

"Guess I really underestimated you," he says.

I'll say.

We are turning back to Matina and Sam and talking about how good the food is and what a great couple Sacha and Rich are, when Greg looks back at me.

"Wait a minute. Did you meet a porn star?" he asks.

It's just like him to focus on the one thing that wasn't mentioned. "No. It's not like I was ever serious about that one anyway," I explain.

He smiles to himself as if gloating.

"Okay, why are you smiling?"

"Oh, nothing."

"Yeah right. You wouldn't be smiling if it were nothing."

"It's just that you didn't really finish the list. Since I've known you, you have never actually *finished* one of your lists."

"You *did* hear me say that I went to a *brothel?*" I can't help but raise my voice. More than a few heads turn and look at me, aghast.

I lower my voice. "Look, Greg, the porn exercise is over. I

proved my point: I am no longer pornophobic. And I'll admit I'm a better person for it. The list is over."

"Even though you didn't finish it," he mumbles, loud enough for me to hear.

The next morning Sam has come over to my place to pick me up for Rich and Sacha's wedding. As I last-minute wrap the fancy wine bottle opener from their registry, and Lou Paget's book *How to Be a Great Lover*, he helps himself to some juice in my kitchen. When I look up, I see him chuckling as he reads my master list, which is still taped to my cupboard door.

"The infamous lists," he says. "But what about the Porn-to-Do?"

"It's on the counter. I was just about to throw it away." I attempted to throw the list away before going to bed last night, but Greg's claim that I've never finished one of my lists was ringing in my head. After sitting in the dark in my kitchen for a half hour, and walking myself through all of the lists I've made over the last decade, I was disappointed to face the fact that he was right. Ne'er a finished list.

"You sure you want to throw it away? You know, we might not have met if it weren't for that," he reminds me.

He's right, but it's hard to imagine putting it in a scrapbook with our photos and other mementos so that we can look at it fondly decades from now with our beautiful children. *Look kids, Mommy went to a whorehouse... and there's Daddy spanking Mommy at a sex party. Yes, that is a dominatrix in the background... Aaaah, the memories...*

"I don't know why I haven't thrown it away already." I grab the list right there, crumple it up, and toss it in the garbage once and for all.

He notices the strange look on my face and plants a comforting kiss on my head while he tenderly massages my shoulders. The gesture totally relaxes me and makes me open up.

"I know it's silly, but it bothers me that there's one thing on the list that I haven't done. I'm just so close." I pause, not wanting to admit the rest, but I do. "I never noticed it before, but Greg is right. I never finish my lists. The master list you see on that cupboard has been up there forever. Maybe I self-sabotage by always putting something on my lists that I know I can't do. Who am I kidding? *Spear fishing?*"

"Doesn't sound that silly to me."

"What was I thinking with 'Meet a porn star'? What's really funny, is that—for some reason I didn't tell Greg—I did actually attempt to meet one. I called Jenna Jameson, because she was the only one I could think of by name. Apparently porn stars are very busy people, because she has not answered my letters to her agent or her publicist. I don't even know why I put it on there."

"Because you were curious about it."

Later we are in the car driving to Palos Verdes for the wedding, but Sam is definitely not taking the Yahoo map route or the MapQuest route. If it were Greg—who always refused to ask for directions—I would have said something already, but the thought of getting lost with Sam is not even remotely annoying. I like having him to myself. Even when we are not talking, I feel completely comfortable.

I stare out the window as Sam points out L.A.'s few surviving architectural treasures on Wilshire Boulevard, such as The

Ambassador Hotel and The El Rey Theatre. My eyes spot a Spearmint Rhino billboard right on the boulevard advertising itself as a gentleman's strip club. This makes my mind wander to the beginning of my porn journey. When I think about it, I went from no porn to mo' porn to mo' better porn.

Looking back, I see that it was a good thing that I didn't have a boyfriend for most of the Porn-to-Do journey. It gave me more time and room to think about what sex and porn mean to me personally. In the end, it turned out not to be merely about using, buying, or learning sexual things to please someone else . . . or even to keep up with social trends. It has really been more about being aware of what is out there, and finding things that might add pleasure or fun to my own life, whether I use the products on someone else or myself.

I remember in the beginning I saw the mainstreaming of porn as something that would corrupt women. Now, I see that this weapon in the hands of women has the power to be a weapon of mass seduction. We women are capable of weeding out what is vulgar and offensive. For those of us who have taken the time to explore it, we realize that, like bad carbs (think chocolate) and good carbs (think broccoli), there is bad porn and good porn.

It's just that, somewhere along the way, the true meaning of the word "porn" was hijacked, or at the very least overshadowed, by hard-core porn. Okay, maybe that's not being fair either. Maybe I prefer kinder, gentler porn, but I can see that there is a place for some legal hard-core stuff too. It probably isn't for most good girls, but men are programmed differently. For one thing, whereas in general, women enjoy analyzing feelings and are better at multitasking and thinking ahead, men typically take things at face value and, thus, do not overanalyze and are better at compartmentalizing and living in the moment. I am confident that I will never be interested in illegal porn, but I am willing to admit that if I didn't overanalyze hard-core porn and just took it at face value, like most men I know, I might be turned on by it.

Somehow, another thing I've learned through this porn journey is that life is not about survival of the fittest or survival of the prettiest, as I have always feared. It's all about survival of the happiest, and good, healthy, enjoyable sex can help you down that road. The biological fact is that we are all programmed for sex and for giving pleasure, but the programming gets tinkered with along the way because life happens. Career. Exhaustion. Break-ups. Death. Marriage. Kids. And more exhaustion. That's where porn comes in. Good porn (such as vibrators, erotic literature, sex enhancement products, and some movies) helps us shift some of the focus back to sex, passion, pleasure, and desire, all of which are natural and wonderful aspects of being human.

When I snap back to the present, I notice that we are driving through downtown Los Angeles.

"Uh, I hate to say this, Sam, but we went the wrong way. Palos Verdes is in the complete opposite direction."

"Actually, I thought you might want to stop here first."

I look out the window. We are parked in front of the L.A. Convention Center. I look back at Sam, confused. "I'm not sure what you are talking about."

He pokes his head out the window and then moves the car up a foot.

Now I see what he is looking at. On the Convention Center

marquee, there are big letters that read: ADULT VIDEO CONVENTION.

I smile at him. His accidental detour was hardly accidental. "Guess I'll be right back," I tell him.

Twenty minutes later, after meeting several porn stars—who were much more approachable than I imagined—I come back out with my own 8-by-10 autographed photo of one of them.

"Mission accomplished?" Sam asks as I re-enter the car.

"The list is complete," I say with immense satisfaction. "Thank you."

The wedding is a beautiful affair. It is set above the Pacific Ocean at a rustic site known as La Venta. And it is definitely putting Sam and me in a very romantic mood.

The fact that Sacha rented a chocolate fountain does not hurt things either.

After the ceremony, Vee runs up to us and squeals, "I think I'm in love! And get this, he doesn't even drive a car."

"Vee, you cannot date someone under sixteen."

She grins at me. "He's fifty, which makes me the younger woman, and he doesn't drive because he has *a driver*." She points across the dance floor to the distinguished older gentleman that she was seated next to last night. He grins at us and raises his glass in a cool gesture. Smiling to myself, I raise my glass back as Vee practically skips back to him.

I spot Greg across the dance floor and excuse myself from Sam for a moment.

As I walk across the dance floor, I can feel Sam watching me with a bemused grin. I love that he is encouraging and supportive of even the silliest of things, and that he is getting a kick out of what I am about to do.

I also sense The Naughty Knitters rooting for me from different parts of the ballroom. Maya is near the bar having an intense discussion about film with a young director who likes her because she is bright, not because she is beautiful. Tricia is flirting with the DJ, who has just dedicated a song to her. Paige and her husband are happily swinging on the dance floor. Yumi is chatting with Sloan, who I just now realize is as funny as Adam Sandler. And Steve is laughing with super Sabine at a candlelit table by themselves.

When I get to the other end of the dance floor, I hand Greg a manila envelope. He opens it and takes out the 8-by-10 glossy photo I got at the convention. I watch him as he looks at it, reading the autographed inscription from up-and-coming adult video star Austyn Moore.

Then unexpectedly he breaks out into laughter. I laugh, too, shake his hand, wish him luck with Matina, and head back to my Sam.

After the wedding, Sam and I stop at the beach in Playa Del Rey and lay in the sand, staring up at a full moon. After being subjected to the loud music at the reception, this silence is sweet. I start to fan my outstretched arms and legs through the sand, making a sand angel. Sam looks over and smiles at the sight of this and then does the same.

I am the first to break the easy silence between us.

"It was great seeing everybody looking so happy tonight."

He completely agrees, and we continue talking about Rich and Sacha's wedding, and how cool it is that they are taking their honeymoon in Thailand. I find out that Sam's favorite food is Thai, which I happen to love to cook. I also find out that, as I suspected, he eats his Kung Pao *with* the peanuts (Mom will be very happy about this). I don't want to give away that my mind keeps wandering to a future with him, but I ask him anyway, "So, where would *you* go on a honeymoon?"

"Batemans Bay, Australia."

"Why Batemans Bay?"

"I hear they have great spear fishing," he says, still staring up at the moon.

This makes me laugh out loud. *How did I get so lucky that making a Porn-to-Do list led me here?*

"You never told me what Ms. Moore"—he is referring to the porn star Austyn—"wrote on the photo for Greg."

I chuckle again as I picture Greg looking at the photo of Austyn in nothing more than a pair of black lace garters, her perky real boobs showing through her long blond hair, and her "come hither" stare.

"She wrote: 'Dear Greg, Ayn is not pornophobic.'"

He laughs out loud again. "That's awesome," he says and then reaches into his pocket and hands me a piece of paper. "Guess you don't need this anymore." It is my crumpled-up Porn-to-Do list that I threw away this morning.

He hands me a book of matches from the wedding. "You want to do the honors?"

I light a match and put it to the piece of paper that Sam is holding. It's like some spiritual purification ritual that signifies fear is behind me and renewal lies ahead.

We watch the list burn bright, until it disintegrates into a hundred tiny embers of light, like fireflies flickering in the night, carried away by the ocean breeze and floating off into the dark night. Those tiny embers of light remind me that the universe is kind. It shines on me when I least expect it.

RESOURCES

The following places, products, and websites did not make it into the book for reasons beyond my control, or are so good they are worth highlighting again. So if you're still curious, check out:

BABELAND—It's true, Babeland is America's premier women-owned-and-operated sexuality boutique. Their L.A. store opened too late for me to review for this book, but a recent visit proves why their retail stores are admired by so many women in Seattle and New York City. Whether you want help figuring out which vibrator to use and how to use it, which porn videos are female-friendly, or which sex-help book might help you through a rough spot, Babeland's seriously-trained female staff will make you feel more comfortable than you would feel in your own living room. And, if you're still too shy for an in-person visit, they have an awesome website (www.babeland.com) that includes customer reviews of products and sex education topics, and info on their new sex toy parties.

WWW.NERVE.COM—a cool online magazine about sex and culture. Makes you feel savvy, not slutty, for wanting to read about sex, and where else can you find daily sex advice from the likes of tiny dog lovers, janitors, and magicians?

HOW TO BE A GREAT LOVER—GIRLFRIEND-TO-GIRLFRIEND TOTALLY EXPLICIT TECHNIQUES THAT WILL BLOW HIS MIND by Lou Paget—Exactly what it says. If you don't live in L.A. or NYC, this is the next best thing to attending Paget's Sexuality Seminar.

WWW.BEAUTIFULAGONY.COM—This website, dedicated to the beauty of human orgasm, is not for the bashful. Everyday people submit video of themselves in the midst of orgasm. Not hard-core because you only see them from the waist up. Guys love this erotic site.

VERY PRIVATE INTIMATE MOISTURE—Despite its corny name, this lotion, formulated to moisturize dry and delicate vaginal tissue, makes for an amazing lubricant during sex. Feels more natural than anything The Naughty Knitters or I have ever tried. Unlike most lubricants, it contains no artificial dyes, fragrance, additives, or hormones, and it is pH balanced to the skin, hypoallergenic, dermatologist, gynecologist, and FDA tested and approved. You can find it at www.loupaget.com

JE JOUE—The world's first programmable (PC or MAC) non-penetrative vibrator. Allows you (or your long-distance significant other) to download pre-programmed or custom massage patterns (a.k.a. "grooves"). In tests, 76 per cent of women reported it was the best toy they'd ever tried. 24 per cent claimed it was better than their lover. Purchase at www.jejoue.com or Babeland.

WWW.THENAUGHTYKNITTERS.COM—Still curious? Log on to read more sex confessions by Good Girls, download a good girl's glossary of porn, learn about the making of *Pornology*, discover awesome sex products, or get relationship advice from The Naughty Knitters and their S.O.B.'s (Significant Others and Boyfriends). What happens on the Web stays on the Web.

Final note: **Relax. It's Just Sex.**

ACKNOWLEDGMENTS

Thank you to Frances Carrillo, Heather Pregerson, Victoria Laviña, DJ Tricia Halloran, Sacha Radford, Robin Schiesser, T.M., Steve H., Amy Tripodi, Julie Carnes, and Yumi Tsujino for their hands-on help, encouragement, or inspiration; to Gray C. Gailey, my good luck charm and mini muse; to Samuel William Gailey for your insight and patience—I forgive you for making me laugh so hard and so often that I have to wear Depends; to Oscar Garza, Yvette Doss, and the *Tu Ciudad* staff for letting me think that I am actually funny; to my talented writers' group, a.k.a., *The Red Herrings:* Tatiana Bliss, Brian Price, Matthew Sloan, Lara Wood, Cody Farley, and especially to Jen Robinson Arellano, who loaned me her brain cells on more than one occasion when mine were nowhere to be found; to Dr. Mark Katz, kind neighbor and proofreader extraordinaire, who offered his assistance just when I was on the verge of collapse—I forgive you for being so good at Sudoku; to Lakota girl for keeping my feet warm for as much as the journey as she could; to Lisa Clancy and the Running Press staff for showing me the ropes (and not in the shape of a noose)—I forgive you for only giving me six months to write this book; to Larry Johnson for introducing me to Amy Schiffman, and to Amy for introducing me to Randi Glass Murray, the rare literary agent who knows how to edit, and whose superhero powers of persistence and laughter helped make this book a reality. Randi, I bestow upon you honorary lifetime membership to The Naughty Knitters, with full stitch and bitch privileges.

And, last, but not least, to Good Girls—and Guys—everywhere …Stay curious!

THE SEX DOCTOR
Fix Your Love Life Fast!

Tracey Cox is a bestselling author, journalist and TV presenter (*The Sex Inspectors*, *Would Like to Meet* and *Under One Roof*). Don't miss her fabulously entertaining and utterly indispensable new book.

No matter how good you think your sex life is, there's always a tip, trick or technique to make it even better. And you won't find a better compilation of libido-lifting, orgasm-orbiting, titillating titbits! *The Sex Doctor* combines the very latest in sex research with hundreds of hot sex tips to guarantee bliss between-the-sheets for everyone. With practical action plans, intelligent advice, how-to's and don't-ever's, prepare to be inspired, amused and, above all, entertained.

- Singles sex and how to get more of it.
- The top five things your new lover's hoping for.
- Foolproof ways to tell how you rate as a lover.
- Find your four new hotspots.
- Discover the seven secrets to giving a hellish hand-job.
- Does cheating count if there's no one around to catch you?
- The latest, greatest sex toys and how to choose and use them.
- Are your parents getting into bed with you?
- Should you stay if the sex isn't any good?
- A sex detox and techniques sex therapists swear by.
- Crucial keys to having fabulous long-term sex.

9780552153409

CORGI BOOKS